SELL AND SELL SHORT

John Wiley & Sons, Inc.

BOOKS BY DR. ALEXANDER ELDER

Trading for a Living

Study Guide for Trading for a Living

Rubles to Dollars:
   Making Money on Russia's Exploding Financial Frontier

Come into My Trading Room

Study Guide for Come into My Trading Room

Straying from the Flock: Travels in New Zealand

Entries & Exits: Visits to Sixteen Trading Rooms

Study Guide for Entries & Exits

SELL AND SELL SHORT

To Matthew —

make money in up & down markets!

Alex Elder

Dr. Alexander Elder
www.elder.com

NY 2009

WILEY

John Wiley & Sons, Inc.

Library of Congress Cataloging-in-Publication Data:

Elder, Alexander
  Sell and sell short / Alexander Elder.
      p. cm. — (Wiley trading series)
  Includes index.
  ISBN 978-0-470-18167-6 (cloth)
  1. Investment analysis. 2. Stocks. 3. Speculation. I. Title.
  HG4529.E465 2008
  332.63′228—dc22   2007050504

Printed in the United States of America.

10 9 8 7 6 5 4 3 2 1

To Inna Feldman,
the manager of elder.com
whose care, kindness, and integrity
have helped shape our company
for the past decade.

CONTENTS

Introduction

There is a time to grow and a time to decline. A time to plant and a time to reap.

That cute puppy bouncing up and down in your living room will some day become an old, decrepit dog whom you will have to drive to the vet's office to put it out of its misery.

That stock you bought with such great hopes and which you enjoyed watching grow has now rolled over and is cutting into your capital instead of increasing it. It is high time to look for an exit.

This is a book about selling.

Buying is fun. It grows out of hope, great expectations, a chest full of air. Selling is a hard, unsmiling business, like driving that poor old dog to the vet for its final injection. But sell you must. And that's what this book is about.

And once you and I talk about selling—that hard, cold reality at the end of almost every trade—we will not stop. We will talk about selling short. Amateurs don't know how to short and are afraid of it, but professionals love shorting and profit from declines.

Stocks go down much faster than they rise, and a trader who knows how to short doubles his opportunities. But before you sell short you must learn to sell and sell well.

So let us take off those rose-colored glasses and learn to sell.

WHY SELL?

We buy when we feel optimistic—or are afraid of missing a good thing. Perhaps you read a story about a new product or heard rumors of a merger. Maybe you ran a technical scan or found a promising chart pattern on the screen. You had some money in your account and called your broker or went online to place a buy order.

You've received a confirmation—now you own this stock. That's when the stress begins.

If the stock stays flat and goes nowhere you feel restless. Did you pick the wrong one again? Others are going up—should you sell yours?

If your stock begins to rise, it creates a different kind of anxiety. Should you take profits now, add to your position, or do nothing? Doing nothing is hard, especially for men, who are told from childhood "Don't just stand there, *do* something!"

When your stock drops, the anxiety becomes mixed with pain—"I'll sell as soon as it comes back to even."

Amazingly, the most psychologically comfortable position for most traders is a slight decline in their stock. It is not sharp enough to be painful, and with the stock near your entry price there is probably not much reason to sell. With no action required, you have a perfect excuse to sit back and do nothing. It feels good not to have to make any decisions! That is how a small loss can gradually become bigger and badder.

If you throw a frog into a pot of hot water, it will jump, but if you heat it slowly, you can cook it alive. Traders with no clear selling plans can end up being boiled alive.

The worst time for making any decision, including the one to sell, is when you feel under the gun. This is why I urge you to write down a trading plan *before* you put on a trade (see *How to Document Your Trading Plan*). A good plan must outline your reasons for entering a trade, and define your entry price, a protective stop, and a profit target. Setting your stop and target levels means making a decision to sell. Making those decisions *before* you enter a trade allows you to use your brain instead of jumping in response to heat like some poor frog.

Psychologists have proven that the quality of decisions we make under stress is lower than those we make in a peaceful and relaxed frame of mind. You are likely to make better decisions, increase your profits, and reduce your losses if you write down your selling plan *before* you buy that stock.

A written trading plan accomplishes an amazing feat—it increases your profits and reduces losses!

So, why not do it?

Two reasons. First of all, most traders have never been taught what you have just read. Beginners and outsiders simply do not have the knowledge.

The other reason is that people like to dream. A written plan cuts into their sweet day-dreaming business. It feels nice to lean back and drift into a vague fantasy of riches. Sitting up straight on a hard-back chair and writing down your specific goals as well as a contingency plan robs you of that vague fantasy.

We all like to daydream, but since you have picked up this book I will assume that you have chosen the pleasure of real money over that of daydreaming. You probably want to learn how to sell, so that you can make more money while risking less.

In that case, we are on the same page. But before you write down your selling plan, let us review some of the key principles of buying. We also need to discuss the two key factors that separate winners from losers—money management and record-keeping. Armed with this knowledge, we will be ready to turn our attention to selling and then to shorting.

SELL AND SELL SHORT

How to Buy, Manage Risk, & Keep Records

Masses of traders crowd into the markets, looking for profits. Every serious trader knows he needs an edge—a method of discovering opportunities and placing orders that gives him an advantage over the majority of competitors. A slight edge, coupled with a lot of discipline, is the key to steady profits.

Every professional knows what his edge is and where the profits are likely to come from. A beginner does not bother himself with such concepts. He may buy today because last night he read about an inverted head-and-shoulder bottom. He may buy tomorrow because of a piece of news that caught his attention. He has no clear concept of buying. He has no edge.

We all go through this stage of initial ignorance. To move beyond it and graduate to trading for a living you need to have a concept of what it is you are trying to buy or sell.

If you find a money-making niche, others may soon crowd into it and drive down the returns. Your profits are always under threat, while the dangers are ever-present. The competition is intense. To keep making money in the markets and to grow equity, you need to define and implement a trading concept that is fairly simple and bulletproof.

THE GAP BETWEEN PRICE AND VALUE

My long search for an edge led me to study the gap between price and value. The concept is quite simple: price and value are not the same. Price can be below value, above it, or equal to it. The distance between price and value may be large or small, increasing or decreasing at any given time. Surprisingly few people are aware of the ever-changing gap between price and value, although when you point it out to them they see it immediately.

The concept is simple, but turning it into a trading method is not that easy.

Everybody knows about price—you read the numbers on a price tag or look up a stock quote on the screen. Any child can tell you the price of candy. We all know price, yet very few people know how to define value and track its changes. If you can do that, your buy or sell decisions are no longer based on price alone. You can buy when value is rising or sell short when price gets too far above value.

Most buying decisions are based on the perception, however vague, that price is below value. Most people buy when they think the crowd does not recognize the true value of their trading vehicle. They think they see ahead of the crowd, and expect to make money after the crowd also sees what they do and drives prices higher. Traders buy when they think that some future event will cause an increase in the value of their trading vehicle.

I became aware of the gap between price and value decades ago, during a brief lecture by J. Peter Steidlmayer. Listening to this Chicago floor trader and sometime author I immediately sensed the value of the concept. I had no idea at the time how many years I would spend looking for a way to implement it in my trading.

Few technical traders ever think about the difference between price and value. Fundamental analysts are much more attuned to the idea, but they do not own it—technicians can use it as well.

It makes sense to buy below value and sell above value.

To implement this idea, we need to answer three questions—how to define value, how to track its changes, and how to measure the distance from price to value.

HOW TO BUY

Successful trading requires confidence; but, paradoxically, it also demands humility. You must realize that the markets are huge and there is no way you can master everything there is to know about them. Your knowledge of the markets can never be complete.

You need to specialize in a certain area of research and trading. You can compare financial markets to medicine; a modern physician cannot be an expert in surgery, ophthalmology, psychiatry, obstetrics, and pediatrics. Such universal knowledge may have been possible centuries ago, but the modern field of medicine has become so huge that all physicians must specialize. They must choose one or perhaps two areas and master them. Outside of those areas they need to know just enough to avoid trouble.

THE THREE GREAT DIVIDES

A serious trader needs to specialize just like a serious physician. He must choose an area of research and trading that appeals to him. Here are some of the key choices every trader needs to make:

- **Technical vs. Fundamental**
  Fundamental analysts study the values of listed companies or the supply-demand equations for commodities. Technicians, by contrast, believe that the sum total of knowledge about any market is reflected in its price. Technicians study chart patterns and indicators to determine whether bulls or bears are likely to win the current round of the trading game. Needless to say, there is a bit

of overlap between the two fields. Serious fundamentalists often look at charts, while serious technicians may have some idea about the fundamentals of the market they are trading.

- **Trend vs. Counter-Trend**
  Most charts show a mix of directional moves and choppy trading ranges. Beginners are fascinated by powerful trends: if they could buy at a bottom, so clearly visible in the middle of the chart, and hold through the ensuing rally, they'd make a lot of money in a hurry. Experienced traders know that the trends, so clearly visible in the middle of the chart, become increasingly foggy as you near the right edge. Riding a trend is like riding a wild horse that tries to shake you off at every turn. Trend trading is a lot harder than it seems. At the same time, one of the few scientifically proven facts about markets is that they oscillate. They continuously swing between being overvalued and undervalued. Counter-trend traders capitalize on this chop of the markets as they fade (trade against) the extremes.

- **Discretionary vs. Systematic**
  Applying your studies and indicators to a chart can be an exciting and engaging process. Discretionary traders keep turning their studies this way and that as they decide whether to buy, sell, or do nothing. Some traders enjoy this game, while others get stressed by this never-ending need for decision-making. System traders prefer to dump market data into a computer, test a set of rules for buying and selling, and then turn the system on and follow its signals.

Another key decision in the markets involves deciding whether to focus on stocks, futures, options, or forex. You may want to specialize even further, by choosing a specific stock group or one or two specific futures. Whatever your trading vehicle, it pays to define your work along the three axes: fundamental/technical, trend/counter-trend, and discretionary/systematic. Being clear about your likes and dislikes will help you avoid flopping around the markets, the way so many people do.

It is important to realize that in each of these great divides both sides are equally valuable. Your choice will depend primarily on your temperament. Professional traders tend to have an open mind. They are always curious about other people's opinions and are respectful towards them. Only arrogant greenhorns look down upon those who have made different choices.

TECHNICAL VS. FUNDAMENTAL ANALYSIS

A fundamental analyst spends his time calculating the value of the business that any given stock represents. He evaluates company earnings, competitive position, management, and other factors. Fundamental analysts of commodities study supply and demand for their markets. For example, when the country's orange-growing regions expect a severe frost, fundamental analysts know that the value of the surviving crop will increase and prices will follow. The big questions then become what portion of the crop is likely to be lost and what will happen to demand in response to a price increase.

A pure technician may not care about the earnings, the frost, or a heat wave. All he wants is the ticker or a symbol and a history of transactions going back some time. He expects to pull some repetitive pattern out of that history and trade it for profit.

Purity and other forms of extremism may attract beginners, but a more mature individual is not likely to see the markets in black and white. It is perfectly normal to feel more attracted either to fundamental or technical analysis. At the same time, an experienced trader, be he a fundamentalist or a technician, does not reject the other point of view but tries to look at the markets with both eyes.

Whether you feel inclined towards fundamental or technical analysis, you have to be curious about how the other side lives. The great Warren Buffett, probably the top fundamental analyst and money manager in the United States, says that people who do not look at prices are like card players who do not look at cards. My own heart is in technical analysis, but whenever I become interested in a stock I like to ask several fundamental questions. I definitely want to know to what industry it belongs. I'd much rather trade a stock in a growth industry, such as nanotechnology or telecommunications, than in some old sluggish group. Also, I tend to stay away from shorting energy stocks and futures, because of my concerns about Hubbert's Peak[1] which calls for a tightness of energy supplies in the coming years.

---

[1]Deffeyes, Kenneth S. *Hubbert's Peak: The Impending World Oil Shortage* (Princeton University Press, 2003)

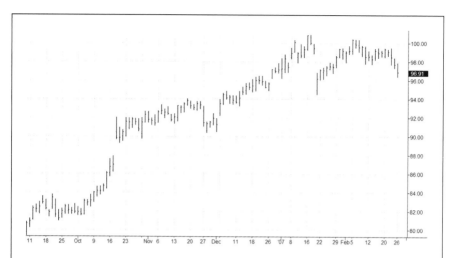

Figure 1.1　The Difficulty with Fundamental Analysis

The fundamentalist's dilemma: this daily chart of IBM shows that while the value of the company is increasing, the uptrend is anything but steady. You can see violent moves in the direction of the trend as well as against it. Day after day, prices change, with the company valued 1% more or 1% less, in the absence of any meaningful news. Prices are attached to values with a mile-long rubber band, making a fundamentalist's lot a hard one!

The problem with fundamental analysis is that values change slowly but prices fluctuate all over the lot. One of my students summed up this problem when he said: "Prices are connected to values by a mile-long rubber band" (see Figure 1.1).

While fundamentalists search for value in the long rows and columns of their spreadsheets, a technician can quickly identify values in any market using a few simple tools. My favorite method for discovering value is to use an exponential moving average—two moving averages, to be exact.

Moving averages identify the levels at which most market participants agree on value (see Figure 1.2). A rising moving average shows that value is increasing, and a falling moving average tells us that value is decreasing.

A trade is an agreement between a buyer and a seller. Since they transact in the midst of the market crowd, their trade represents a mo-

Moving Averages

A single price does not tell you whether the crowd is bullish or bearish—just as a single photo does not tell you whether a person is an optimist or a pessimist. If, on the other hand, someone brings ten photos of a person to a lab and gets a composite picture, it will reveal that person's typical features. If you update a composite photo each day, you can monitor trends in that person's mood.

A moving average serves as a continuously updated composite photograph of the market—it combines prices for several days. The market consists of huge crowds, and a moving average identifies the direction of mass movement.

The most important message of a moving average is the direction of its slope. When it rises, it shows that the crowd is becoming more optimistic—bullish. When it falls, it shows that the crowd is becoming more pessimistic—bearish.

From *Trading for a Living* by Dr. Alexander Elder,
John Wiley & Sons, Inc.,1993

mentary consensus not just between the two persons but for the crowd as a whole. If every tick on your screen represents a momentary consensus of value, then a moving average represents a composite photograph, a longer-term consensus.

A faster moving average represents a short-term consensus. A slow moving average represents a longer-term consensus. I call the area between the two lines "the value zone."

Using moving averages to identify value helps differentiate between two different types of trading. A trend-following trader wants to buy when prices pull back towards a rising moving average. A counter-trend trader recognizes when the prices get too far away from the value zone, and gets ready to trade the snap-back.

TREND VS. COUNTER-TREND TRADING

Take a look at the chart in Figure 1.2, and the arguments for and against trend or counter-trend trading will leap at you from the page. You can easily recognize an uptrend: when prices run from the lower left corner to the upper right corner, you do not need to be a technician

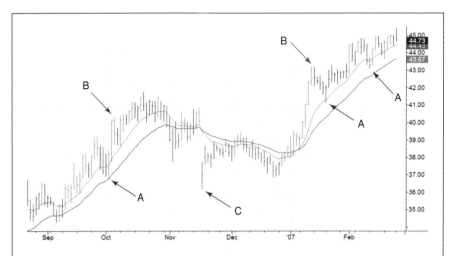

Figure 1.2   Moving Averages Identify Value
Daily chart of MW, 26-day and 13-day EMAs

A. Pullback to value in an up-   **B.** Price far above value—Sell!
  trend—Buy!   **C.** Price far below value—Buy!

The slow EMA (exponential moving average) rarely changes direction; its angle identifies the increase or the decrease of value. The faster EMA is more volatile. When prices dip into the zone between the two lines during an uptrend, they identify good buying opportunities. Prices are attached to values with a rubber band; you can see that prices almost always get only so far away from the EMA before they snap back. When a rubber band extends to the max, it warns you to expect a reversal of the latest move away from value.

to identify a bull market. It seems simple enough to buy and hold—until you realize that this trend, just like any other, is clear only in retrospect. If you had a long position, you'd be wondering every day, if not every hour, whether the uptrend was at an end. Trying to ride a trend is like trying to ride a high-strung horse that keeps trying to shake you off and at times rolls on the ground to get rid of you. Sitting tight requires a great deal of mental work!

Counter-trend trading has its own pluses and minuses. You can see how prices keep outrunning themselves time after time. They keep getting away from value, only to snap back to it. Buying below value and shorting when prices rise too far above value has a different attraction:

the trades tend to last only a few days. They require less patience and make you feel much more in control. On the minus side, the profit potential of each trade is smaller.

This is the choice you need to make: you can trade in the direction of a long-term moving average or you can bet on prices returning to their moving average after they become overextended. The first approach is called trend-following; the second, counter-trend trading.

In his brilliant book *Mechanical Trading Systems: Pairing Trader Psychology with Technical Analysis*, Richard Weissman draws a clear distinction between three types of traders: trend-followers, mean-reversal (counter-trend) traders, and day-traders. They have different temperaments, exploit different opportunities, and face different challenges.

Most of us fall into one of these trading styles without giving it much thought. Very few of us make a conscious business decision. For example, when I began to trade, many serious and intelligent people told me I had to be a trend-follower. I did it for many years, but my heart was not in it. After years of trying to be a trend trader, I came to realize that what I really wanted to do was counter-trend trading. I have been happier and much more profitable ever since. Many of my friends, on the other hand, only trade trends and would not touch a counter-trend trade. You have to figure out who you are, and trade accordingly.

DISCRETIONARY VS. SYSTEMATIC TRADING

This is another great divide in trading, and you need to know very clearly on which side of it you stand. Both are perfectly acceptable, but there is an abyss between them. You can bridge it, but please do not try to jump across while you are in a trade.

A discretionary trader looks at a chart, reads its signals, and places an order to buy or sell short. He monitors the chart and at some point realizes that the signals that prompted him to go long or short have disappeared or reversed. He decides to place an order to exit and completes his discretionary trade.

A systematic trader cannot tolerate this degree of uncertainty. He does not want to keep making decisions every step of the way. His solution is to study historical data, design a system that would have performed well in the past, fine-tune it, and turn it on. From now on he lets his system track the market and generate buy and sell signals.

Neither discretionary trading nor system trading will guarantee success. Beginners lose money with both, but in different ways. When a beginning discretionary trader shows me certain signals on his charts, he is likely to overlook other, just as strong or even more powerful signals that point in the opposite direction. A beginning systematic trader is very likely to fall into the sin of curve-fitting. He spends time polishing his backward-looking telescope until he has a system that would have worked perfectly in the past—if only the past repeated itself perfectly in the future, which it almost never does.

I am attracted to discretionary trading because of its freedom. I find it extremely attractive to approach the market like a blank slate, study broad indexes and industry groups, and decide whether to trade from the long or short side. It is a pleasure to establish entry and exit parameters, apply money management rules, determine the size of a trade, and finally place my order. There is a sense of responsibility and thrill in monitoring the trade and deciding to exit as planned, jump a little sooner, or hold a little longer. I am also attracted to counter-trend trading, but most methods described in this book can also be used by trend-followers.

Systematic traders try to capitalize on repeating patterns in the markets. The good ones know that while things repeat, they do not repeat perfectly. The most valuable quality of a good system is its robustness. A system is called robust when it continues to perform reasonably well even when market conditions change. There is a body of literature on system development, and a good starting point is Robert Pardo's *Design, Testing and Optimization of Trading Systems*. Shortly after writing it, Bob became a noted money manager by implementing his methods in the real world. Not too many authors can make that claim.

The decision to be a discretionary or a systematic trader is rarely based on cost-benefit analysis. Most of us decide on the basis of how we feel about choices in life in general. When I interviewed Fred Schutzman for my book *Entries & Exits*, he said:

> System trading works for us because it takes the emotion out of trading. I am not good at making live decisions. I am more of a researcher, a scientist. I can talk to the computer and it can do the trading for me.... if we can program concepts, I can continue as an analyst and the computer will trade unemotionally. I am doing

the analysis, and the computer trades off my inputs. It pulls the trigger if the conditions exist.... System trading is not for everyone—a lot of people do not like handing the power over to a computer. They want to retain responsibility for the decisions.

Paradoxically, at the top end of the performance scale there is a surprisingly high degree of convergence between discretionary and systematic trading. A top-notch systematic trader has to keep making what looks to me like discretionary decisions: when to activate System A, when to pull back System B for underperformance, when to add a new market to the list of those he trades, or when to drop a market from the list. At the same time, a discretionary trader like me has a number of firm rules that feel very systematic. For example, I will absolutely not enter a trade against the weekly Impulse system, described below, and you couldn't pay me to buy above the upper channel line or short below the lower channel line on the daily charts. The systematic and the discretionary approaches can be bridged—just do not try to do it in the middle of an open trade. Do not change your horses in the middle of the stream you're trying to cross.

ONE TRADER'S TOOLBOX[2]

When I put on my first trade ever, the worst possible thing happened. I made money. That lucky break created the delusion that trading was easy. I began jumping into other trades—with a predictable outcome.[3]

As I recovered and rebuilt my devastated account I knew I had to educate myself. I began to read voraciously about the markets. I looked up sources and references in every book I read, and then read those books as well. In those faraway, pre-Internet days I was fortunate to find a gentleman in Los Angeles by the name of Donald Mack who ran a business called The Investment Centre Bookstore. I must have become

---

[2]This section presents a brief version. For full details, please see *Come into My Trading Room*, John Wiley & Sons, Inc., 2002.

[3]I recently volunteered to teach a course "Money and Trading" in a local high school. One of the best things to happen in that class was that we lost a few dollars on our first trade. The kids got upset, but it made everyone more alert and served as a good start for the year.

his biggest customer. My fantasy was that if I read everything there was to read and learn about every method, I'd surely find a good money-maker.

Once again, the outcome was predictable, and it was back to my day job, working and saving to rebuild my tiny account. Even though I lost money, all that reading left me with something positive—a good overview of the field.

Over the years, as I continued to trade and study the markets, it became increasingly clear to me that in this field "less is more."

Whenever we look at a chart, we deal with only five pieces of data—each bar has an open, high, low, and closing prices, plus volume. If you trade futures, add open interest. It makes no sense to use a long list of tools and indicators to analyze these five numbers. An abundance of tools only increases the level of noise and adds to the confusion. I established a rule of "five bullets to a clip"—allowing me to use no more than five indicators on any given chart. You may use six if you desperately need an extra one, but never more than that. For myself, I do well with four: moving averages, envelopes, MACD, and Force Index.

This does not mean that you should use the same indicators. You should feel perfectly comfortable using others—just be sure to understand how your indicators are constructed, what they measure, and what signals they give. No one can master everything in the markets, just as no physician can master all of medicine. You need to choose a small handful of tools that feel comfortable to you.

Market newcomers often become fascinated by technical trading tools. They imagine that if they get the "right" software, the "right" indicators, and the "right" settings the profits will just roll in. Nothing could be further from the truth! While technical tools are important, they are responsible for only a small share of any trader's success. You also need to focus on trading psychology, money management, and record-keeping. Each of those factors is like a leg of a chair, and technical analysis is just one of them. A chair that has only one leg is useful only for firewood.

Beginners' childish faith in the power of technical analysis is often coupled with a great deal of laziness. Each week I receive e-mails from people who ask for "the exact settings" of moving averages, MACD, and other indicators. Some say that they want to save time by taking my numbers and skipping on research so that they could get right on to trading. Save the time on research, my elbow! If you do not do your

My Toolbox

My approach is based on the Triple Screen trading system which I developed in the 1980s and continue to improve to this day. Since every market can be analyzed in several timeframes, Triple Screen insists that you begin by defining your favorite timeframe in which you like to work, such as daily, hourly, or weekly chart. Once you know what your favorite is, do not look at it! You must first go to the timeframe one order of magnitude higher, make your strategic decision there, and return to your favorite timeframe only to make a tactical decision—where to buy or sell—and then trade only in the direction of the longer timeframe.

Since my favorite timeframe tends to be the daily, I use weekly charts to make my strategic decisions, and return to dailies to implement them. The weekly and daily charts are my first two screens. The third screen is the entry method, for which you can either use an intraday chart or simply place an order using a daily chart.

MOVING AVERAGES

Price is a consensus of value at the moment of a trade. A moving average (MA) reflects an average consensus of value in its time window. If price is a snapshot, a moving average is a composite photograph. It provides two important messages to traders. First, its slope identifies the direction of change in the public's mood. A rising moving average reflects growing optimism (bullish), while a falling MA reflects growing pessimism (bearish).

Another important role of the MA is differentiating between what I call "value trades" and "greater fool theory" trades. If you buy near the moving average, you're buying value. A person who buys well above the moving average is in effect saying—"I'm a fool, I'm overpaying, but I hope to meet a greater fool down the road." There are very few fools in the financial markets, and a person who keeps buying above value is not likely to win in the long run. He may get lucky once in a while, but buying near value is a much more sensible strategy. I like using two EMAs on my charts, one showing a longer-term, and another a shorter-term, consensus of value. I call the area between them "the value zone." There are several types of moving averages, but I always use exponential ones. EMAs are more sensitive to incoming prices and less sensitive to old prices.

ENVELOPES OR CHANNELS

One of the very few scientifically proven facts about the markets is that prices oscillate above and below value. You could say that markets are manic-depressive—rising too high and falling too low, only to swing back to the normalcy of the value zone.

There are several types of channels, and my favorite is a straight envelope—the lines above and below the EMA, both parallel to it. A well-drawn channel fits like a good shirt, covering the body of prices, with only the most extreme prices—the neck and the wrists—sticking out. Amateurs love to buy breakouts, but professionals tend to look for buying opportunities near the lower channel line and shorting opportunities near the upper channel line.

Some traders like to use standard deviation channels, often called Bollinger Bands, which expand and contract in response to market volatility. They are only useful for options traders because volatility is a key factor in option pricing. If you trade stocks, futures, or forex, you are better off with straight envelopes.

MACD LINES AND MACD-HISTOGRAM

Moving Average Convergence-Divergence (MACD) is an indicator whose fast line represents the short-term consensus of value, and the slow line the long-term consensus. When the fast line rises above the slow line, it shows that bulls are dominant, and when the fast line is below the slow line, the bears are in charge.

MACD-Histogram measures the power of bulls and bears by tracking the difference between the two MACD lines. When their spread increases, it shows that the dominant market group is becoming stronger—it is a good time to trade in that direction. Divergences between peaks and bottoms of MACD-Histogram and price are among the strongest signals in technical analysis.

MACD-Lines and MACD-Histogram are derived from three exponential moving averages of closing prices. Their settings—12, 26, and 9—have migrated into trading software and become default settings in many packages. In writing my books, I used those settings to illustrate this indicator.

What settings should you use? If you want to use the same ones as everyone else, use 12, 26, and 9 because the crowd is basically lazy and uses the default values. You can also choose settings that are a little faster or a little slower. Think about it and experiment with the values, or use the defaults.

FORCE INDEX

Everybody watches prices, but it is volume that moves them. Volume reflects the intensity of traders' commitment, the heat of their exuberance, the depth of their fear. Instead of looking at a plain plot of volume, I use

Force Index, which links volume with price changes. Divergences between Force Index and prices tell me when a trend is becoming weak and ready to reverse. By contrast, new highs of Force Index tell me that the trend is strong and likely to continue.

THE IMPULSE SYSTEM

This system identifies bullish and bearish phases in any market or timeframe by combining two indicators. The slope of the fast moving average identifies the inertia of the market, while the slope of MACD-Histogram identifies the push of the bulls or bears. The Impulse system gives a buy signal when both the EMA and MACD-Histogram rise, and a sell signal when both decline. When the two indicators get in gear, they mark especially bullish or bearish periods. Just as importantly, the Impulse shows when bulls or bears start slipping, and a trend starts growing weaker.

One of my Traders' Camps graduates, a brilliant programmer named John Bruns, programmed the Impulse system for several popular software packages, coloring each bar in accordance with the Impulse system. When the EMA and MACD-Histogram rise at the same time, the market is in gear to the upside and the bar turns green. When both fall, bears are in control and the bar is red. When the two indicators point in opposite directions the bar is blue.

The Impulse system	The slope of EMA	The slope of MACD-Histogram	The trading message
Green	Up	Up	Long or stand aside; no shorting
Red	Down	Down	Short or stand aside; no buying
Blue	Up	Down	Either long or short
Blue	Down	Up	Either long or short

The Impulse system works best as a censorship method. When the Impulse is green, you may buy or stand aside but absolutely no shorting is permitted. When the Impulse is red, you may go short or stand aside but buying is prohibited. I wait for the Impulse system to go "off green" before shorting and "off red" before buying.

Some programs do not allow users to change the color of their bars on the basis of conditional formatting, but you can still identify green or red Impulse by noticing the slope of the EMA and MACD-Histogram.

Adapted from *Entries & Exits* by Dr. Alexander Elder,
John Wiley & Sons, Inc., 2006

own research, you will not have the necessary confidence during the inevitable drawdown periods.

I believe that successful trading is based on three M's—Mind, Method, and Money. Your Method—the indicators and tools—is just one component of this equation. Equally important is the Mind—your trading psychology—and the Money, or risk control. Record-keeping ties all of these three M's together into a firm, working structure.

In a moment we will talk about the Mind, the Money, and the Record-Keeping. But before we move on, let us stay a little longer with the trading tools and review what I think is the best leading indicator of the stock market—the New High–New Low Index.

THE NEW HIGH–NEW LOW INDEX

Most traders pay attention to the key market indexes that are given to them ready-made, such as the Dow, the Nasdaq, and the S&P. There is one additional market indicator that is much more forward-looking. I believe that the New High–New Low Index (NH-NL) is the best leading indicator of the stock market. I look at it every day to confirm my bullish or bearish stance. NH-NL takes a bit more work to construct, although its formula is very simple.

$$\text{NH-NL} = (\text{New Highs}) \text{ minus } (\text{New Lows})$$

NH-NL is very easy to track by hand, since the raw data is published daily in all major newspapers. For example, yesterday there were 51 new highs in the market and 98 new lows, giving us NH-NL of minus 47. The day earlier we saw 43 new highs and 130 new lows, resulting in NH-NL of minus 87. Plotting these numbers on a day-to-day basis gives us three lines: New Highs, which I like to plot in green, New Lows, which I plot in red, and daily NH-NL which I plot in some neutral color.

Plotting the weekly NH-NL is a bit more tricky, as you have to decide when your week ends. I used to plot this indicator by adding daily numbers for the past week, but last year switched to plotting weekly NH-NL as a 5-day running total of daily NH-NL.[4] For example, as I write this on a Wednesday morning, my weekly NH-NL for the past night

---

[4]This change reminds me of a sentence with which I ended my first book: "I continue to learn, and like any trader, I reserve the right to be smarter tomorrow than I am today."

New High–New Low Index

A stock appears on the list of new highs when it is the strongest it has been in a year. This shows that a herd of eager bulls is chasing its shares. A stock appears on the list of new lows when it is the weakest it has been in a year. It shows that a crowd of aggressive bears is dumping its shares.

The New High–New Low Index tracks the strongest and the weakest stocks on the exchange and compares their numbers. It measures the balance of power between the leaders in strength and the leaders in weakness. This is why NH-NL is a leading indicator of the stock market. The broad indexes, such at the S&P500, tend to follow the trend of NH-NL.

You can visualize the stocks on the New York Stock Exchange as a regiment. If each stock is a soldier, then new highs and new lows are the officers. New highs are the officers who lead the attack up a hill, and the new lows are the officers who are deserting and running downhill. There are no bad soldiers, only bad officers, say military experts. The New High–New Low Index shows whether more officers lead the attack uphill or run downhill.

When NH-NL rises above its centerline, it shows that bullish leadership is stronger. When NH-NL falls below its centerline, it shows that bearish leadership is stronger. If the market rallies to a new high and NH-NL rises to a new peak, it shows that bullish leadership is growing and the uptrend is likely to continue. If the market rallies but NH-NL shrinks, it shows that the uptrend is in trouble. A regiment whose officers are deserting is likely to turn and run.

A new low in NH-NL shows that the downtrend is likely to persist. If officers are running faster than their men, the regiment is likely to be routed. If stocks fall but NH-NL turns up, it shows that the officers are no longer running. When officers regain their morale, the whole regiment is likely to rally.

From *Trading for a Living*, by Dr. Alexander Elder,
John Wiley & Sons, Inc., 1993

sums up the daily NH-NL for Monday and Tuesday of this week, as well as Wednesday, Thursday, and Friday of the previous week.

Surprisingly few software vendors supply the New High and New Low numbers, but even when they do, those numbers alone are not enough. They need to be processed in a manner described above to make them useful for analysts and traders. Some software vendors process their data in strange ways whose logic eludes me. Kerry Lovvorn, my co-manager of the Spike group, has spent a great deal of time and energy to develop a proprietary method of locating this data and transferring it into TradeStation. He sends out a nightly NH-NL update to all members of our Spike and Spike Spectator groups, and when he is busy I do it for him.

I like to track NH-NL for all listed stocks on the weekly and daily charts (see Figures 1.3, 1.4, and 1.5). The weekly NH-NL helps identify major tops and bottoms, while the daily chart is useful for shorter-term timing.

Another extremely important feature of this weekly chart is that its bearish divergences signal traders when to sell their long positions and

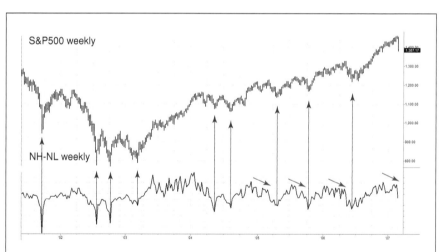

Figure 1.3   Weekly S&P500 and New High–New Low Index

Green arrows—downspikes. Red arrows—bearish divergences.

This chart tracks the behavior of weekly NH-NL during the 2003–2007 bull market. It has two striking features. The first is that every bottom of any importance is identified by a downspike of NH-NL. When NH-NL spikes several thousand below zero, it identifies the end of a bear market and the beginning of a new bull market. This chart shows only three such occurrences, but one can see more of them on a very long-term chart (not shown). In an ongoing bull market, a weekly downspike below −1,000 (minus one thousand) identifies the end of a downtrend and a great buying opportunity. The upspikes carry no such meaning.

go short. Notice that tops are broader than the bottoms and the signals to sell and go short are less precise than the buy signals near the bottoms.

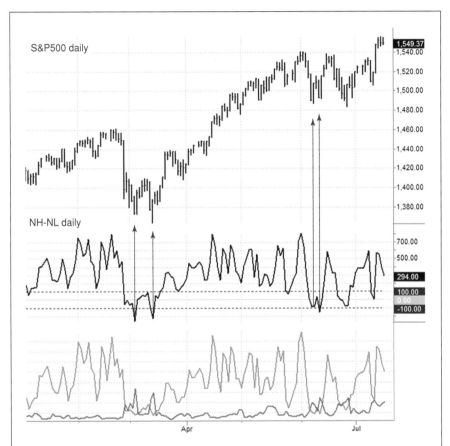

Figure 1.4 Daily S&P500 and New High–New Low Index

Red line—new highs. Green line—new lows. Blue—NH-NL.
Green arrows—downspikes.

This chart tracks the behavior of daily NH-NL in 2007. Whenever the daily NH-NL falls below zero, while the bull market is going on, it gives a buy signal. When it becomes negative it marks a brief imbalance in favor of the bears during an overall bull market. That is the time when many people become fearful and bearish, but NH-NL helps counteract their psychological pull. You can see that the daily chart of NH-NL provides excellent buy signals during a bull market but is not too useful for identifying market tops.

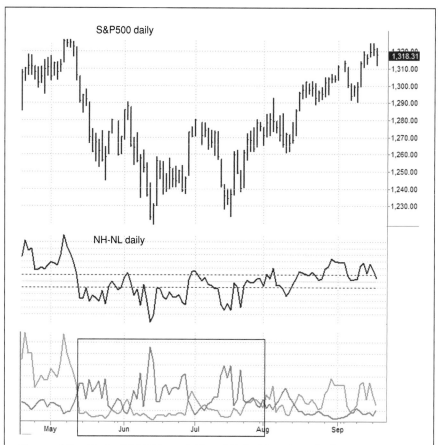

Figure 1.5   Daily S&P500 and New High–New Low Index

The box marks the summer 2006 bottom—new lows stayed above new highs for nearly three months.

The length of time NH-NL stays below zero provides an important indication of the durability of the uptrend to follow. Strong uptrends grow out of solid bottoms, when NH-NL stays negative for two or three months. If NH-NL spends only a few days below zero, it shows that the bottom is not too solid. Even if it leads to a rally, that rally, built on a poor foundation, is likely to end in a severe break.

Another message of these charts is that it pays to keep good notes—a visual diary of your trading and research. You must remember what has gone on before in order to profit in the future.

CHAPTER 2

TRADING PSYCHOLOGY AND RISK MANAGEMENT

What trading tools do you use? You probably have a computer, some software packages, and databases. You probably visit several trading-related websites and may have a shelf of trading-related books. If you think that these electronic and physical objects are all the tools that support your trading, you overlook a hugely important trading instrument.

YOUR MIND AS A TRADING TOOL[1]

Your mind is a much more important tool than any computer or book.

Your emotions, hopes, and fears have an immediate and lasting impact on how you trade. If your computer freezes while you're doing your homework or if your Internet connection goes dead in the midst of a busy trading day, you'd immediately recognize those events as severe obstacles to trading. Meanwhile, what goes on inside of your own head has a greater impact on the success or failure of your work than any technology.

Your mind is constantly at work, but it is humanly impossible to process all the signals that enter it from all directions. The input you receive through your eyes and ears is so immense that your mind must do a lot of automatic filtering to save itself from being flooded, overloaded, and shutting down. With a waterfall of sensations coming at you from life in general and from markets in particular, your mind must automatically sort out what to see and what to filter out. Most people

---

[1]This section presents a brief version. For full details, please see *Trading for a Living*, John Wiley & Sons, Inc., 1993.

are unaware of this filtering process. In fact, what you think are the objective signals from the markets tend to be highly filtered messages.

Once you become aware of this largely unconscious filtering process, you can see that most traders respond not so much to the markets but to the contents of their own heads. When people trade on the basis of their fears and fantasies instead of the reality of the markets, the results are likely to be poor. This explains why so many traders lose money and wash out of the markets.

To illustrate this unconscious filtering process, let us step away from the markets for a moment and take a look at what happens at the highest levels of the government.

The President of the United States has virtually unlimited sources of information—but there is no way one person can process everything available to him. He ends up depending on trusted assistants, such as cabinet ministers, to process the data in their area of expertise and give him their summaries. Those ministers, in turn, depend on their assistants in the narrower areas of expertise to process information and feed it to them. It is a logical system, designed to work well. It fails when the man at the top tells the men below what information he believes is correct. This influences them to serve up the information that confirms his preconceived notions.

For example, think of Iraq—instead of true information percolating up from the field, intelligence agencies were told to look for weapons of mass destruction. As it turned out much later, those did not exist, but overeager agencies produced enough flimsy "evidence" for the President to authorize the invasion. We are still dealing with the consequences of that highly flawed decision-making process.

What can we do as traders to avoid fabricating our own evidence? How can we avoid the trap of buying or selling because we "see" something that we want to see in the markets, when it is not actually there?

Much of this book is dedicated to the recognition of good trading signals. Before we proceed, I want you to recognize the hugely important fact that your mind is a part of the decision-making process. Your fears, wishes, and fantasies have a greater impact on your trading than all moving averages and trendlines combined. You have a great capacity for deluding yourself—but your success depends on seeing the truth.

If your mind is a trading instrument, we will need to set up a system for processing information. Your decision-making process must be transparent and unbiased. Then you will be able to learn from your experience and become a better trader going forward.

ON BEING DISCIPLINED

Whenever I run a Traders' Camp, there are campers who ask for help in acquiring discipline. I sometimes joke about tying people to the palm trees for physical discipline. Jokes aside, the question remains how to maintain discipline after one graduates from a Camp or finishes reading a book. Let us consider several essential points:

- **Some traders are destined to fail**
  The markets produce endless temptations. People with a history of poor impulse control are likely to get nothing but grief when they try to trade. Those who are actively drinking or using substances are highly unlikely to succeed as traders. They may have a few lucky trades, but their long-term forecast is grim. I have written about applying the principles of Alcoholics Anonymous to trading in my first book, *Trading for a Living*. If your drinking, eating, or some other behavior is out of control, you are better off not trading until you resolve your addiction problem. Obsessional nit-pickers or greedy people who cannot tolerate losing a dime are unlikely to do well in trading.

- **Keeping records: actions are more important than promises**
  It is easy to talk about discipline on a weekend, when the markets are closed, but let me see you in front of a live screen when the markets are open. All your promises and good intentions will not amount to a hill of beans—unless you act to implement them. This is why I keep repeating that good records are essential for successful trading. You must write down your trading plans and compare your performance with those notes. We are just about to discuss a simple system of record-keeping. Your ability to follow that system will be an excellent predictor of your success or failure. If you keep good trading records, you will be very likely to succeed. If you fail to keep good records, your chances of successful trading will be slim to none.

- **Solitude is essential**
  Many people feel stressed by the markets. They respond by huddling with others, following them, and aping what other people do.

To become a successful trader you must make your own decisions. You will need to insulate yourself from others while you make
your trading plans and implement them. This does not mean becoming a hermit—it is a good idea to network with other traders.
But you may not talk about your trading plans while you are making and implementing them. Stay alone with your trade, learn all
you can, make your own decisions, record your plans, and implement them in silence. You can discuss your trades with the
people you trust after those trades are closed—but not a moment
sooner. Many people fear solitude, but you need it for trading.

As my late grandfather used to say, "The road to Hell is paved with
good intentions." Even a responsible person can lose his bearings in
front of a live screen. It is not enough to promise to be good and disciplined. You need to write down a plan and follow it when you trade.
You need to complete a trading diary after each trade and record the
consequences of your actions. It is also important to remember that
if your discipline occasionally fails, it is not the end of the world, but
a reminder to return to the right track. If you slip up while trying to
stay on a diet, it does not mean that you can drop the plan and pig
out. Just correct your slip and return to the original plan.

ON BEING KIND TO YOURSELF

It may seem as if undisciplined traders are having fun, but that is usually a false appearance. Losers can be extremely harsh and shockingly
abusive towards themselves. They keep breaking the rules and hitting
themselves, breaking and hitting.

For example, a trader finds a stock that he likes and buys it. The
stock rallies, but a few days later it stalls and appears ready to reverse.
The novice sells at a profit—and feels good about it for about a day.
Then the uptrend resumes and the stock shoots up. Now the trader
feels a great pain because he is no longer onboard. Had he continued
to hold, his profit would have been so much larger. How does he react?
Probably by beating himself over the head!

Instead of congratulating himself for having correctly identified the
trend and taken some money out of it, he feels disappointed and angry.
In his next trade he probably will take greater risks and overstay the

trend. Afterwards, he will beat himself up for that and then probably get out from the next trade too soon.

This poor guy should be celebrating that he got two out of three right, instead of beating himself up. He was right on the market and right on the entry—but premature on his exit. With two correct decisions out of three resulting in a profit, he is well ahead of the majority of market participants. He should pat himself on the back and then create a good record of his trade, documenting his entry and exit. He should revisit his record in a month and then again in two months, updating his diary with fresh charts. He should celebrate his achievement and take full advantage of that trade as a learning experience.

Beating yourself up will not make you a better trader.

Think of another situation: a trader notices an attractive stock, studies it, and makes a mental note to continue to watch it and probably buy. Soon he loses track of that plan. As the joke goes, a "mental note" is not worth the paper on which it is written! A few weeks later he glances at the stock again and sees that it had a big run-up. His pick was right but his attention wavered.

What does the trader do? He kicks himself, as if that would do him any good.

A healthier approach would be to congratulate himself on his superior stock-picking skill. He deserves a pat on the back for finding that wonderful stock. He can probably find another one just as good, and the next time he will be more alert and not miss the signal to buy. He would benefit from fixing his deficient record-keeping. This trader needs a system for documenting his discoveries and keeping them in his view in an actionable form, something that we will discuss later in this book. The fact he found that stock is great—all he needs now is to catch up on the record-keeping.

You need to stop beating yourself up when your trades go awry. You have to celebrate your achievements and soberly take stock of your shortcomings. Keeping good records will help you identify and correct your mistakes, and allow your accomplishments to shine even brighter.

Beginners underestimate the importance of psychology. Your mind is an essential component of your success (or lack thereof). You would not throw your laptop on the floor if it froze on you and caused you to miss some quotes. In the same spirit, please do not hit your poor head when it misses something—treat it kindly and nicely, and it will serve you better!

While working on this chapter, I received an e-mail from Nils Gajowiy, a trader and a teacher of traders in Germany:

> At a seminar for beginning traders we spoke about the importance of a written trading plan and the negative impact of emotions on trading. Suddenly one of the participants asked: "Can you tell me anything positive about emotions? I keep hearing that they mislead us to take wrong decisions, to deviate from the trading plan, etc. But do they have any positive aspects?"
>
> I kept thinking that positive emotions are a strong motivator which increase our strength in many other areas. We have a saying in Germany, "When you are in love, you can move mountains." I looked through all my books and saw that nobody has ever written a word about the positive impact of emotions on trading. Do you have any suggestions about that topic?

I hope that my earlier comments on treating yourself kindly and celebrating even partial successes will help answer Nils' question. Let me list several additional points:

- **It is better not to trade when you are in foul mood.**
  Remember that even a good trader has only a very narrow edge in the market. Anything that reduces that edge will shift the balance of power against you. Feeling calm, relaxed, and in a pleasant mood is extremely important for your success. If you have a severe toothache or if a problem with a spouse or one of your kids has you very upset, you would be better off taking a break from the markets.

- **If you feel stressed or preoccupied, stand aside from the markets until your personal stress clears up.**
  The markets require you to think and act fast. You need to get into the flow of things and make quick intelligent decisions, without ruminating or worrying. The markets send out a torrent of information which you must process and act upon as swiftly as if riding a surfboard.

- **Successful traders love the game more than the profits.**
  On Sundays, with my weekend homework completed and plans for the next week drawn up, it is a pleasure to think of the next day's opening. A surfer probably has a similar feeling in the

evening, knowing he'll be going to the beach in the morning. This good feeling comes from being prepared. Even if the ocean becomes stormy and tosses my plans out of the water, it can only scrape me a bit but not hurt me!

When I began interviewing people for *Entries & Exits,* it came as a surprise to me how many men wanted to talk about their love for their wives. One after another talked with great feeling about the trust, support, and encouragement he felt at home. A person with a happy personal life has an advantage, while someone with a stormy personal life finds himself doubly stressed. A person who goes home to a smiling, loving spouse and does not need to spend an ounce of mental energy on figuring out the angles of a tense personal relationship is in a much better position when he or she sits in front of the computer to analyze charts and make decisions.

RISK CONTROL[2]

When the stakes of a game go up, spontaneity and ease go out the window. When the stakes become dangerously high, people become stiff with tension and their performance deteriorates.

The edge that the winners have over losers in the financial markets is very narrow. If you start putting on trades whose size makes you tense, your performance will decline, and you will begin losing. One of the key goals of money management is to put your mind at ease by providing a safety net for your account. Intelligent money management is a reflection of healthy trading psychology. It allows you to concentrate on trading instead of worrying about losses.

Imagine what would happen if you came to my office and I offered you twenty bucks to climb on a conference table, walk its length, and jump off at the far end. You would probably be surprised, laugh, and collect the money. That smile would quickly disappear if I raised my offer to $2,000 but challenged you to walk not on a table but on a sturdy plank as wide as that table, connecting the roofs of two office buildings. Even if the day was very calm and windless, your legs would

---

[2]This section presents a brief version. For full details, please see *Come into My Trading Room,* John Wiley & Sons, Inc., 2002.

probably tremble and you would feel extremely tense. Physically, the task would not change, but the new offer would greatly raise your risk. That fear would prevent you from accomplishing your task.

As a trader sinks into worry or fear, he becomes more stiff, less adaptable, and more prone to making bad decisions. When you start playing for stakes outside of your comfort zone, you will begin losing money.

Trading is like walking on a high wire. To feel at ease, to feel playful, adventurous, and ready to explore the nooks and crannies of trading, you need a safety net. If you happen to take a wrong step, stumble and fall, the net will catch you. You'll suffer no damage—just a minor scrape. Having a safety net will reduce danger and improve your trading performance.

One of the most common problems among traders is fear of pulling the trigger. I've heard enough people complain about it to devote an entire chapter in *Entries & Exits* about how to overcome it. In a nutshell, fear of pulling the trigger is the result of trading too large a size. If you had something like $20 riding on a trade, you would squeeze that trigger fast and hard, without hesitation. A trader afraid of pulling the trigger must take a break from trading and sharply reduce the size of his trades. He can build up that size only slowly and gradually.

The financial markets are infested with loud vendors whose vulgar advertisements imply that making money is easy if only you buy their merchandise. In fact, the market is a very dangerous place, where most traders lose money. An account that has lost half its value is as good as dead. You may fund a new account, but the old one is finished. Most accounts get demolished in one of two ways: by a shark bite or a piranha bite.

A shark bite is a single disastrous loss that mauls the account so badly that it has virtually no chance of recovery. A poor beginner who loses one-third of his equity would have to generate a 50% return on the remaining capital simply to come back to even. The victim of a shark attack almost always loses much more than money. He loses his confidence, becomes fearful, and cannot pull the trigger again. Whatever your trading method and style, you must do everything in your power to protect yourself from a shark bite.

Following the 2% Rule will keep any loss in your account to a relatively small, livable size.

A piranha is an aggressive fish that lives in the rivers of South America. Its main danger comes from the fact that it travels in packs.

A careless bull who stumbles into a piranha-infested river gets reduced to a collection of bones floating downstream. A smart bull would have fled after the first few bites.

The 6% Rule will define a series of losses after which you must exit the markets and wait on the shore.

The two pillars of money management are the 2% and 6% Rules.

Beginners are often fascinated by technical indicators. They tend to spend the bulk of their time looking at charts and trying to recognize patterns. Experienced traders know full well that psychology and money management are just as important. Professionals tend to spend almost as much time calculating money management angles as performing market analysis.

THE 2% SOLUTION—PROTECTION FROM SHARKS

The 2% Rule prohibits you from risking more than 2% of your account equity on any single trade.

When beginners first hear about this rule, many misunderstand it. They take it to mean that a person with a $100,000 account may buy only $2,000 worth of a stock. That is completely wrong! This Rule does not limit your position size—it only limits your risk.

Of course, if you are planning to hold your position down to zero, then its maximum size would have to be capped at $2,000. On the other hand, if you do a much more sensible thing and use a stop, your risk per share will decrease, and your permitted size will increase.

- The distance from your entry price to the stop level defines your maximum dollar risk per share.
- The 2% Rule defines your maximum risk for the entire position.
- Knowing the risk per share and the total permitted risk makes it easy to calculate the maximum number of shares you may trade.

For example, you may decide to buy a stock at $12.48 and put a stop at $10.98. This means you'll be risking $1.50 per share. Assuming you have $100,000 in your account, applying the 2% Rule tells you that the maximum permitted risk is $2,000. Dividing this total permitted risk of $2,000 by $1.50 risk per share means you may trade 1,333 shares. You should round this number down to 1,300 or even lower. Keep in mind that your commissions and slippage have to fit under the 2% total risk

The 2% Rule

The ability to find good trades does not guarantee success. No amount of research will do you any good unless you protect yourself from the sharks. I've seen traders make 20, 30, and (once) even 50 profitable trades in a row, and still end up losing money. When you're on a winning streak, it's easy to feel invincible. Then a disastrous loss wipes out all profits and tears into your equity. You need the shark repellent of good money management. The single most important rule is to limit your loss on any trade to a small fraction of your account.

Limit your loss on any trade to 2% of equity in your trading account.

Suppose you're trading a $50,000 account. You want to buy XYZ stock, currently trading at $20. Your profit target is $26, with a stop at $18. How many shares of XYZ are you allowed to buy? Two percent of $50,000 is $1,000—that is the maximum risk you may accept. Buying at $20 and putting a stop at $18 means you'll risk $2 per share. Divide the maximum acceptable risk by the risk per share to find how many shares you may buy. Dividing $1,000 by $2 gives you 500 shares. This is the maximum number, in theory. In practice, it has to be lower because you must pay commissions and be prepared to be hit by slippage, all of which must fit under the 2% limit. So, 400 rather than 500 shares are the upper limit for this trade.

Poor beginners often think 2% is too low. Professionals, on the other hand, often say 2% is too high and they try to risk less. Good traders tend to stay well below the 2% limit. Whenever amateurs and professionals are on opposite sides of an argument, you know which side to choose. Try to risk less than 2%—it is simply the maximum permitted level.

Adapted from *Come into My Trading Room*, by Dr. Alexander Elder,
John Wiley & Sons, Inc., 2002

limit. You may buy a smaller position if you wish, but never go above the 2% limit! We will return to this concept in the chapter on stops and the Iron Triangle.

Two years ago I volunteered to teach a class called "Money and Trading" at a high school near my office. To make the experience more real for the kids, I opened a $40,000 account which we traded in class. I told the kids that if by the end of the school year we lost money, I'd eat the loss. But if we made a profit, I'd donate half of it to their school and divide the other half among the members of the class. Then I laid down the law—the 1% Rule. Since we began trading with $40,000, I told the kids the maximum risk on any trade would be $400. For example, the kids got excited about Nokia and wanted to buy it at $18, with a stop at $16.75 (risking $1.25 per share). The 1% Rule told them we could trade a maximum of 300 shares. As our account grew, the permitted risk grew with it, but it could never exceed 1% of our current capital.

A trader with a larger account may vary the 2% Rule depending on his level of confidence in a trading idea. For example, he may define a small, medium, or large commitment as risking 0.5%, 1%, or 2% of his account. Then he may risk only 0.5% on an average trade, 1% on a more important trade, and reserve the 2% of risk only for the most promising trades.

THE 6% RULE—PROTECTION FROM PIRANHAS

As markets go through stages, rallies give way to declines or trading ranges. Your style of trading may be in tune with the current market stage or out of tune with it. This is why you need to protect yourself from the possibility of a series of losing trades damaging your account.

You may follow the 2% Rule, and even reduce it to 1%. Still, when losses begin to pile up, your account may begin to sink. The natural human tendency is to push harder when things go badly and put on more trades. In fact, a much better response is to step back and take some time off. The 6% Rule forces you to do just that, by capping the maximum monthly loss in your account.

The 6% Rule requires you to stop trading for the rest of the month after your cumulative loss for that month reaches 6% of your account equity.

Every good trade must begin with this money management question—does the 6% Rule allow me to trade? You know how much you have already lost during the month. You also know how much money you have exposed to the risk of loss in your open trades. Now add up the two and ask—do I have enough available risk left in my account to put on another trade?

If your losses for the current month plus your risk on existing trades expose you to a total risk of 6% of your account equity, you may not put on another trade. When I taught the high school class, risking 1% per trade, the 6% Rule meant we could never have more than six open

---

The 6% Rule

Most traders on a losing streak keep trying to trade their way out of a hole. Losers often think that a successful trade is just around the corner. They keep putting on more and bigger trades, digging themselves ever deeper holes. The sensible thing to do would be to reduce your trading size and then stop and review your system. A trader keeps sharks at bay with the 2% Rule, but still needs protection from the piranhas. The 6% Rule will save you from being nibbled to death.

Whenever the value your account dips 6% below its closing value at the end of last month, stop trading for the rest of this month.

Calculate your equity each day, including cash, cash equivalents, and current market value of all open positions in your account. Stop trading as soon as your equity dips 6% below where it stood on the last day of the previous month. Close all positions that may still be open and spend the rest of the month on the sidelines. Continue to monitor the markets, keep track of your favorite stocks and indicators, paper trade if you wish. Review your trading system.

You may have more than three positions at once if you risk less than 2% per trade. If you risk only 1% of your account equity, you may open 6 positions before maxing out at the 6% limit. The 6% Rule protects your equity, based on last month's closing value, not taking into account any additional profits you may have made this month.

Whenever you do well, and the value of your account rises by the end of the month, the 6% Rule will allow you to trade a bigger size the following month. If you do poorly and the size of your account shrinks, it will reduce your trading size the next month. The 6% Rule encourages you to increase your size when you're on a winning streak and stop trading early in a losing streak.

Adapted from *Come into My Trading Room*, by Dr. Alexander Elder,
John Wiley & Sons, Inc., 2002

---

positions at any given time. The class traded very carefully and never hit the 6% limit.

The 2% Rule and the 6% Rule provide guidelines for pyramiding—adding to winning positions. If the stock you bought rallies, you can move your stop above breakeven and then you may buy more of the same stock. You must handle each addition as a separate trade and make sure the risk of the new position is no more than 2% of your account equity and your total account risk stays under 6%.

Most traders go through emotional swings, becoming elated at the highs, gloomy at the lows, and losing money to sharks and piranhas across the board. If you want to be a successful trader, the 2% and the 6% Rules will convert your good intentions into the reality of safer trading.

ON KEEPING RECORDS

Whenever you put on a trade, you must have two goals. The first, of course, is to make money. The second is to become a better trader.

You can reach the first goal in some trades but not in every trade. There is a fair bit of randomness in the markets, and even the best planned trades can go awry. Even a top trader cannot win in every trade—this is a fact of life.

On the other hand, becoming a better trader is an essential and very reachable goal for every trade. Whether you win or lose, you must become a better trader at the conclusion of each trade. If you haven't, the trade has been wasted. All the energy and time you put into analysis, all the risks you took with your money—wasted. You must keep learning from your experience, otherwise you are just playing at being a trader and not being serious. The absence of records exposes a wannabe trader as a dreamer and an impostor.

GOOD RECORDS LEAD TO GOOD TRADING

The best way to learn from your experience is to keep good records.

Keeping good records allows you to transform fleeting experiences into solid memories. Your market analysis and your decisions to buy or sell become deposits in your data bank. You can draw on those memories, re-examine them, and use them to grow into a better trader. Writing your notes makes you focus and use your "extracranial memory." A human mind has a limited amount of memory that is instantly available (what the computer people call RAM).

The rules of money management we have just discussed will help you survive the inevitable rocky times. The record-keeping methods I am about to share with you will put your learning into a solid uptrend, and your performance will follow. Money management and record-keeping, taken together, create a rock-solid foundation for your survival and success. The rest—the analysis and the techniques—you can pick from this book, my other books, or those written by other serious authors.

Almost anyone can make an inspired trade, hit the market right, and watch profits roll in. No matter how inspired, a single trade or even a handful of trades will not make you a winner. You need to build a pattern of trades that on balance are successful over a long period of time.

The proof of a successful strategy is growing equity. Seeing your equity grow quarter after quarter and year after year is the true proof of trading prowess. Trading is a hard job. We tend to become a little arrogant and careless after a big win or a string of wins. That's when, feeling invincible, we start feeding our equity back into the markets.

Any trader, even the worst gambler and loser, will occasionally hit it right and score a profit. A single profit or even a handful of profits does not prove anything or matter in the long run. Even a monkey throwing darts at a stock page can occasionally pick a winner. Our most important challenge is to maintain a positive slope of our equity curve.

For that you need to keep good records.

You need two sets of records. All the numbers relating to your trades must go into a spreadsheet and the visual record of your trades must go into your diary.

TRADER'S SPREADSHEET—BASIC ACCOUNTABILITY

Whenever I talk with traders, it amazes me how few people maintain records of their trades in spreadsheets. Many rely on their brokers, but while your brokerage house is probably very accurate, its statements do not provide the necessary level of information. This is why I recommend using your own spreadsheet. My company, www.elder.com, offers the basic spreadsheet shown below at no charge, as a public service to traders. You can e-mail us at info@elder.com and ask for the template.

Basic spreadsheet literacy is highly desirable for traders. If beginners took 10% of the time they spend staring at indicators and invested that time in learning basic Excel, their payoff would be much greater. You do not need to become a spreadsheet expert, but a simple ability to manipulate numbers will give you a much greater degree of control over your trading (Figure 3.1).

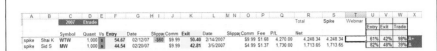

Figure 3.1 A Basic Record-Keeping Spreadsheet

A. Source, group. I always want to know where my picks come from—my own research, the Spike group, mentioned earlier, webinars, etc. Of course I process all input from others through my own system and accept full responsibility for every trade.

B. Source, individual. If the pick came from a group, such as Spike or a webinar, I want to record the name of the individual whose pick I traded. Some people have an excellent track record, while others, seemingly very smart, lead me to losses. I want to track the quality of the tips that come my way.[*]

C. Symbol. One could also add a column for the name of the stock.

D. Quantity. If I exit this position not at once but in two or more trades, I insert a row following this one and split my purchase between two or more rows, depending on the number of exits.

E. Long or short. I use Excel's Auto-Format to color a cell depending on whether it is a long (l) or short (s). Professionals are just as comfortable shorting as they are buying.

F. Entry price.

G. Entry date.

H. Entry order (leave blank if your entry was at the order price). If you did not use a limit order and/or were filled at a price different from your order level, put the price at which you placed your order here.

I. Entry slippage. Calculates dollars won or lost and colors the cells a shade of red or green depending on the result. Using limit orders occasionally leads to positive slippage.

J. Entry commission. If you insert a line later (see point D), remember to split the commission.

K. Exit price.

L. Exit date.

M. Exit order (similar to column H, above).

N. Exit slippage (similar to column I, above).

O. Exit commission.

P. Fee. Assessed on selling, so if you go short, fill in this cell after receiving a confirmation that you sold short; otherwise fill in after selling your long position.

Q. P/L. Gross profit or loss, before commissions and fees, but after slippage, if any.

R. Net. Net profit or loss after commissions and fees.

S. Net, Spike. So many of my trades come from the Spike group that I have a special column in my spreadsheet for them.

T. Net, webinars. Same idea as column S.

U, V, W, X. These four columns show performance grades on every trade; we will explore them in a later chapter.

[*]The Spike Spectator group and the webinars are open to the public—there is nothing secret about receiving such picks. For more information, see www.elder.com.

The previous figure shows the headings as well as a few lines from my own spreadsheet, with my own trades. The text explains the meaning of every column.

This basic spreadsheet takes just a minute to update after every trade. What you see above is a single tab. In my own spreadsheet I have a tab for every account and a summary tab where I record the value of every account on a weekly basis to track my equity curve.

If you would like a more high-end spreadsheet, I recommend *Trader's Governor,* programmed by my old friend James (Mike) McMahon. It calculates risk, evaluates trades, tracks capital, and much more. It is extremely powerful, but takes longer to learn than this simple spreadsheet.

TRADING DIARY—YOUR KEY TO LASTING SUCCESS

People who like to explore and learn always make mistakes. Curious and intelligent people inevitably make errors. Someone who never makes a mistake is a narrow-minded individual who stays in his shell, never does anything new and always repeats himself. Whenever I hire people, I tell them that I expect them to make mistakes—it is a part of their job description! I also tell them that what makes me really angry is when people repeat mistakes.

Making mistakes is a sign of learning and exploring. Repeating mistakes is a sign of laziness, carelessness, or some neurotic problems. There is a nice piece of advice in an old Russian saying: "Do not step on the same rake twice!"

The best way to learn from your trading mistakes and victories is by keeping a Trading Diary. It allows you to convert the joy of successes and the pain of losses into the bankable gold of experience.

A Trading Diary is a pictorial record of your trades (see Figure 3.2). It documents your entries and exits by using charts marked up with arrows, lines, and commentaries. I create a diary entry for every purchase or sale. To make sure my diary is always current and up to date I have a rule—no breakfast until my diary for the previous day is completed. This encourages me to update the diary before the market opens and a new trading day begins.

It is important to document every trade. The only exception to this rule is very active day-trading. If you make a dozen trades each day, you can allow yourself to create a diary entry for just every third or fourth trade.

Why a pictorial diary, in addition to the spreadsheet?

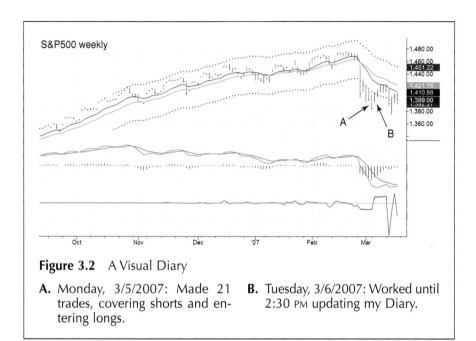

Figure 3.2 A Visual Diary

A. Monday, 3/5/2007: Made 21 trades, covering shorts and entering longs.

B. Tuesday, 3/6/2007: Worked until 2:30 PM updating my Diary.

You probably carry with you photos of people and things you care about. In your wallet, purse, or on your desktop you have photos of your wife, girlfriend, husband, children, dog, house, car. Now I also want you to carry the pictures of your trades, so that you get to know them intimately and understand them better than before. Creating and maintaining a Trading Diary is the best way to learn from your experience.

In February 2007 a variety of signals which we will discuss later in this book led me to become extremely bearish on the stock market. I went heavily short stocks and index futures, as well as long index puts. When the stock market collapsed, I was loaded with shorts. When my indicators signaled that a bottom was at hand, I spent hours taking profits, covering shorts. The next day, instead of going to the office, I worked from early morning until 2:30 PM documenting the trades I had just closed out. If I had to choose between my profit from catching that swing or having my Diary, I would choose the Diary! I can always make more profits if I continue to use my Diary, but without it profits can quickly turn to losses.

To maintain a Trading Diary, I suggest using two inexpensive and widely available programs. You can add them to whatever programs you already use for market analysis. One of them will help you capture and edit images, while the other will let you store and retrieve your diary records.

The best tool for taking pictures of your charts and making notes on them is a program called SnagIt. It makes it easy to capture images from any charting program, draw and write on them and paste them into your diary. Windows provides a PrintScreen utility for taking screen-shots, but nothing compares to the ease, versatility, and the sheer pleasure of using SnagIt (www.snagit.com). I use it almost daily for up-dating my Diary or sharing trading ideas with friends. Whenever we shoot each other an e-mail, we tend to send charts captured and marked up with SnagIt instead of writing long messages.

My program of choice for keeping a trading diary is Microsoft Out-look.[1] This is a fantastically powerful program, but most people scratch its surface by using it only for e-mail. I've come to believe that Outlook is the best program for keeping myself organized, focused, relaxed, and in control—and not only in the markets, but for life in general.[2]

The instructions for using SnagIt and Outlook are included with both programs. The following comments touch upon just a few features of these programs.

Go to the Calendars tab in Outlook, create a new Calendar, and name it Trading. You can view any Calendar in a daily, weekly, or monthly for-mat. I prefer a monthly format, which serves as a table of contents for all of my trades, both open and closed (see Figure 3.3). Lately, I have begun keeping two calendars—one for regular trades and another for long-term positions which stay open for months or even longer.

---

[1] I began keeping my first trading diary years ago in a large notebook. I used to print out black-and-white charts on a dot-matrix printer, cut them out and paste them into the notebook with double-stick tape, then mark up trading signals with colored pens. Years later I graduated to an electronic diary, creating a Word file for every trade. I found both diaries cumbersome to keep, and it was difficult to find something in Word when I wanted to look for an old trade. Finally, Kerry Lovvorn (www.kerrylovvorn.com), a camper who be-came my co-manager of the Spike group, showed me how to implement my diary using the power of Microsoft Outlook. It put me completely in control of my trading history. Later I met a number of traders who kept their diaries in a program called Lotus Notes.

[2] If you feel as if your work and paperwork are out of control, there are two books I highly recommend. In *Getting Things Done*, David Allen teaches a system for bringing simplicity and clarity into your life. In *Total Workday Control*, Michael Linenberger shows how to implement those principles in Outlook. I have read both books several times, took extensive notes, and implemented many of their recommendations. They had a strong positive impact on my life.

Trading					
Monday	Tuesday	Wednesday	Thursday	Friday	Sat/Sun
February 12	13	14	15	16	17
E-minis research	E-minis trade and rese:	E-minis research	E-minis research	E-minis research	
Sugar Long (Entry grac	Wheat long (Entry gra:	OEX put	Sugar sold (Mar 07) (E:	Sugar, add to longs (E:	
WTW short (Entry grac		STTS sold (Exit 64%, T			18
		Sugar long (Entry grad			
		Wheat long (Entry gra:			
19	20	21	22	23	24
holiday	E-minis research	E-minis research	E-minis rsearch	Cotton long (Entry 72%	
	MW short (Entry 82%)		ENR short (Entry 40%)	E-minis research	
			Wheat sold half 497.5		25
					CPST long-term
26	27	28	March 1	2	3
E-minis research	CPST long (Entry)	CHTR sell (Exit 77%)		OEX put sell (Exit 60%)	
ENR add to short twice	OEX put sell (partial) (:			S&P short (Entry 26%)	
MW add to short (Entr)				Sugar sold (Exit 80%,	4
5	6	7	8	9	10
AEOS cover (Exit 38%	OJ short (Entry 48%)	Cocoa cover (Exit 70%	Cotton sell (Exit 56%,	E-minis day	
CI short (Entry 28%)		Coffee add L (Entry 34	E-minis day		
Cocoa short (Entry 35!		DECK add S (Entry 63!	OJ add L (Entry 28%)		11
Coffee Long (Entry 13!		E-minis Day (24% of r:			
CPST add long (Entry 3		MT add S (Entry 35%)			
12	13	14	15	16	17
CI cover (Exit 94 % Tr	Cocoa S add (Entry 71	CPST L add (Entry 33%	E-minis day	E-minis day	
Cocoa short (Entry 28!	E-minis day (1 good 2 b	DECK cover (Exit 76%,		IKN sell (Exit 69%, tra:	
Coffee add (Entry 93%	IKN long (Entry 31%)	E-minis day			18
E-minis research		F L add (Entry 80%)			
HNT cover (Exit 20%,		MT cover (Exit 35%, T			

Figure 3.3   A Trading Diary in Outlook
See the description of the meanings of colors in Figure 3.4.

Together with two trader friends mentioned elsewhere in this book, Kerry Lovvorn and Jeff Parker, we have created an Outlook add-on for keeping a Diary which we named AK-47. Initially, the three of us built it for ourselves, but then we offered it to the public, and you can see its description on www.elder.com.

Whenever you click on a calendar to create a new record for a trade, Outlook allows you to label that entry. The labels show up in the monthly view, and if you set a system of rules for coloring labels, each of them will carry a message (see Figure 3.4).

Most of my Diary entries include two charts—a weekly and a daily. Depending on the trade, I may also add a monthly or intraday chart. Figures 3.5 and 3.6 show a recent example of a Diary entry.

Figure 3.4 Labeling the Entries in a Trading Diary

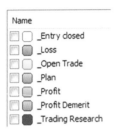

The calendar in Outlook gives you a list of colors—you can assign a name to each color, making your labels immediately recognizable. Here are the colors I've chosen, but you may well select different ones:

None. Entry into a trade that has been closed. Whenever I exit a trade, I do two things. I create a new diary entry, documenting that exit, but I also return to the record of my entry into that trade and change the label to "None."

Red. Exit that resulted in a loss.

Yellow. Open trade. When I first enter a trade, I set its label to yellow. Whenever I glance at my diary in Outlook, the yellow labels call attention to themselves, reminding me that these trades are open and I need to manage them.

Purple. Planned trade. Once implemented, I drag the icon into the box of the day on which I traded and change the label to yellow for an open trade.

Green. Profit.

Blue. Profit Demerit. I made money on this trade but less than I should have, or I violated my own rules.

Brown. Research (a paper trade).

A trader without a Diary is like a senile person. The poor man cannot learn anything: you can show him today how to zip his pants, but tomorrow he will forget again. Most losing traders are stuck, repeating the same mistakes over and over again. A Trading Diary helps you break out of that vicious circle. Maintaining and reviewing a Trading Diary will lift you to the level of a thinking and learning human being.

Now, before we move on to the next chapter, would you like to see my exit from that trade, shorting DB? We have already looked at my entry, but what if I told you I forgot how I exited? What if I waved my fingers in the air and told you that DB went down and I covered? How useful would that be to you?

Not very.

I hope that by now I have convinced you that it is essential to keep a Trading Diary. Will you promise to keep one? If so, I'll open

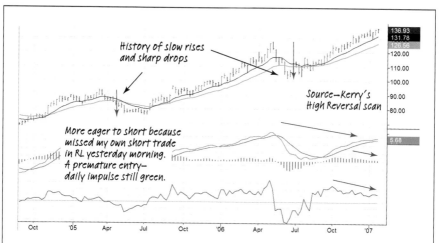

Figure 3.5 Trading Diary—DB, Entry, Weekly Chart

The weekly chart shows the source of a trading idea—an e-mail from a friend who ran several market scans and shared the results with me. Diagonal red arrows mark bearish divergences. Thin vertical arrows show that the stock is prone to sharp drops. There is also a remark chiding myself for being a little too eager to enter. I was very bearish on the stock market and restless after missing an entry into a trade that came from my own scan.

my Outlook again and bring up the exit diary. Take a look at Figures 3.7 and 3.8.

You can see that the exit is also graded. Its 45% rating was not that great, but the trade grade was very nice. Taking over $9 profit on 1,000 shares was a good payday. See the note—"keep an eye on it to maybe short again." The trade does not have to end when you exit a position. There is a lot to review, much to learn, and you can continue to make plans for the future. I hope that this exercise has helped convince you that it is important to keep a Trading Diary. You need to document your successes and failures and learn from both.

HOW TO DOCUMENT YOUR TRADING PLAN

I believe that the best format for creating a trading plan is similar to the Diary we have just reviewed. When you scan a large number of stocks, you can keep brief notes on the potentially interesting ones in a spreadsheet or on a notepad with three columns: Date, Ticker, and Comment. The idea is to narrow down your search to a few action-able stocks. Once you have a handful of candidates, it is time to work them up and create an action plan for each promising one.

When you find a stock that you think you may want to trade in the days ahead, create a plan for it using the same format as the Diary, shown above. Capture a weekly chart using SnagIt, mark its signals with arrows and lines and write on it. Paste the chart with all the markings into a newly created entry in your Calendar within Outlook. Now capture a daily chart, mark it up, and paste it into the same Out-look entry, below the weekly chart. Name that Calendar entry after the

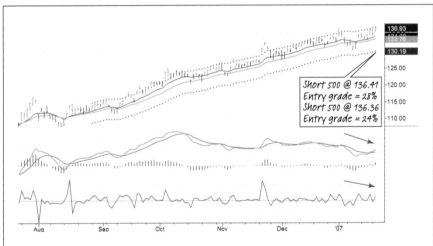

Figure 3.6   Trading Diary—DB, Entry, Daily Chart

The daily chart shows more bearish divergences and a false upside breakout (a hugely important trading signal we will discuss later). It documents my entry into the trade and grades the quality of my two sell orders on a 100-point scale. We will discuss grading buys and sells in a subsequent chapter. Having these charts in front of me today brings the experience of that trade back to life and allows me to learn from it. What did I do right? What did I do wrong? How could I have improved my entry into the trade?

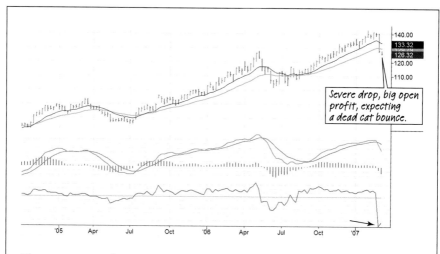

Figure 3.7 Trading Diary—DB, Exit, Weekly Chart

The weekly chart shows that the price dropped below the value zone, underneath both moving averages. A severe downspike of the Force Index marks a potential bottom. MACD-Histogram has declined close to the zone where upside reversals tend to occur.

stock and label it as a planned trade so that you can easily recognize it. Save and close your newly created entry.

Go to your brokerage house website and place an order or orders for your planned trades. Make sure your broker sends you an alert immediately after your order is filled. Once you know you are in a trade, it is a good idea to place your stop-loss and profit-taking orders using an OCO (one cancels other) order. The exact mechanics of placing orders are outside the scope of this book—this is something you need to discuss with your broker.

Once you have created a plan for trading a stock, add its ticker to your monitoring list in the quote window of the program you use for market analysis. The size of the computer screen limits the size of the quote window, which is actually a good thing. I want to monitor only as many stocks as can fit into a single screen, without dividing my attention between dozens of tickers. I like this window (Figure 3.9) to show the key market indexes, such as the S&P500, as well as separate

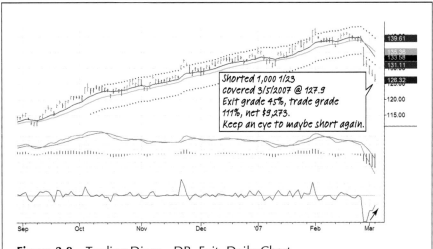

Figure 3.8　Trading Diary—DB, Exit, Daily Chart

The daily chart shows that prices are severely overextended to the downside, having fallen out of their channel. At the same time, there is a bullish notch in Force Index. The bears had a great ride, but all rides must come to an end. The odds of this one continuing are not that good.

sections for my long, short, and futures positions. I named the bottom section Monitor, and put there the stocks I am considering trading.

I also write down the key trading messages on my charts, especially the price and size of my entry as well as the target and stop. When the markets become active, it is easy to lose track of things. This is why writing on the chart is very helpful, as illustrated in Figure 3.10.

Once you execute your plan and enter a trade, move its Outlook Calendar entry from the day when you made the plan to the day when the trade took place. Update the chart and add an intraday chart if you like. Add a few relevant comments—the size of the trade, the entry grade (we will discuss that in a moment), any comments on the quality of your entry, or the feelings the trade evoked. Change the color of the label from purple (Planned Trade) to yellow (Open Trade), then click Save and Close. The entire process of changing a plan into an entry record should take just a few minutes.

Most beginning traders feel out of control and overwhelmed by the markets. This system for creating plans and monitoring trades is a tool that will help you control your trading. When your work becomes better organized, you will be in a much stronger position to take profits from the markets.

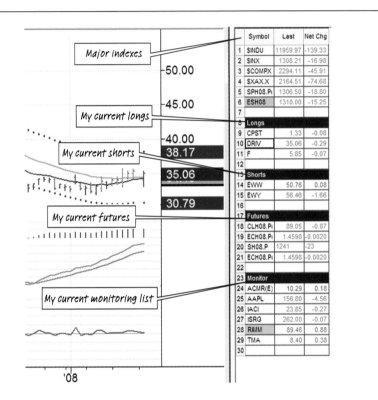

Figure 3.9 The Quote Window in My TradeStation

My quote window always tracks the latest prices and the net changes for the day.

This is the setup I want to see whenever I open my trading program. It shows all the important data at once: the key indexes, my long and short positions in stocks, my futures positions, and my monitoring list. The chart (truncated in this picture) is on the left, the list on the right. I have set up my TradeStation so that whenever I click a symbol in the quote window on the right, its chart automatically appears in the window on the left.

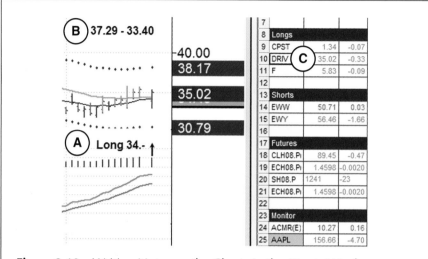

Figure 3.10 Writing Notes on the Charts in the Quote Window

A. Shows the purchase day and price
B. Reminds me about the target and stop
C. The trade in question

Even a faulty plan is better than no plan at all, as long as you record it. If you keep good records, you will be able to recognize any flaws in your method and fix them. Keep doing this long enough, and you may start running out of mistakes! That's when your equity curve will be ready to turn up.

MARGRET'S METHOD—PUT IT ON THE WALL

In addition to the fairly high-tech diary we just reviewed, I want to give you a low-tech method for keeping track of planned trades.

You may look at a chart and see a beautiful trade starting to come together—only it is not there just yet. You may notice a stock sinking on low volume towards its multiyear support zone. You may say to yourself, "If it comes down a bit more and this support holds, I will buy it." Sounds like a good plan, but what are the chances of you remembering it three weeks later, when the stock actually does what you expected? By that time you'll be looking at other stocks and dreaming of other trades, oblivious to the fact that your first pick is doing exactly what you expected it to do. You may notice it only many weeks later, when you accidentally glance at its chart and then it hits you—you missed another fantastic buy!

The best trades come together slowly. You notice them from far away and have to wait for more pieces of the puzzle to emerge before you can pull the trigger and place an order to buy or sell short. Meanwhile, you have to keep an eye on the developing trade.

Years ago I became very impressed by a low-tech system my good friend Margret used for keeping track of her trade ideas. Margret, who died last year, was a terrific trader. I invited her to be interviewed for my book *Entries & Exits,* but she declined. She was modest, even shy, kept a low profile, lived in the Caribbean, and did not want to draw attention to herself.

"My niece gave me $18,000 to trade for her," Margret said to me once, "and I turned it into $60,000. Now she thinks I may know what I am doing." "Your niece is right!" I said.

On one of my first visits to her tropical penthouse I noticed that her desk stood in a niche, the size of a small room, facing out into the hall. That niche had a few shelves with Margret's books and papers but also several large bulletin boards, with charts pinned to them. Margret explained that whenever she saw a trade starting to come together, she printed out the chart and marked it up with a red pen, showing what the stock had to do in order for her to buy it. Margret pinned those charts to the walls of her trading niche. Whenever she walked to her desk she saw the charts with her own hand-drawn action signals. There was no way this woman, who grew up poor, was going to let a good trade pass her by.

If you decide to implement Margret's method, be sure to take the charts down from the wall after you enter the trade or decide to pass it up. Make sure the visual records on your wall are fresh and up-to-date.

FRED'S METHOD—A CHIHUAHUA TRADE

I learned this method for implementing trading plans from an old friend who came to teach at one of our Traders' Camps. Fred Schutzman is a CTA (commodity trading advisor), and even though he came to teach, he also liked to sit in on my classes. One day I was showing a trade that was coming together, saying that I was going to place an alert with my electronic broker. I wanted to receive a message when that stock reached a certain predefined level.

"Why don't you place a small order there instead of an alert?" asked Fred.

It hit me that placing an order and receiving a fill had an entirely different emotional meaning than receiving an e-mail. One more e-mail in the midst of a busy day only added to that day's clutter. It would be a completely different matter to receive a fill for a few shares of stock. Suppose I was planning to trade a 1,000-share lot and placed an order for 10 shares at the trigger level. Once I owned those 10 shares, I'd have to re-analyze the charts and make a decision—to buy another 990 shares, bringing the trade to its full size, or to sell those 10 shares, taking a tiny loss because my view of that stock has changed.

There is a big difference between looking at a picture of a woman and hugging a real one. There is a difference between reading an e-mail about a potential trade and holding a real position, no matter how small.

I liked Fred's suggestion very much and implemented it immediately. Years later I came up with a name for this method—a Chihuahua trade. A Chihuahua is a tiny dog, so small you can put it into your pocket, but it is a real dog nonetheless. I met a woman in the Dominican Republic who kept a pack of big dogs for security at her estate. The big dogs slept much of the day, but she also had a few Chihuahuas who were always alert. Whenever they heard someone approaching the fence, they began barking, and then the big dogs would wake up and rush in to investigate.

This is why when I am away from the screen and need to place an alert for some future trade, I prefer to place a Chihuahua-sized order. Recently a friend gave me a present—a photo of a Chihuahua at the feet of a Great Dane. I have the picture on my bookshelf and continue to use trigger orders instead of sterile alerts.

HOW TO GRADE YOUR PERFORMANCE

A person who trades without measuring and grading his performance is like someone who calls himself a competitive runner but does not own a stopwatch. Only a recreational runner can jog around the block without a stopwatch, to get some exercise and enjoy the scenery. A person who claims to be a competitive runner but has no stopwatch and keeps no records is a joker.

How to Grade Your Performance

Imagine two friends taking a college course. Both have similar abilities and backgrounds, but one takes a test each week, while the other waits for the final. All other factors being equal, which of them is likely to get a higher grade on the exam? The one who waited or the one who took weekly tests?

Most educational systems test students at regular intervals. Testing prompts people to fill the gaps in their knowledge. Students who take tests throughout the year tend to do better on their finals. Frequent tests help improve performance.

The markets keep testing us, only most traders don't bother to look up their grades. They gloat over profits or trash confirmation slips for losing trades. Neither bragging nor beating yourself up makes you a better trader.

The market grades every trade and posts results on a wall, only most traders have no clue where to look. Some count money, but that's a very crude measure, which does not compare performance in different markets at different prices. You may take more money from a sloppy trade in a big expensive market than from an elegant entry and exit in a difficult narrow market. Which of them reveals a higher level of skill? Money is important but it doesn't always provide the best measure of success.

From *Come into My Trading Room*, by Dr. Alexander Elder,
John Wiley & Sons, Inc., 2002

There is no "recreational trading" in the markets. There is competitive trading and there is losing, and not much else in between. If you are serious about winning—and if you aren't you shouldn't be in the markets—you must get yourself a stopwatch before you run another lap.

There are many ways to measure performance. I suggest grading your trades on three scales: your buy grade, your sell grade, and—most importantly—the overall trade grade.

HOW TO GRADE YOUR ENTRIES AND EXITS

The two most basic ratings for every trade are the buy and sell grades, which measure the quality of your buying and selling. Tracking them will help you increase your level of competence in entering or exiting trades, whatever their outcome.

You can measure the quality of your buying and selling by comparing your transaction price to that day's range. When you buy, you want to trade as close to the low of the day as possible. When you sell, you want to trade as close to the high of the day as possible.

$$\text{The Buy Grade} = \frac{\text{the high of the day minus buy price}}{\text{the high of the day minus the low of the day}}$$

The result is expressed as a percentage: if you buy at the low of the day, your grade is 100%, and if you buy the top tick, your grade is 0. Grades below 25% are poor, above 75% superb, and between 25% and 75% satisfactory.

$$\text{The Sell Grade} = \frac{\text{the sell price minus the low of the day}}{\text{the high of the day minus the low of the day}}$$

The result is expressed as a percentage: if you sell at the top tick of the day, your grade is 100%, and if you sell at the bottom tick your grade is 0. Here too, you want to score above 75% for an excellent grade, while anything less than 25% is poor.

Whenever I trade, my goal is to score above 50% on my entries and exits. This means buying below the midpoint of the day and selling above the midpoint.[1] A non-trading market analyst said to me once that a person who placed his trades at random would average 50% of the day's range. Far from it! An entire industry of professional traders makes a living from buying low and selling high. When the insiders and the professionals take the lowest buys and the highest sells, the public is left to buy high and sell low. Grading your entries and exits makes you focus on your executions, and that leads to a better performance over time.

If you now return to Figure 3.1, you will understand the meaning of columns U and V. They grade the quality of my entries into and exits from the trades shown in that spreadsheet. Just keep in mind that in

---

[1]Trading tends to attract smart people, but occasionally one runs into exceptions. I recently presented this grading system at an institutional conference where a young man raised his hand and asked whether I decided on my entry point during the day or after the close. After regaining my breath, I answered that I am still looking for a broker who would accept my orders to trade at the prices of the previous day.

long trades the entry is a buy and the exit a sell, while in short trades the sequence is reversed—first a sell, then a buy.

It may seem like an easy task—to buy in the bottom half of a bar and sell in the upper half—but it is surprisingly hard to accomplish. Psychologically, it is easy to buy high and sell low. Keeping a score of your entries and exits and following their trends to measure your progress makes you a sharper, more demanding, and more successful trader. Knowing that at the end of the day you will have to grade your trade helps restrain you from chasing intraday rallies or selling into intraday declines.

HOW TO GRADE YOUR TRADES

The goal of trading is to make money, but can you use money to measure the quality of every single trade? I believe that the amount of profit or loss provides only a very crude measurement of a trade's quality.

The amount of money in your account at the end of a month or a quarter is extremely important for plotting the equity curve. That curve provides an accurate measure of your performance as trader. Money does not provide a good measure of any individual trade because the amount you make or lose in a single trade heavily depends on the trade's size as well as the market's current volatility.

The best way to rate your performance in any single trade is to measure the number of points gained or lost against the market's recent volatility. What has been the normal swing of that market in recent months? What percentage of that swing did you catch in the latest trade? Answering these questions will provide a good measure of your performance in that trade.

What yardstick should we use to rate a trade's quality? A well-drawn channel on the daily chart serves as an excellent reflection of that market's recent volatility. Our trade grade will show what percentage of the channel we have managed to capture.

For swing trades, I use a channel around the longer moving average on the daily chart. For day-trades, I use a channel on a 5-minute chart, also centered around the longer moving average.

One of the few scientifically proven facts about the financial markets is that they fluctuate above and below value. As a psychiatrist, I can say that the market is manic-depressive. When it becomes manic, prices rise above the upper channel line. When it becomes depressed, prices fall below the lower channel line. While prices keep swinging

---

Channels

A moving average reflects the average consensus of value, but what is the meaning of a channel?

The upper channel line reflects the power of bulls to push prices above the moving average—the average consensus of value. It marks the normal limit of market optimism. The lower channel line reflects the power of bears to push prices below the average consensus of value. It marks the normal limit of market pessimism. A well-drawn channel helps diagnose mania and depression.

Most software programs draw channels according to this formula:

Upper Channel Line = EMA + EMA × Channel Coefficient
Lower Channel Line = EMA − EMA × Channel Coefficient

A well-drawn channel contains the bulk of prices, with only a few extremes poking out. Adjust the coefficient until the channel contains approximately 95 percent of all prices for the past several months. Mathematicians call this the second standard deviation channel. Most software packages make drawing them very easy.

Find proper Channel Coefficients for any market by trial and error. Keep adjusting them until the channel holds approximately 95% of all data, with only the highest tops and the lowest bottoms sticking out. Drawing a channel is like trying on a shirt. Choose the size in which the entire body fits comfortably, with only the wrists and the neck poking out.

Adapted from *Come into My Trading Room,* by Dr. Alexander Elder, John Wiley & Sons, Inc., 2002

---

between mania and depression, I rate the quality of each trade by the percentage of the channel it captured.

$$\text{The Trade Grade} = \frac{\text{exit price minus entry price}}{\text{the upper channel line minus the lower channel line}}$$

I measure the channel height—the upper line minus the lower line—on the day of the entry into a trade. If you look at Figure 3.1, you will see that column W tracks the percentage of a channel captured in every trade. This is the most important ranking for every trade. Even if you score 100% on your entry and exit but get a low single-digit or even negative number for your trade grade, the trade is a failure. Not a total failure, of course—as long as you keep good records, you are learning from losing as well as from winning trades.

And what about column X in Figure 3.1? Here I fall back on the old school system and call every trade that captures 30% or more of the channel an A trade. Sometimes there are even A+ trades. Any trade that captures 20% to 30% of a channel gets rated B; 10% to 20%, C; below 10%, a C–; and below zero it becomes a D trade. If you now return to Figure 3.3, showing my Outlook Calendar, you will understand why the labels for some winning trades are colored green (Profit) and others blue (Profit Demerit). It is not enough to make profits—it is just as important to earn a good performance grade.

Grading every entry and exit as well as every trade will lead you to adopt a demanding and tough-minded attitude towards your work. As a private trader, you have no manager. To win, you must become your own manager, and that's what trade ratings help you accomplish.

If you like the rating system I've shown you, you can expand it even further. For example, you may want to add a column to your spreadsheet measuring the cost of your trades—the total cost of commissions, fees, and slippage divided by the gross profit from that trade.

TWO TYPES OF BUYING

I once heard a phrase that stayed with me for years—a man who owned a flower shop said that he had to "buy well to sell well." Flowers have to be sold quickly, before they wilt. Buying at a low price gives the shop owner more pricing power. If business becomes slow, he can drop his selling price and still be profitable. Buying well—getting a low price—helps him sell well.

As we near the end of our brief discussion of buying, we need to discuss its two main types. One is value buying: "buy low, sell high." The other is momentum buying: "buy high, sell even higher."

A value buyer tries to identify value and buy near or below it. He wants to sell when prices become overvalued. To help define value I put two moving averages on a chart and call the space between them the value zone (see Figure 3.11). To help define overvalued and undervalued zones I add channels to my daily and intraday charts. The space above the upper channel line identifies the area of mania, and the space below the lower line the zone of depression.

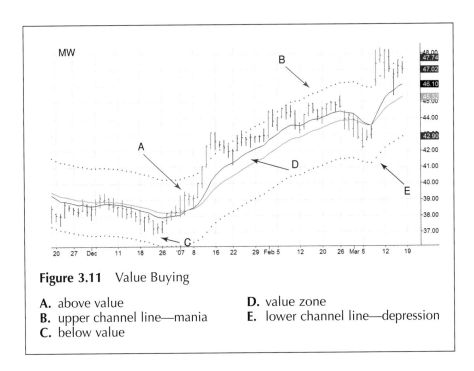

Figure 3.11   Value Buying

A. above value   **D.** value zone
B. upper channel line—mania   **E.** lower channel line—depression
C. below value

In trading, we do not have the luxury of shooting at a standing target—the target keeps moving. Prices move very fast, but the value zone moves at a much slower rate. The concept of a value zone gives a trader a target that moves a little slower than prices.

We will discuss the tactics of selling using the concept of value in a later chapter, but even a quick look at Figure 3.11 will show that the concept of buying at or below value and selling in the overvalued zone makes logical sense.

Momentum trading calls for a completely different approach to buying and selling. The chart in Figure 3.12 shows how a stock, after spending several months in a narrow trading range, broke above its resistance line and accelerated to the upside. Several weeks later, after a half-hearted pullback that did not even reach its former resistance line, the stock accelerated and went up at an even sharper angle than before.

Here, the time to buy was whenever the stock showed renewed strength by taking out the previous day's high. But where would you

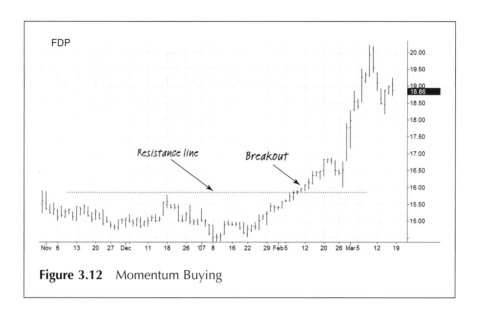

Figure 3.12   Momentum Buying

sell? In retrospect, that point would have come during the false break-out above $20—but this became clearly visible only several days later. How would you decide when to sell at the right edge? Our next chapter is dedicated to the questions of selling.

The two charts we have just reviewed show that the way we sell will depend on why and how we buy. Are you primarily a value trader or a momentum trader? And how do you make this decision?

This tends to be one of many instances where people make market decisions on the basis of emotions rather than hard facts. We make some of the most important decisions in life this way, and it is not necessarily a bad thing. Some of us are temperamentally drawn to buying low and selling high, suspicious of runaway trends. Others scan the markets, looking for runaway trends, jumping aboard and trying to hop off before a significant reversal.

Only you can decide whether to be a value or a momentum trader. I cannot make this choice for you. Whatever you decide, please keep in mind that having a written plan for buying and selling will put you miles ahead of your competitors. Whatever your method, a person with a plan has a clear advantage in trading.

Remember, your mind is a trading instrument. When it gets clouded in the heat of action, as it often does, the quality of your decisions will deteriorate. Having a written plan will keep you rooted in the cooler, calmer times before the trade, when you were in a much better position to make decisions.

When you come to the market to sell, knowing whether you are a value or a momentum trader and having a written exit plan will give you a terrific advantage over the masses of impulsive traders.

Remember—buy well to sell well!

PART TWO

How to Sell

We have discussed how to buy, manage risk, and keep records. It will take a lot of work to implement these lessons—but this is exactly the kind of work that will put you ahead of the market crowd!

Now is the time to move on to selling.

If every trade is a journey, you are better off traveling with a map. It will help you find your way to the target or return to the starting point and close out your position. A map does not guarantee success, but it will help you recognize when you get off track and must go back. A trader without a map is more likely to meander and waste energy and capital.

Putting a plan on paper has a powerful psychological effect on most people. It reduces stress and increases profitability. We make our best decisions when we feel relaxed. Writing down a plan and executing it from a sheet of paper helps you reduce tension by separating the two jobs you have: analyzing and trading.

Give your "analyst" the luxury of peace and quiet, as he thinks and writes down his plan. Give your "trader" the luxury of simplicity in the midst of action—give him a map and let him run with it, focusing only on implementing decisions. Keep the two jobs separate. Let the analyst think. Let the trader execute. Let them work as a team instead of stepping on each other's toes in some crazy dance.

The Psychotic Mr. Market

Warren Buffett, one of the most successful investors in America, is fond of saying that when you buy a stock you become the partner of a manic-depressive fellow he calls Mr. Market. Each day Mr. Market runs up to you and offers to either buy you out or sell you his share. Most of the time you should ignore the man because he is psychotic. Occasionally Mr. Market becomes so terribly depressed that he offers to sell you his share for a pittance—and that's when you should buy. At other times he becomes so manic that he offers a crazy price for your share—and that's when you should sell.

Buffett's idea is brilliant in its simplicity, but hard to implement. Mr. Market sweeps most people off their feet because his mood is so contagious. They want to sell when Mr. Market is depressed and buy when he is manic.

We need to keep our sanity. We need objective criteria to decide how high is too high and how low is too low. Buffett makes his decisions on the basis of fundamental analysis and a fantastic gut feel. Traders can use technical analysis.

Adapted from *Come into My Trading Room*, by Dr. Alexander Elder, John Wiley & Sons, Inc., 2002

You can view this section of the book as a menu for sellers. You may choose just one item that appeals to you and make a good living from it. Or you may choose several approaches to selling and combine them.

Some of the menu choices are more appropriate to different market conditions. Some methods will be easy to combine—such as using both a profit target and a stop-loss order. Other tactics cannot be readily combined—you can sell at a nearby channel line or at a faraway resistance zone, but not at both. Just as in the kitchen, some items on the menu will go well together, while others will not. This is why you need to be clear in your mind as to what method you'll use for selling. It will pay to write down your plan.

You also need to be clear about your timeframe for selling. Are you putting on a position trade whose duration will be measured in months, a swing trade that will last a few days, or merely a day-trade?

If this is a day-trade, you've got to have your finger on the trigger as you sit in front of the live screen. One of the worst mistakes of chronic losers is to a convert a day-trade gone bad into a long-term position. On the other hand, watching a live screen is usually counter-productive for a position trade. A trader who watches a live screen almost always loses his position by getting out too early on some minor signal, and misses the big trend he was aiming to catch. Clarity is a virtue in trading.

THE THREE TYPES OF SELLING

Whenever you plan to buy a stock, ask yourself whether you plan to own it for the rest of your life and leave it to your heirs. Since the most likely answer is "no," the next question must be: *What will prompt you to sell this stock?*

Obviously, you buy because you expect the stock to rise. How high does it need to fly for you to say "Enough!" and sell it? Do you have a specific price target or a range of targets where you will seriously consider selling? Is there a price or indicator pattern that will tell you the uptrend is at its end and it is time to take profits? Needless to say, the best time to answer such questions is before you enter a trade.

What if you are wrong about the rally, and the stock slides instead of rises? How low does it have to fall for you to pull the trigger and shoot the puppy? The worst time to make such decisions is when you own the falling stock. As it keeps sliding lower and lower, there will be signs of the stock being oversold, of the decline being at its end and about to reverse. If you are unwilling to take a loss, you can delude yourself for a long time and suffer serious damage. The best time to make a decision on when to get rid of a stock is before you buy it.

Finally, you may decide to sell if a stock does not move within a specified period of time or if it traces a suspicious price or indicator pattern. What does this stock have to do to challenge your bullish outlook? I call this type of selling "acting in response to engine noise." As you become more experienced, your ears will become more attuned to such noises.

In summary, you can divide selling choices into three main categories:

1. Sell at a profit target above the market.
2. Be prepared to sell below the market, using a protective stop.
3. Sell before the stock hits a target or a stop—because market conditions have changed and you no longer want to hold it.

Let us now review these choices one at a time. Remember, trading is a huge field, and no one can master every method. It pays to be aware of many methods. You will need to select what appeals to you and train yourself to become good at it.

CHAPTER 4

SELLING AT A TARGET

Y ou buy a stock when you expect it to rise. If you thought you
could get it cheaper, you would have waited to buy it at a lower
price later.

Once you select a buy candidate, you need to ask several questions:

1. What do you think the profit target is—how high is this stock
   likely to rise?

2. How low does it need to fall to convince you that your decision
   to buy was incorrect and the time has come to cut losses?

3. What is this stock's reward-to-risk ratio, meaning what is the relationship between its potential reward and risk?

Professional traders always ask these three questions. Gamblers do
not bother with a single one.

Let us begin by tackling the first question: What is the stock's profit
target?

A good way to set a target for a swing trade is to use either a moving average or a channel. A good way to estimate a profit target for a
long-term trade is to look at long-term support and resistance.

Putting on a trade is like jumping into a fast-moving river. You can
walk up and down the shore, looking for a spot to jump in. Some people spend a lifetime on the shore, paper-trading their way through life.
You are safe on the shore: your skin is dry and your cash is earning
interest in a money market account. One of the very few things in trading you can totally control is the moment you decide to jump in. Do
not allow restlessness or anxiety to push you in sooner than you need
to, before you find a good spot.

While you are on the shore looking for a place to jump in, there is another important area to scout. You must look downstream, where the current rips over boulders, creating rapids. You need to scan the distant shore for what may be a good place to get out of the water. You must set up a profit target for your trade.

Decades ago, when I first began to trade, I had the misguided notion that I was going to get into a trade and get out when "the time was right." I was afraid to set a profit target because that would reduce my potential profit. An amateur who gets into a trade with no clear idea of a profit target is pretty certain to become confused and lose his bearings. Not surprisingly, there was very little profit for me in those days, but no shortage of losses.

Kerry Lovvorn hit the nail on the head when he said during his interview for *Entries & Exits*: "People want to make money but do not know what they want from the markets. If I am making a trade, what am I expecting of it? You take a job—you know what your wages and benefits are going to be, what you're going to be paid for that job. Having a profit target works better for me, although sometimes it leads to selling too soon."

In this chapter I will show you several trades from my diary, including an entry, an exit, and a follow-up. Since this is a chapter about selling, I will focus on the exits from long trades, while covering the entries just enough to provide a general idea of the reasons for a trade.

Before we begin, let me comment on the follow-up charts in this book. Some of them may look impressive, with my exit nailing the top, but often you'll see that more money was left on the table than taken from it.

Beginners who look at charts are often mesmerized by powerful trends. Experienced traders know that big trends look clear only in retrospect. All trades are perfectly visible in the rearview mirror, but the future is vague, changeable, and unclear. Putting on a trade is like riding a wild bronco at a rodeo. As you shoot out of the gate, you know that if you can stay on horseback for 50 seconds you'll be considered a very good rider and earn a prize. The time to ride a long distance will come later and on a different horse. We will discuss selling long-term positions later in this chapter.

As you look at these trades, most of which come from my personal trading diary, please pay attention to several features. Notice that I grade every trade in three ways—for the quality of my entry and exit and, most importantly, for the overall quality of the trade. I always write down my source for the trade idea. It can be my own homework, a Spike pick, or something from a webinar. I have cells in my record-keeping spreadsheet that trace a total P&L for every source of ideas, for obvious reasons. I want to know who to listen to in the future and who to ignore.

Now we are ready to begin setting profit targets. Let us discuss the tools available to us. My favorites are:

1. Moving averages
2. Envelopes or channels
3. Support and resistance zones
4. Other methods

SELLING AT A MOVING AVERAGE

Robert Rhea, a prominent market technician during the first half of the twentieth century, described the three stages of a bull market. During the first stage, prices recover from the oversold excesses of the preceding bear market—they rise from deeply undervalued levels back to value. During the second stage, rising prices reflect improving fundamentals. Finally, during the third and final stage, prices rally on enthusiasm, optimism, and greed—people buy "because prices have always gone up." Rhea, who had done a great deal to popularize the Dow Theory, was writing about bull markets that lasted several years. I found that I could apply his concept to shorter timeframes.

We have already discussed how moving averages reflect a longer-term consensus of value. When prices crash below a moving average and drag it down, a bear move is in progress. When prices stop declining and the moving average flattens out we need to become alert to the possibility that the bear may be dead.

The markets run on a two-party system. When the bear party loses power, we can anticipate that the next election will go to the bulls. The first target for a bullish move would be a rally back to value, up to the moving average.

This approach to buying below value and setting the profit target in the value zone works especially well with the weekly charts. The Triple Screen trading system (see "My Toolbox" on pages 15–17) calls for making strategic decisions on the weekly charts and implementing them on the dailies, where you can make tactical choices on buying and selling.

I recently received an e-mail from a trader friend about a stock he has been trading. Kerry pointed out that the stock had recently broken below its multiyear low and had stabilized. Whenever I look at a stock I haven't seen in a while, I pull up its weekly chart (Figure 4.1) and compress it so that the entire history fits into a single screen. I want to see at a glance whether the stock is cheap or expensive, relative to its own history. EXTR, with a high above $120 and a low near $3, was trading below $3.50, giving an absolutely clear answer to this question.

Next, I open up the stock's weekly chart and review its history over the last two or three years (see Figure 4.2). This format allows me to identify long-term price and indicator patterns. Here you can see that the stock's price has recently broken below long-term support at $4.05. The decline had stalled and the trend had changed from down to sideways. Both MACD-Histogram and Force Index are trending higher—a bullish sign. I decided that a rally was likely to occur and carry prices into the value zone on the weekly chart. That zone was between $3.67 and $3.96, between the two moving averages.

At the right edge of the daily chart (see Figure 4.3), EXTR shows a false downside breakout—one of the most bullish signals in technical analysis. It is confirmed by a bullish divergence of MACD Lines. In addition, the bullish divergence of Force Index is sending an important

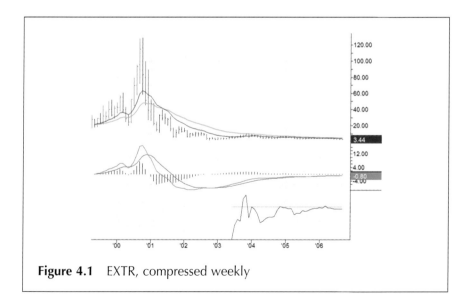

Figure 4.1   EXTR, compressed weekly

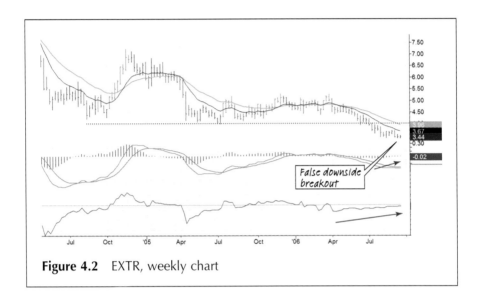

Figure 4.2 EXTR, weekly chart

message—the attempted downside break had no power. Decision—go long EXTR, with a stop at 3.31 and a target of 3.81, above the upper channel line. The distance from the latest closing price to the target was 37 cents, down to the stop 13 cents. The reward-to-risk ratio was nearly 3:1—not the greatest ratio but certainly a very acceptable one.

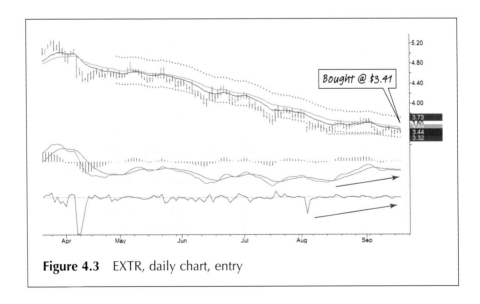

Figure 4.3 EXTR, daily chart, entry

EXTR			Upchannel	Downchannel	Day's High	Day's Low	Grade
Entry	$3.45	20-Sep-06	3.74	3.31	$3.50	$3.41	56%
Exit							
P/L						Trade	

It was a nice entry on a quiet day—buying in the lower half of the daily bar, for a 56% entry grade. The day after I bought EXTR it weakened, and the following day it touched a new low. It must have triggered some stops, punishing those who like to place their stops immediately below the latest low. It is important to make an allowance for the normal noise of the markets and place your stop a little farther away, in an area where you do not expect the prices to go.

The following week EXTR exploded to the upside, almost reaching its upper channel in a single day. It closed near the high, but the following day it had a narrow range and could not rise any higher. I saw this is a sign of resistance and sold at 3.63 (see Figure 4.4).

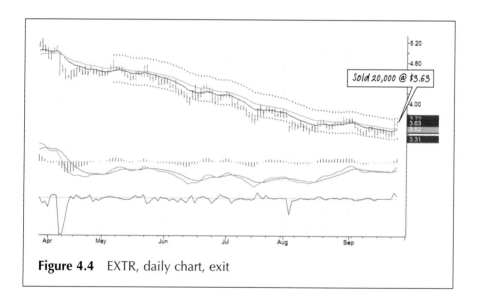

Figure 4.4   EXTR, daily chart, exit

EXTR	20-Sep-06	Date	Upchannel	Downchannel	Day's High	Day's Low	Grade
Entry	$3.45	20-Sep-06	3.74	3.31	$3.50	$3.41	56%
Exit	$3.63	27-Sep-06			$3.66	$3.56	70%
P/L	$0.18					Trade	42%

I chose not to hold out for more than the market seemed willing to give. I treat a selling target as a working estimate. If the market appears very strong, I will try to ride the price move beyond the target. If it appears weak, I will get out earlier.

This was a very nice exit, selling near the high of the day, for a 70% exit grade. Even more rewarding was the trade grade. Taking 18 cents out of a 43-cent channel produced a 42% trade grade—an A+ trade. I bought below value and sold near the overvalued level.

One of the essential values of keeping a Trading Diary is that it encourages you to return to every closed-out trade a month or two later (see Figure 4.5). It makes you re-evaluate your performance with the benefit of hindsight. If you keep learning from your experiences, you will become a better trader tomorrow than you are today!

In retrospect, I could have held much longer—but at the time of the exit there was no clear way of knowing that those rallies would come. There are two sure-fire ways to nail every bottom and top. One is to paper-trade using old charts; the other is to lie about your performance. As for the real traders, risking real money, fast dimes are better than slow dollars.

You have to develop a style of trading that feels comfortable and follow it without regrets. Regret is a corrosive force in trading. If you kick

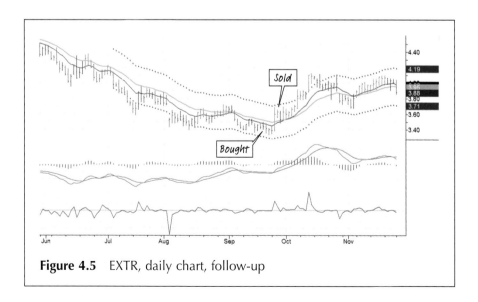

Figure 4.5 EXTR, daily chart, follow-up

yourself for leaving some money on the table today, you will reach out too far tomorrow—and fail.

And now let us review another trade.

One of the advantages of the futures markets is that there are so few of them. You can easily review a couple dozen key futures markets as part of your weekend homework. This is how I became aware of the following pattern in the gold market.

At the right edge of the daily chart (Figure 4.6), gold has broken below the support line but closed above it. I learned from David Weis, a frequent guest instructor in our Trading Camps, that a false downside breakout is one of the most bullish signals in technical analysis. The Impulse system on both the weekly chart (not shown) and the daily chart has turned blue, saying that the worst of the downtrend was over, permitting buying.

Notice a severe downspike of Force Index several days prior to the right edge. Such downspikes identify the areas of panic and a washout of weak longs, clearing the air for an advance. A bullish divergence of both MACD Lines and MACD-Histogram between September and October bottoms delivered a powerful buy signal. I bought December 2006

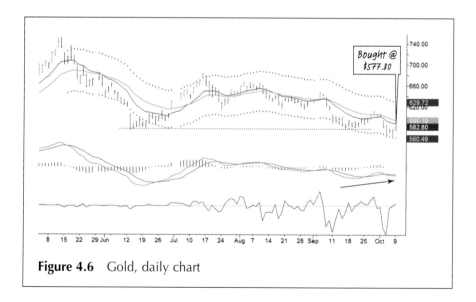

Figure 4.6 Gold, daily chart

gold on 10/10/2006 at $577.80, with the target near the weekly value zone, above $630 and a stop just below the recent lows.

		Upchannel	Downchannel	Day's High	Day's Low	Grade
Entry	$577.80	628	559	$580.80	$573.00	38%
Exit						
P/L					Trade	

The entry day's high was 580.80, low 573, making my entry rating 38%—just about a passing grade. My target: a move across the EMAs, towards the upper channel line.

I sold gold three days later, on Friday 10/13 (see Figure 4.7). On the technical side, I did not like the fact that it had a very narrow range on the day it hit its slower moving average on the daily chart. The value zone serves as natural resistance for both upmoves and downmoves. The narrow range showed a lack of progress in an area where resistance could be expected. On the psychological side, I had an incentive to sell that had nothing to do with the market. I had a ticket to fly to

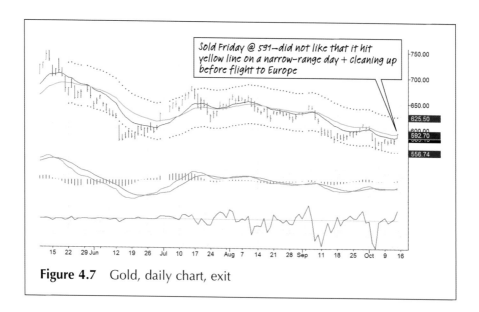

Figure 4.7 Gold, daily chart, exit

Europe the following week and wanted to reduce my market positions to a minimum. I did not want to hold anything that might require time, attention, and babysitting. I guess you could say I was looking for a reason to get out.

		Upchannel	Downchannel	Day's High	Day's Low	Grade
Entry	$577.80	628	559	$580.80	$573.00	38%
Exit	$591.00			$594.20	$587.60	52%
Trade						19%

My exit grade was 52%, meaning that I sold just above the midpoint for the day. My trade grade was a B–, as I took $13.20 out of a $69 channel. Quite a decent grade, but it certainly left room for improvement.

Now, without a Diary, one would close out this trade and move on. The Diary allows us to look back—how good was this trade in retrospect? Let us revisit gold two months later (see Figure 4.8).

When we look back with the benefit of hindsight, we must be careful not to be swept off our feet by the powerful trends that are clearly visible only in retrospect. Four days after my exit, gold reached a top and collapsed right back to my entry level. It made two more very tradeable swings from the value zone between the EMAs to the overvalued

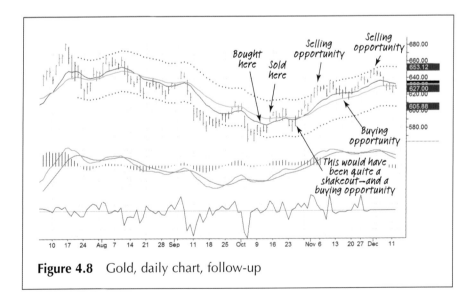

Figure 4.8 Gold, daily chart, follow-up

zone near the upper channel line on the daily charts. I had bought below value and sold above it—it was a very reasonable sale, considering the fact that gold was just coming out of its bear market and one
had to be very cautious betting on the bulls. When in doubt, get out!

SELLING AT ENVELOPES OR CHANNELS

We have seen how moving averages on the weekly and daily charts
present good profit targets for the rallies that jump off the bear market
lows. Later, after a bullish trend has established itself, you will rarely—
if ever—see such targets. As prices keep chugging higher, moving averages start lagging behind them. This is why moving averages do not
make good targets during steady uptrends.

Before we continue our search, let us take a look at an important
pattern on this weekly chart (see Figure 4.9). It shows one of the most

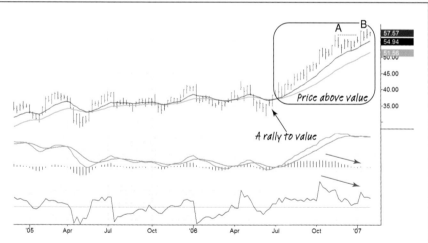

Figure 4.9 INFY, weekly chart

This weekly chart of INFY shows a rally to value early in 2006; that's
when a weekly moving average would have worked as a target. It was
followed by a powerful upmove during which prices stayed above value
for months. Clearly, a moving average would not have provided a target
under these conditions. We need to find a better tool for targeting exits
during uptrends.

powerful signals in technical analysis—a bearish divergence between prices and weekly MACD-Histogram. Following peak A, MACD-H declined below zero—I call this "breaking the back of the bull." The stock rallied to a new bull market high at point B, but the indicator traced out a much lower, almost non-existent peak. That was a loud warning to the bulls. This signal was confirmed by a multitude of other bearish signs: a breakout of prices to a new high with no follow-through; a bearish divergence of Force Index; and completely flat MACD-Lines.

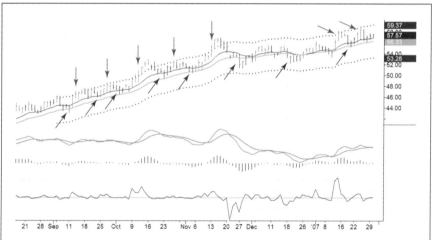

Figure 4.10   INFY, daily chart

While the weekly chart of INFY shows prices running above their moving average for months, this daily chart of the same stock during the same time period shows a very different pattern. Prices keep running higher within their price channel, as if on invisible rails. Such orderly patterns are fairly typical in steady uptrends. A stock keeps moving up, fluctuating between value (its moving average) and the overvalued level at its upper channel line.

When a stock is rallying in this fashion, the space between the two EMAs, the value zone, is a good place to buy. The upper channel line shows where that stock becomes overbought and marks a good zone for profit-taking.

We can see the shorter-term action on the daily chart, shown in Figure 4.10. Trading a stock in such an uptrend—repeatedly buying at value and selling at the upper channel line—may feel like going to a cash machine (although I'm reluctant to use the phrase because nothing in the markets is as simple as going to an ATM). Still, you can see a steady repetitive pattern, as the stock oscillates between its value zone, which keeps rising, and the overvalued zone, which keeps rising as well. This pattern gives traders a good profit target—selling at the upper channel line.

If moving averages help define value, then channels or envelopes drawn parallel to those averages help define overbought and oversold zones. Ideally, we want to buy below value, below the moving averages, and sell at an overvalued level, near the upper channel line. We will grade our performance by the percentage of the channel we can capture in our trade, keeping in mind that anything above 30% will be considered an A trade.

During one of my monthly webinars, a trader named Jeff Parker brought CEGE to my attention (see Figure 4.11). I run these webinars

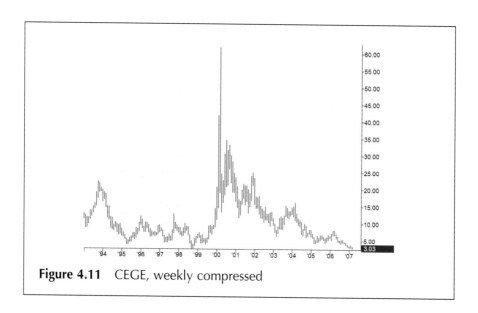

Figure 4.11   CEGE, weekly compressed

once a month, and each consists of two sessions a week apart. A couple of dozen traders gather in a virtual classroom to review the markets and specific stocks. Many participants bring up their picks for me to review. If I like a pick very much, I announce that I will probably trade it the next day. That was the case with CEGE, which immediately attracted my attention.

Compressing the weekly chart of CEGE into a single screen, you can see that the stock had rallied above $60 in the happy days of the 1990s bull market. It then crashed and burned, tried to rally a few times, but sank below $3 near the right edge of the chart. By then it had lost over 95% of its peak bull market value. I call stocks that have fallen more than 90% "fallen angels" and often look for buy candidates among them. My entry into CEGE is shown in Figures 4.12, and 4.13.

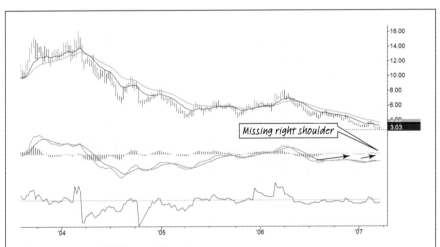

Figure 4.12   CEGE, weekly chart

Opening up the weekly chart, you can see a powerful combination—a false downside breakout accompanied by a bullish divergence of MACD-Histogram. The Impulse system has turned blue at the right edge, allowing buying. The latest bullish divergence was of a "missing right shoulder" type, meaning the indicator could not even decline below zero. It showed that bulls were growing strong, as bears were running out of breath.

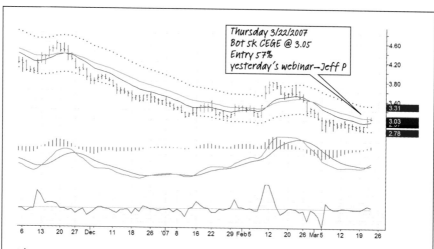

Figure 4.13   CEGE, daily chart, entry

The daily chart showed that the first rally from the oversold lows had already taken place. Prices were in the value zone on the daily chart. The upper channel line on the daily chart presented an attractive target for the next leg of the rally. At the same time, there was a good possibility that prices could overshoot this target, in view of a very bullish pattern of the weekly chart.

When the webinar resumed the following week, we revisited CEGE. Jeff, whose pick it was, spoke about it being very overbought. Prices had shot up towards the upper channel line, without quite reaching it, and stalled for two days. MACD-Histogram reached an overbought level. Since I had a number of long positions at the time, I decided to prune my holdings by selling CEGE shortly after it opened the following day (Figure 4.14).

My exit grade was only 6%, as the stock rallied sharply after I sold. It was a poor grade, but one cannot score highly on every single sale—the important thing is to try to keep the average grade above 50%. My trade grade, however was an A—I took 36% out of this stock's channel.

A few days after I exited, Jeff called, kicking himself for having sold too soon (see Figure 4.15). I tried to humor him—look, by having sold early we freed ourselves from the stress of having to decide what to do with the super-profits of a runaway trend! Seriously, though, this trade provided several important lessons.

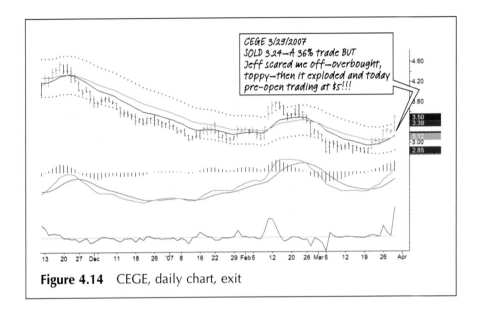

Figure 4.14 CEGE, daily chart, exit

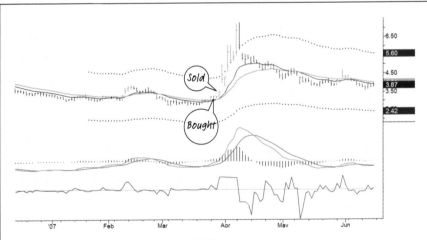

Figure 4.15 CEGE, daily chart, follow-up

The follow-up of this trade is a mixture of comedy and pain. The stock exploded after I sold, and I heard from several webinar participants who sold a day or two after me and scored much greater profits. And then it exploded again. And again.

First of all, it is important to have confidence in your profit targets and not sell too soon. Second, it does not pay to kick yourself over a missed opportunity. This will only lead to reckless trading down the road. I told Jeff that he had to congratulate himself for having picked such a good stock. If you keep buying good stocks, eventually some of them will bring you windfall profits.

In Figure 4.15, notice how much wider the channels are on the follow-up chart than on the one preceding it. I use a program called Autoenvelope which automatically draws channels that contain approximately 95% of the recent price data. When prices jump, an Autoenvelope becomes wider. This is a reminder that in trading we never shoot at a stationary target—the target always moves, making the game harder. Here I took profits near the channel wall—but a few days later the "wall" moved!

CEGE returned to narrow daily ranges after its brief price explosion. It began to sink back towards the base where we had bought, working its way towards becoming an attractive buy once again.

Holding Out for More

When it comes to dealing with the good things in life, the majority of people always want more—a bigger house, a shinier car, perhaps even a newer and better spouse. I remember being stopped dead in my tracks at a party where I talked to a couple; the husband had just received an important promotion and the wife spoke of wanting to "upgrade our friendships." The entire advertising industry pushes us to reach for ever more. No wonder so many people spend their lifetimes in a mindless race, like caged animals chasing their tails. This endless race tends to become very dehumanizing.

When people who have bought into the rat race come to the market they also tend to reach for more, more, more. Even a profitable trade brings them no joy; it burns them to see that they neither bought at the low, nor sold at the high, but left some money on the table. This bitterness drives them to either buy too early or sell too late. People who keep reaching for more usually gain a lot less than those who follow their tested methods.

Those who reach out for more than the market is willing to give often end up with much less.

The power word in life, as well as in trading, is "enough." You have to decide what will make you happy and set your goals accordingly. The pursuit of your own goals will make you feel in control. To always crave more is to be a slave to greed and advertising. To decide what is enough is to be free.

Do not get me wrong—I am not suggesting you take a vow of poverty. I like flying business class, living in a nice place, and driving a powerful convertible as much as any other guy. What I am saying to you is this: find the level at which you will be satisfied and be happy when you get there. This is so much better than always feeling off-balance, short, chasing after an ill-defined "more."

And what to do if "more" somehow falls into your lap? What if one month you hit the market just right, and super-profits drop into your account? The experience of super-profits unhinges most people. Craving even more, they climb farther out on a limb and take wild risks the following month until their super-profits turn into super-losses. In order to stay cool and calm you need a personal plan for managing profits—we will return to this topic in the chapter on the personal dividend.

For a trader who craves more and more, the idea of taking profits near the upper channel line can feel very stressful. Some trades do not reach their target while others overshoot it.

You cannot become fixated on the channel as an iron-clad profit target. If the market starts acting weak, there is nothing wrong with accepting less than your initial target. Neither trade shown above quite reached the upper channel line. EXTR missed it by a bit, gold by a wide margin—but both ended up being very profitable. Paradoxically, being willing to accept less often gives you more. See a recent trading example in Figures 4.16 and 4.17.

An even greater source of stress for greedy traders comes from powerful moves that overshoot their targets and keep on going. A trader looks at a market from which he exited with a nice profit and starts kicking himself as that market continues to move in the same direction—only now without him.

Let us review another trading example. In January 2007 I became very bullish on sugar, on the basis of weekly charts (not shown). I began building a long position in the March 2007 contract, eventually taking profits and rolling over into May (see Figures 4.18 and 4.19).

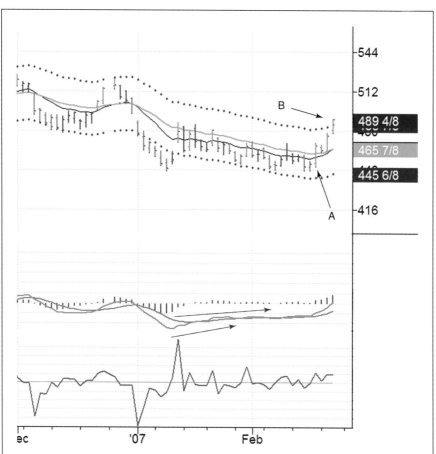

Figure 4.16   Wheat, daily chart

A. Bullish patterns on weekly and daily charts—go long.
B. Took profits on 1/3 of the position, held the rest.

This chart of wheat shows a very nice purchase near the lows, following
multiple bullish divergences. Prices accelerated and punched above the
upper channel line. I was so bullish on wheat at the time (based on
the weekly charts—not shown) that I took only partial profits. I violated
my rule and did not sell above the upper channel line.

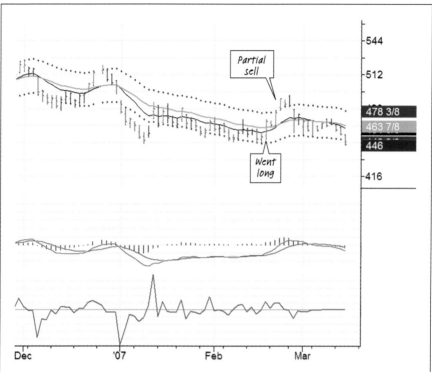

Figure 4.17   Wheat, daily chart, follow-up

Wheat continued to reward greed for two more days after my partial exit.
Prices kept hovering above the upper channel line but then collapsed. I
had to scramble as my open profits melted away. The entire profit for this
wheat trade would have been much greater had I gratefully accepted
what the market was giving me, instead of reaching for more.

I am sure that we could find many examples of prices rising above
the upper channel line and continuing "to walk the line," rising with
the line. Of course it happens, but that is not the point. My point is that
"enough" is better than "more." It leaves you feeling calm and in control—and these feelings lead to greater profitability in the long run.

This brief discussion raises one other important point, which we
already discussed in Chapter 2, page 26 "On Being Kind to Yourself."
Not all my trades are successful—some lose money while others, such
as the ones shown above, earn much less than what was available.

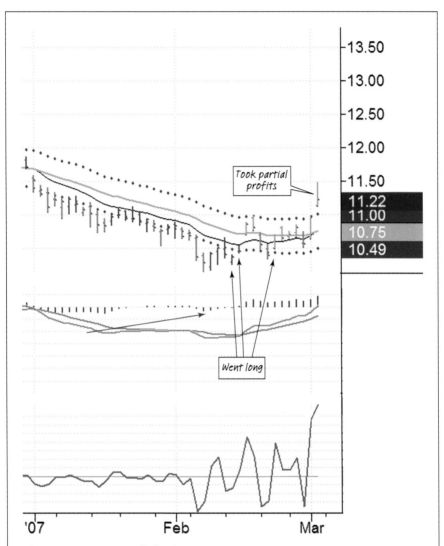

Figure 4.18 Sugar, daily chart

Sugar prices jumped soon after the rollover. The chart above shows that the entire day's bar popped above the upper channel line. In the face of such great strength I took only partial profits on my longs, but held the remaining two-thirds of my position. I was so impressed with sugar's strength—which confirmed my bullish forecast—that I ignored the fact that the bar above the upper channel closed near its low—a suspicious sign of weakness.

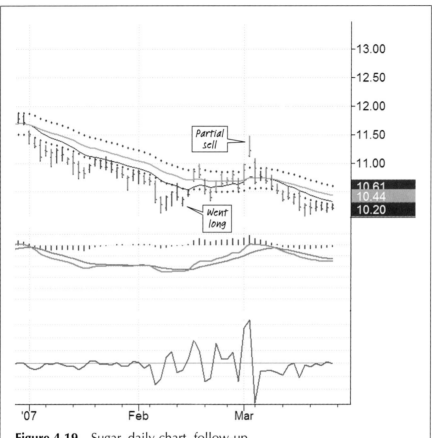

Figure 4.19   Sugar, daily chart, follow-up

The following day, sugar prices collapsed and I had to scramble. My total profit on this trade would have been much higher had I sold the entire position on a break above the upper channel line. I missed a great opportunity by taking only a partial profit.

When I recognize that I have made a mistake, I do not beat myself over the head. I create a diary entry, analyze what happened, and learn as much as I can from my failings. I accept my imperfections, and as long as I learned something from a trade, that trade was a good, productive experience.

A Rally Stumbles

What if you set a profit target for your trade at the envelope but later come to believe that the rally has even greater potential? How much longer can you hold? Experience has taught me that it is better not to overstay trades. Still, occasionally situations occur in which a rally rockets higher, and it feels tempting to hold on for a bit more than initially planned.

Once prices blow through your initial target, where will you take profits? There is an option that appeals to me because it feels the least stressful. I wait for the first day when the price fails to reach a new high for this move and sell either near the day's close or soon after the opening the following day.

Here, as with everything else in trading, it is important not to try to reach for extremes. The top tick of a rally is the most expensive tick in the market—fortunes have been lost hunting for it. The logic behind the "no-new-high" tactic for a fallback target is straightforward. When a super-powerful move cannot reach a new high, it gives you a sign

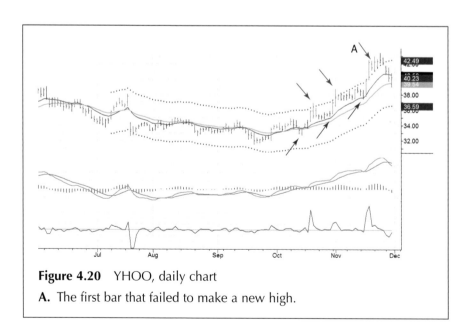

Figure 4.20   YHOO, daily chart

A. The first bar that failed to make a new high.

that the bulls are starting to run out of breath. Of course, they may regain their breath and reach even higher, but I have long ago given up on trying to catch the absolute top. Remember, the top tick is the most expensive tick of every rally.

Figure 4.20 shows a YHOO rally that began in October. At first, it moved like so many other trades—below value in October, followed by a rally to the upper channel line, then a drop back to value in October, followed by another rally to the channel. Following the second rally, prices barely declined, showing that the bulls were very firm and not giving way to the bears.

After prices touched their value zone in November, they staged an explosive move to the upper channel line. They reached the line within one day and rocketed higher the following day. On the third day of this rally, the bulls appeared to either have lost confidence or taken a rest. The range on the third day was narrow and the volume thin, reflected by falling Force Index. Even more important, the bulls failed to lift prices to a new high for this rally. That was the signal to sell.

Prices did rally a little higher on subsequent days, but the bulk of the upmove was over. Three days after the "no-new-high" day, prices began to sink back towards value. Selling early beats selling late. Only someone with a crystal ball can call the top of every move, but those who live by a crystal ball must get used to swallowing a lot of ground glass. It is important to trade without regrets about missed opportunities. Remember—the power word is "enough."

SELLING AT RESISTANCE LEVELS

Moving averages can provide targets for rallies from deeply oversold levels. Channels or envelopes can provide targets for short-term traders. These tools help catch short-term swings—but such moves seem puny to long-term position traders. We used to call such people investors, before the whole world accelerated and everyone became a trader of one sort or another. Long-term traders, whose time horizon is measured in months or even years, need bigger targets. A deer hunter needs a bigger gun and a different scope than someone who goes out shooting rabbits.

Support and resistance zones provide better targets for long-term trades. We can identify support and resistance by looking for price levels where a great deal of trading has taken place, clearly more than the areas immediately above or below.

In order to have confidence in any technical tool we must under-stand how it works and what it measures. To put our money on the line, we need to go deeper than merely drawing lines on charts. If we are going to rely on support and resistance, we need to understand the economic or psychological factors they represent.

Each price tick reflects an agreement between a buyer and a seller, but it also represents something greater—the opinion of the crowd that surrounds these two people. Had the crowd disagreed with either the buyer or the seller, someone would have stepped in and snapped away that trade at a different price level.

The more transactions that occur at a certain price level, the more people believe that level represents value. A congestion zone on a chart tells you that many market participants consider that level a fair value and are prepared to buy or sell there.

If you look at any chart, you'll notice that prices very seldom move in a steady and orderly way for any great length of time. They almost never move in a straight line. Instead, prices stay within a range, swirl-ing behind an obstacle like water behind an earthen dam. Once the dam breaks, the stream of prices surges until it finds another basin. It will now spend a long time filling that basin, until it breaks a new dam and surges again.

If each tick represents a transaction between a buyer and a seller, then a trading range represents a general consensus of value between masses of buyers and sellers. When prices lap at the edges of a range, amateurs become excited. They expect breakouts and buy new highs or sell new lows. Professionals know full well that most breakouts are false and are followed by retracements. They tend to trade in the oppo-site direction, selling at the upper edges of congestion zones and buy-ing at their lower edges. Once in a blue moon the amateurs win, but in the long run it pays to trade with the pros.

This back-and-forth action of prices draws trading ranges on many charts. A range is a horizontal pattern with fairly clear upper and lower boundaries which identify support and resistance. A price range rep-resents a huge financial and emotional commitment by masses of buy-ers and sellers. If you glance at the average daily volume inside the range, multiply it by the number of days in that range and then by the average price of the stock during that time, you will immediately real-ize that a trading range for a single stock can quickly run into billions of dollars.

Support and Resistance

When traders and investors buy and sell, they make an emotional as well as a financial commitment. Their emotions can propel market trends or send them into reversals.

The longer a market trades at a certain level, the more people buy and sell. Suppose a stock falls from 80 and trades near 70 for several weeks, until many believe that it has found support and reached its bottom. What happens if heavy selling comes in and shoves that stock down to 60? Smart longs will run fast, banging out at 69 or 68. Others will sit through the entire painful decline. If losers haven't given up near 60 and are still alive when the market trades back towards 70, their pain will prompt them to jump at a chance to "get out even." Their selling is likely to cap a rally, at least temporarily. Their painful memories are the reason why the areas that served as support on the way down become resistance on the way up, and vice versa.

Regret is another psychological force behind support and resistance. If a stock trades at 80 for a while and then rallies to 95, those who did not buy it near 80 feel as if they missed the train. If that stock sinks back near 80, traders who regret a missed opportunity will return to buy in force.

Support and resistance can remain active for months or even years because investors have long memories. When prices return to their old levels, some jump at the opportunity to add to their positions while others see a chance to get out.

Whenever you work with a chart, draw support and resistance lines across recent tops and bottoms. Expect a trend to slow down in those areas, and use them to enter positions or take profits. Keep in mind that support and resistance are flexible—they are like a ranch wire fence rather than a glass wall. A glass wall is rigid and shatters when broken, but a herd of bulls can push against a wire fence, shove their muzzles through it, and it will lean but stand. Markets have many false breakouts below support and above resistance, with prices returning into their range after a brief violation.

A false upside breakout occurs when the market rises above resistance and sucks in buyers before reversing and falling. A false downside breakout occurs when prices fall below support, attracting more bears just before a rally. False breakouts provide professionals with some of their best trading opportunities.

From *Trading for a Living* by Dr. Alexander Elder,
John Wiley & Sons, Inc.,1993

Have you ever noticed that people tend to become a little emotional about money?

Do you think that a crowd with a billion dollars' worth of commitments might be inclined to act when those commitments are threatened?

Support and resistance are built on two powerful emotions—pain and regret. People who have bought in the range only to see prices drop feel a lot of pain. They are waiting for prices to return so they can "get out even." Their selling, driven by pain, is likely to put a lid on any advance. People who sold short in the range are also waiting for a pullback. They regret that they did not short even more. Their regret will lead them to sell short when prices return to the level where they shorted, resisting the advance. Pain and regret will put a damper on a rally into a trading range or a decline into that range.

Let us review examples of support and resistance on the charts of some well-known markets: IBM and the Euro.

In 2005 IBM (see Figure 4.21) fell into the $73–$78 zone, spent about three months there, and then erupted into a rally. Half a billion shares

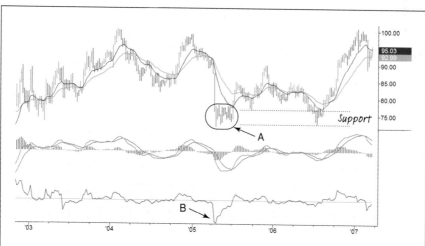

Figure 4.21   IBM, weekly chart

A. Half a billion shares traded at approximately $75—about 37 billion dollars within this range.

B. Notice how downspikes of Force Index tend to identify important market bottoms. Can you find two more downspikes on this chart?

were traded in that zone, with an approximate value of $37 billion. You can begin to imagine how much emotion was attached to that huge pool of money! When IBM fell back into that zone a year later, there were enough buyers who regretted that they had missed the boat earlier. They soaked up the supply and pushed IBM back up, up, and away.

How can we set good targets for massive rallies? Looking into IBM's history on the same chart you can see that in recent years whenever the stock got into the $95–$100 zone, heavy selling drove it down. Think of those poor folks who bought near $100 in 2004. After sweating and suffering through the bear trend, don't you think they were waiting for IBM to rise back to their purchase price, so that they could "get out even?"

Yet of course, "even" is never really even. Think of the lost interest, the depreciation of money, and the loss of opportunity because the money was tied up in IBM at $100 a share. Think of the psychological burden of sitting on a losing position and not being able to concentrate on better opportunities. The losers are waiting, ready to dump millions of shares when the stock finally returns to their purchase price. If you were one of the smart traders who bought near $75, wouldn't you expect the rally to stall near the $100 level? That zone of overhead resistance would have been a very sweet level for placing your profit target.

The Euro (Figure 4.22) erupted from the gate soon after its listing in 2001, rising from 85 cents to $1.36 within three years. A severe bearish divergence in 2005, marked by a red arrow on the chart, capped the uptrend and sent prices lower. The Euro found support near the 2004 lows, then dipped below that level, frightening the bulls.

It is important to keep in mind that support and resistance are not made of plate glass. They are more like wire fences, and bulls and bears can push parts of their anatomy through them. As a matter of fact, some of the best buy signals occur after the bears manage to push prices slightly below support. This sets off stops and takes out the weak holders before the bulls resume control and lift prices again. We already discussed the signals from false breakouts in an earlier chapter.

At the right edge of Figure 4.22 we see a bullish divergence. The last bar on the right edge has turned blue. This change of the Impulse system tells us that the bears are slipping and buying is now permitted.

If we go long here, what will be the target for the upmove? It would be rational to expect resistance in the congestion zone of the 2005 top, between 1.3 and 1.35.

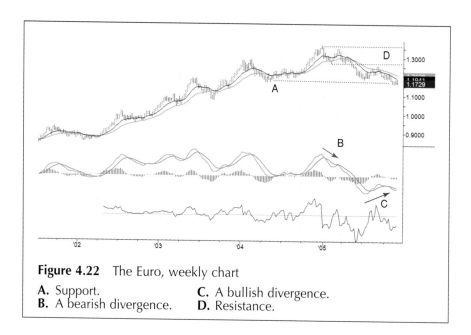

Figure 4.22 The Euro, weekly chart
A. Support.   **C.** A bullish divergence.
B. A bearish divergence.   **D.** Resistance.

Currencies are notoriously hard to trade since they move nearly 24 hours a day. You may be peacefully asleep in your bed while your competitors halfway across the globe are picking your pockets. You wake up to discover that the price move you've expected to see has already occurred. If you are a swing trader, looking to catch price moves that last a few days to a few weeks, you are better off staying away from currencies. Leave them to day-traders and to long-term position traders. These people can benefit from the currencies' well-established tendency to run in long trends.

To follow up on the chart of the Euro, in Figure 4.23 we see a combination of signals—a bullish divergence of MACD, a false downside breakout, the Impulse system turning blue on the weekly chart. They confirmed each other in area B and generated an especially strong message to buy. The entry into this long trade in the Euro worked out extremely well. The buy signal allowed us to set a reasonable long-term profit target—at the resistance in the trading range of the 2005 top.

After the Euro hit resistance at point C it stalled and went flat for several months. At the same time, the behavior of MACD-Histogram in area C indicated that prices were likely to rise higher. The new MACD-H

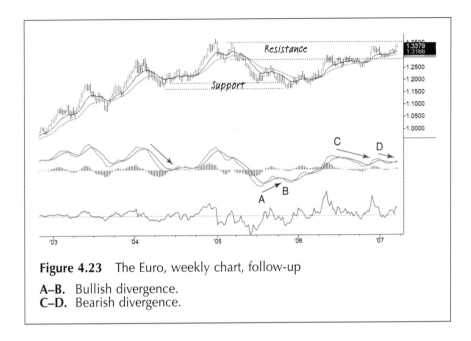

Figure 4.23   The Euro, weekly chart, follow-up

A–B. Bullish divergence.
C–D. Bearish divergence.

peak C, the highest in over a year, showed that bulls were at a record strength. This meant that the price level associated with this indicator peak was likely to be exceeded.

That's exactly what happened near the end of 2006 and again in early 2007, but on those occasions MACD-Histogram was giving different messages. Its bearish divergences signaled that the upmoves were nearing their ends.

Looking at support and resistance helps you set reasonable targets for long-term moves. The great value of such long-term targets is that they help you fix your eyes on a remote but reachable goal. This helps you hang on to a long-term move and not get thrown off your horse by the short-term action of prices or indicators or both.

Another benefit of having a long-term target is that it reminds you to sell in a predetermined zone. If you buy low, it would be useful to have a reminder to help you sell high. Many traders become more bullish near the tops, along with the rest of the market crowd. A target tells you when your goal has been reached. It may not be a perfect goal, but it is your target. You have set it, and now it tells you to take profits, go home, take a nice vacation, and look for the next trade.

Psychologically, it is much harder to trade long-term trends than short-term swings. In short-term trading you are active, watching the market every day, ready to adjust your stops and profit targets, add to your position, take partial profits, or exit the trade altogether. Many of us find this feeling of control psychologically satisfying. The emotions tend to be very different in long-term trading. There are weeks and even months when you do nothing. You recognize short-term tops and bottoms but restrain yourself from doing anything, as you wait for your long-term target to be hit. That's why having a price target is so important—it increases your psychological holding power.

To conclude this chapter on setting profit targets at support and resistance, I will share with you another trade from my diary (see Figure 4.24). It will illustrate techniques, as well as some psychological points. It will show why it is harder to hold a long-term position than a short-term trade. And it will allow us to discuss several important issues relating to the management of a trade, beyond simply setting a profit target.

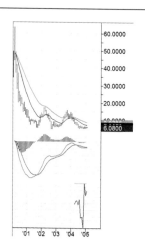

Figure 4.24   STTSY monthly

My attention was drawn to STTS, since renamed STTSY, during a monthly webinar in November 2004. One of our most active participants at the time was Jackie Patterson, a Californian who had left her job to become a full-time trader. She was a good stock-picker, but no stock she brought up had gotten me as excited as STTSY.

This computer-chip testing company traded above $60 in the happy days of the 1990s bull market but fell below $6 during the bear market. It was one of those "fallen angels" we have already discussed. The idea, of course, is to buy after a stock stops declining. It is OK to buy cheap but not OK to buy on the way down.

The weekly chart appeared extremely attractive. It showed that after the stock crashed from above $60 to below $6, it bounced above $17. Another fall, below $5, was followed by a bounce to nearly $16. This puppy's behavior made it clear that even after it lost over 90% of its value it had no desire to die. A stock that has survived a bear market becomes a prime buying candidate for the next bull market.

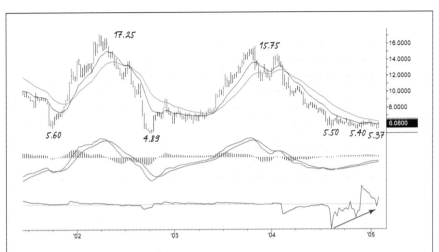

Figure 4.25   STTSY weekly

At the right edge of the chart STTSY fell again, below $6. The price level below $6 emerged as a very strong support zone. In looking at the chart, it became evident that the zone near $16 provided very strong resistance. Whenever STTSY rose to that level, it seemed to hit a ceiling and come tumbling back down to the floor.

Zooming into the right edge of the weekly chart (Figure 4.25), the picture became even more attractive. The stock established three lows during the past six months at $5.50, $5.40, and $5.37. This pattern told me several things. First of all, the support was solid. Even when the stock was pushed to a slightly lower low, it refused to accelerate to the downside, but instead recoiled and came back up. Furthermore, the fact that STTSY kept stabbing to lower lows looked tremendously bullish to me. Those quick stabs seemed to indicate that some powerful interests were trying to push the stock a little lower in order to frighten holders into selling so they could buy up their shares. David Weis, a very experienced trader, jokingly called such interpretations "a paranoid view of the markets."

The bears were so weak that MACD-Histogram stayed above zero during the latest decline. Force Index, in the bottom pane of the chart, showed three stabs to the downside—each more shallow than the next, confirming that the bears were becoming weaker.

When the Impulse system went blue at the right edge of the chart, it removed the last prohibition against buying. I bought 10,000 shares at $5.99. My plan was to hold until STTSY reached $16, which I figured might take a couple of years. I was looking to clear a $100,000 profit on this trade.

As the stock began to move in my favor, I added another 5,000 shares at $6.13, but a few weeks later offloaded that lot at $6.75, clearing 62 cents and booking a quick profit on that side bet. My plan was to hold for the long haul, but this turned out to be much more stressful than quickly trading in and out.

STTSY briskly rallied to $8.16, then sold off back to my buying point. I was convinced that my initial plan was correct and continued to hold. STTSY rallied again, this time to $8.85. I saw multiple signals of a top, including a bearish divergence of weekly Force Index, marked with a red arrow on the chart (Figure 4.26). Focusing on my target of $16, I clenched my teeth and held. The decline quickly wiped out nearly $30,000 of paper profit and the position briefly went negative as STTSY dipped below my entry point. I held on to my original plan, focusing on the bullish details, such as a "kangaroo tail"—a one-bar stab towards the lows. It was accompanied by a bullish divergence of Force Index,

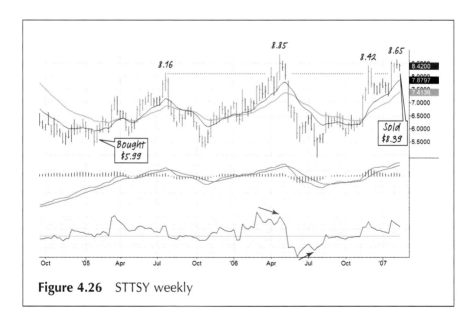

Figure 4.26   STTSY weekly

marked with a green arrow on the chart. STTSY rallied again, this time up to $8.42, but holding long-term was becoming less and less fun.

During this trade I made a multitude of shorter-term swing trades in other stocks. Trading short-term was a lot more fun and profitable. I also held a handful of other long-term positions, similar to STTSY, as my plan was to teach myself to hold for the long haul. Still, my position in STTSY was starting to feel like a headache. I'd had enough of those rallies into the $8–$9 zone, followed by declines back down to the purchase point, with no profit to show for my work or patience.

In February 2007, two years after I bought STTSY, the stock rallied to $8.65, slightly better than its previous high of $8.42. There the rally stalled and the weekly ranges became narrow. Such signs often precede price declines. I felt the weight of STTSY on my shoulders and gave an order to sell, getting out of my 10,000 shares at $8.39. Instead of hitting my $100,000 target, I cleared less than $24,000 on this trade—$27,000, taking into account a side bet on STTSY early in the game. I was happy to be out of STTSY, liberated from having to look at the stock as it gyrated up and down. Still, I had gotten into such a habit of watching it that I kept an eye on it (see Figure 4.27). What I saw turned out to be highly amusing, to say the least.

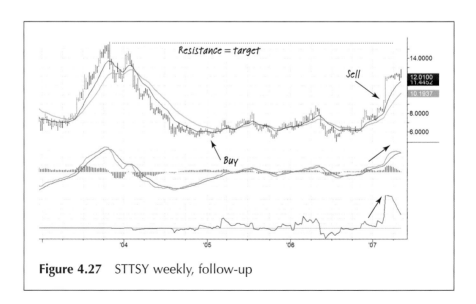

Figure 4.27   STTSY weekly, follow-up

Just a few days after I got relief from selling STTSY, the stock stood on its hind legs and roared. Two weeks later it traded near $12. Most indicators confirmed the great strength of the bulls by reaching new record highs. They signaled that whatever brief weakness may intervene, the bulls were very strong and that $12 was likely not the final peak in STTSY. The stock appeared ready to go higher, and the initial target of $16 looked very realistic.

Did I buy it back? Of course not! My two-year entanglement with STTSY was over. The relatively small profit I took out of its ongoing spectacular move would be the only money I'd make out of it—much less than what was available. So why show this trade here? Is there anything we can learn from it? Yes, quite a lot. Here are the lessons, in no particular order:

1. As we said earlier, whenever you put on a trade, you have two goals: to make money and to become a better trader. You may or may not reach the first goal, but you must reach the second. If you do not learn from your trades, you are wasting your time and money. During this trade, I kept good notes, both in a spreadsheet and in a visual format in my diary, allowing me to extract lessons from the experience. The money profit was relatively small, but the trading lessons were multiple and rich.

2. First of all, my entry into this trade was excellent. I had correctly identified an important bottom and acted in good time. Second, my profit target for the trade appears to have been on track even though I could not hold long enough to get full benefit from my analysis.

3. This trade confirmed to me that I am temperamentally better suited for shorter-term trading. Since I am determined to learn to hold long-term, I must adapt by adding some elements of short-term trading to my long-term positions. I decided that in future long-term trades I will establish a core position that I will hold from start to finish—its smaller size will produce less stress. At the same time, I will put on larger short-term trades in the direction of my long-term trade. Looking back on Figure 4.26, there would have been every reason to buy extra on the way up, sell when tops were formed at the upper dashed line, and buy again whenever the stock fell back to its original buy zone near the lower dashed line.

4. This trade reminds us that it is important to treat yourself well. Your mind is a trading instrument, and abusing yourself for mistakes, such as getting out too early, would be like slapping your computer—it does not improve performance. My goal is to learn from my mistakes, not to punish myself for them.

5. Last but not least, I want you to see that even experts make mistakes. I still make them. You will continue to make them. The idea is to weed out gross mistakes, such as not using a diary or violating money management rules. Once you've done that, you can concentrate on the lesser ones.

As I write this book, I have several long-term trades going. There is a major U.S. industrial concern whose stock, I believe, wants to rise from $7 into the $20+ range. I am even more excited about a little Nasdaq number that trades for a bit over a dollar. It traded near $100 in the 1990s—this fallen angel lost over 99% of its value in recent years. I acquired the bulk of my position below $1 and expect to hold it until the stock reaches $20 a couple of years from now. With both stocks, I have a core position that I do not touch and a bigger short-term position that I keep putting on and taking off, actively trading in the direction of the trend. The lessons of STTSY are continuing to help me.

CHAPTER 5

SELLING ON A STOP

If you compare buying a stock to getting married, using a stop is like signing a prenuptial agreement. If your happy relationship hits the rocks, the prenup will not take away the pain, but it will reduce the hassle, the uncertainty, and the expense of the separation. What if you are a happy bull but discover that your beloved stock has been sneaking out and getting between the sheets with a bear? Any breakup is going to hurt, but the best time to decide who gets what is when you still tenderly hold each other's hands.

Price targets help you hold on to the stocks that move in your favor. Stops help you sell when the stocks turn against you. Even a profitable trade deserves to have a protective stop. Some traders also like to ride runaway trends by using trailing stops that follow rapidly moving prices.

A stop provides an essential reality check for any trade. Yes, you love this stock. Yes, you have great expectations. But what if it doesn't work? Have all your previous stock ideas worked out well? Or has there been one or two that did not? More than one or two? Many? Is there any doubt then that you need a stop? You need to examine the chart and decide where you want to get out if that trade starts going against you.

Once you put on a trade, a pernicious "ownership effect" will set in, making it much harder to decide when to sell. The best time to make that decision is before you enter a trade.

Think of that old-fashioned jacket that hangs in your closet. You cannot bring yourself to throw it away—because it is yours, you are used to having it, you've always had it. At least that useless jacket does not cost you anything beyond taking up space in your closet. (And in your mind, I might add—holding a useless possession creates a tiny dead spot—and after a while many little dead spots merge into bigger dead zones). At least you won't have to pay rent for the jacket that hangs there. On the other hand, having a dead trade in your account can become very expensive. It can become downright ruinous.

A single bad trade, if large enough, can punch a hole in your account. A group of bad trades can destroy it.

Another side effect of not using stops and holding on to bad trades is that they interfere with making good trades. Just as a toothache interferes with your thinking and prevents you from planning new and exciting things, a losing trade grabs more of your attention than it deserves. It prevents you from seeking out new and better trades. Whenever a trade that's gone against you has your nerves tied in a knot, it makes it harder for you to get into a new trade. Even when it looks promising, you find excuses not to buy. Holding on to a losing trade costs you money, pain, and missed opportunities.

A trading system without stops is not a system—it is a joke. Trading such a system is like racing a car without seatbelts. You may win several races, but the trouble is that the very first crash could end your career.

If you are a discretionary trader, stops are your link to reality. You may have beautiful ideas of profits, but deciding where to put a stop forces you to look at the possible downside. It makes you ask the essential question: *Is the potential profit worth the risk?*

Every trade deserves a protective stop. Follow this simple rule: you may not put on a trade unless you know exactly where you will place your stop. You must make that decision before you enter a trade. In addition to the stop you need a profit target to evaluate that trade's reward-to-risk ratio. A trade without a target is like a chip tossed on the green felt of a casino table.

About 20 years ago one of my friends hit a rough patch in his market career and went to work as a broker. I moved one of my accounts to him, and whenever I called to place an order, he would not let me get off the phone until I also gave him a stop. My friend has since grown into a successful money manager, but I remember him as the most disciplined broker I ever had.

And what about moving stops? Markets change, prices change, and your outlook on a stock may change. You may become more bullish, more bearish, or less certain. As your perception of risk and reward changes, you may want to move your stop. How can you do it? In a market where everything is permitted—most of all losing money—what rules will you set for moving stops?

The absolutely essential rule of moving stops is that you may move them only one way—in the direction of the trade. When you go long and place a stop below the market, you may move it up but never down. When you go short and place a stop above the market, you may move it down but never up.

You buy a stock because you expect it to go up. If it starts going down, it tells you that your decision was poor. Had you expected that stock to go down, you would not have bought it. Moving your stop farther away to accommodate your mistake would only compound the error. Don't do it. Using stops is a one-way street. You may tighten them but never loosen them.

Let us summarize what we have discussed so far:

- You need stops; a trade without a stop is a gamble.
- You need to know where you'll put your stop before you enter a trade (if the reward-to-risk ratio is poor, do not enter that trade).
- Everybody needs hard stops; only expert discretionary traders are allowed to use soft stops, discussed below.
- Whenever you change a stop, you may move it only in the direction of the trade.

If you have any doubts about these points, please go back and reread this chapter. If you agree, let us move forward and discuss how to place stops. As they say in real estate, "there are three key factors in this business: location, location, location."

An important footnote about stops—it is perfectly fine to re-enter a market after it hits your stop. Beginners often make a single stab at a stock and leave it alone after it kicks them out. Professionals, on the other hand, see nothing wrong with trying to buy or sell short a stock again and again, like trying to grab a slippery fish, until they finally get it by the gills.

THE IRON TRIANGLE

The main purpose of using a stop is to protect yourself from an adverse move by limiting the loss on a trade to a predetermined amount. The secondary purpose is to protect paper profits. With loss control being the key purpose of stops, it is no wonder that setting stops is tightly linked with money management.

The process of risk control works in three steps:

1. Set a stop on the basis of chart analysis and calculate the dollar risk per share by measuring the distance from the planned entry price to the stop level.

2. Use your money management rules to calculate the maximum amount you may risk on a trade in your account and decide how much you will risk.

3. Divide the number of dollars in line 2 by the number of dollars in line 1 to find out how many shares you may trade.

I call this sequence the Iron Triangle of risk control. One side is your risk per share, another your total permitted risk per trade. The third side, derived from the first two, gives you the maximum trade size.

Stop placement is tightly linked with trade sizing. Once you decide what to trade, you need to decide how big a position you will put on. Most people make this decision on the basis of some vague gut feel. They trade bigger after a few successful trades or smaller after getting slapped around by the market. Many approach the sizing decision from the wrong angle. Some trade the same number of shares every time, others invest the same percentage of their account in every trade. These common approaches make little logical sense.

Size, as the joke goes, does not matter. What matters is risk.

As a trader, you do not really trade IBM or EBAY or soybeans—you trade money and you deal in risk. This is why you must set your position size on the basis of risk. It is risk, rather than any external factors like number of shares or the cost of a position, that matters.

Compare buying 1,000 shares of a $20 stock and placing your stop at $17 to buying 2,000 shares of a $40 stock and placing your stop at $39. Even though the size and the cost of the second position is greater, the amount of risk is lower.

Let us review the three steps outlined above, followed by a few trading examples:

1. **Calculate dollar risk per share**.
   Suppose you decide to buy a stock that is trading at $18. Now suppose that your chart analysis indicates that if this stock falls

below $17 it will cancel the bullish scenario. You decide to place a protective stop at $16.89. Your risk per share then will be $1.11. It could become even higher in the case of slippage, but $1.11 is a reasonable estimate.

2. **Calculate dollar risk per trade.**
   Suppose you have $50,000 in your trading account and follow the 2% money management rule, as explained in Chapter 1. This means that your maximum risk per trade is $1,000. That is actually quite a lot of risk for a modest account. Many traders decide to risk less than 1%.

3. **Divide your risk per trade by risk per share.**
   This is how you find the maximum number of shares you may trade. If your maximum permitted risk per trade is $1,000 and the risk per share in the planned trade is $1.11, your maximum number of shares is below 900. Remember, the $1,000 maximum allowed risk per trade must cover commissions and slippage. Also, there is no law that says you must go up to the maximum permitted risk on every trade. You are not allowed to risk more, but you are perfectly welcome to risk less.

What if you have big expectations for that $18 stock? You may want to give it some extra room and place a stop as far away as $15.89, but then your risk per share would be $2.11. Since the maximum permitted risk for the trade would remain the same, your maximum purchase would drop to 470 shares.

On the other hand, if you sit in front of the screen, watching that stock like a hawk, you may put a stop at $17.54, and risk only 46 cents per share. Your maximum permitted risk will remain $1,000, but now you will be able to trade a 2,170-share block.

Decisions about stops are tightly linked to decisions regarding profit targets. You must weigh the amount of risk you are willing to take against the potential reward you are trying to reap. As a rule of thumb, I am attracted to trades with reward-to-risk ratio of 3:1 or better. I would be very reluctant to enter a trade whose reward-to-risk ratio is 2:1 or lower.

Using stops is an essential practice. Before we discuss the wide variety of stops available to you, let us clarify two extremely important distinctions. We must choose whether to use market or limit orders for our stops. We also need to look into the rarely discussed choice between soft and hard stops.

MARKET OR LIMIT ORDERS

All orders can be divided into two broad groups—market and limit orders. A market order is filled at what brokers like to call the best price—but what is in fact any price and often the worst price. An alternative to a market order is a limit order. It demands an execution at a specific price—or no execution at all. A limit order helps you avoid slippage.

A market order guarantees you an execution but not the price. A limit order guarantees you the price but not the execution. You must choose one or the other because you cannot have both in the same trade. You have to decide what is more important to you—an execution or an avoidance of slippage? You may answer this question differently at different times, depending on what you are trying to accomplish.

Suppose you've bought 1,000 shares of a $19 stock, and your research indicates that if it declines to $17.80, the uptrend will be over. You call your broker or log into his website and place a stop order to sell 1,000 shares at $17.80, good until cancelled. Normally, a stop order is placed below the market as an MIT order—"market if touched." If you put your stop at $17.80, it will become a market order to sell 1,000 shares the moment that stock trades at $17.80. Your position is now protected. You can go about your life and feel less worried about that stock.

A market order is a slippery thing. In a quiet market, you may get filled at $17.80. Occasionally, you may get very lucky, and if prices bounce after touching $17.80, you may get filled at $17.81 or $17.82. What is much more likely to happen, however, is that during a sharp downdraft the stock does not linger long enough at $17.80. You put your MIT stop at $17.80, but when you get your fill, it is at $17.75. This slippage on 1,000 shares has just cost you $50—probably several times larger than your commission.

Prices move smoothly only in quiet markets but they can jump across several price levels when the action heats up. Putting an MIT order at $17.80 does not guarantee you'll be filled there. In a fast decline you may suffer slippage and get filled at $17.78, $17.75, or even lower. If a sudden piece of very bad news hits your stock, it may gap all the way down to $16, or even lower.

A stop is not a perfect tool for protecting your profits or reducing losses—but it is the best tool we have.

Stung by slippage, some traders switch to limit orders. They order to sell only at a specified price, using a limit order for their stop. I strongly disagree with this tactic.

I almost always use limit orders for entering trades and taking profits at target levels. A limit order says, in effect, "my way or the highway." I will only do business at a level that suits me, and will not accept slippage on an entry or on profit-taking. If I miss entering a trade as a result of a limit order, I do not complain—there will be many other trades in the future. If you try to enter a trade using a limit price and do not get filled, you lose nothing.

The situation with protective stops is completely different. If you miss an exit from a trade, you can get caught in a waterfall decline. A trader can lose a lot while fiddling with limit orders, trying to save a few pennies. When the trouble hits, run without haggling. That is why I use limit orders for entries and profit-taking but switch to MIT orders when using stops.

HARD AND SOFT STOPS

A hard stop is an order you place in the market. A soft stop is the number you keep in your mind, prepared to act as soon as the market reaches that level. The distinction between them is extremely important, but I am a little reluctant to discuss soft stops here. It is a topic for professional and semi-professional traders, and I am concerned that some beginners may misunderstand and misuse it. For most beginners, a soft stop is like no stop at all.

This reminds me of a TV commercial I once saw—a company advertised a soft drink by showing people on small motorbikes zooming up and down steep slopes. Splattered across the bottom of the screen in big white letters was a warning: "All tricks performed by trained professionals. Kids: do not attempt to duplicate at home!" And that's exactly what I'd like to say about soft stops.

If the topic is so dangerous, why not leave it out of the book altogether?

Because I want this book to be useful for the people who are rising to a higher level of trading who may find hard stops too rigid. I want to put control into your hands, trusting you to make reasonable decisions.

Just remember that hard stops are for everybody, but soft stops are permitted only for the pros or serious semi-pros.

Whatever method you use for setting stops, in the end you will come up with a number—the level at which your stop belongs for the next trading day. Will you make that number a hard or a soft stop?

A hard stop goes into the market as a specific order—you actually give it to your broker. The big plus of a hard stop is that it allows you to take your eyes off the market. It is perfect for those who cannot be in front of the screen during trading hours and who do not like making decisions in real-time. Beginners must use hard stops because they have neither the expertise nor the discipline to make decisions in real-time and carry them out.

Professional systematic traders use hard stops, but professional discretionary traders may use either hard or soft stops. A pro can do his research, come up with a number for a stop and enter it into his record-keeping system—but he may not necessarily give that order to his broker. He may watch that level, prepared to exit if prices get near it, but give himself a bit of latitude at the same time.

Using soft stops requires two things—iron discipline and full-time attention to the screen. You have no business using soft stops if you are not in front of the screen, ready to execute a trade when the market hits your level. You also need absolute discipline. A beginner who freezes in fear and keeps hoping for a lucky break when the market turns against him should not be using soft stops.

Soft stops can provide a terrific benefit by allowing more flexibility than hard stops. As the market starts heading down towards your stop level, you may decide that the stock looks heavy and get out earlier; you may cut losses sooner and save more money. Alternatively, you may decide that a decline on low volume could be a fakeout move and hold the stock a little longer, giving it a chance to recover. Needless to say, in all of these situations you need to know exactly where your stop is and exactly how you are deviating from it. An experienced professional can benefit from the flexibility of a soft stop, but too much freedom is deadly for beginners.

A trader has no right to use soft stops until he or she has traded profitably for one full year. Even then you may adopt soft stops only slowly and continue to use hard stops when you are away from the screen.

Since the decision-making process for establishing stop levels is the same for hard and soft stops, I will not be making any further distinction between them in this chapter. We will discuss how, where, and when to place your stops. You will need to decide whether those will be hard or soft, depending on your level of expertise.

A BAD PLACE

Among the many misconceptions about stops one stands out as the worst. It has cost investors and traders billions of dollars and will, undoubtedly, cost them more. This misconception is that one should place stops on long positions immediately below the latest low.

This idea has been around for so long that it has acquired the look and feel of received truth. It became popular because it is so simple, feels comfortable, and does not require much thought. Even I took this advice early in my trading career and passed it on to others—until, as so often happens, reality hit me on the head.

There is one major problem with placing a stop immediately below the latest low—it very likely will lose money. The trouble with such stops is that markets very often trace out double bottoms, with the second bottom slightly lower than the first. I could fill a book with charts showing this pattern. The level immediately below the latest low is where amateurs cut and run and where professionals tend to buy.

Whenever prices approach a bottom area, I become very alert to the possibility that they could penetrate to a lower low. If prices fall to a new low, while the indicators fall to a more shallow low, creating a bullish divergence, I wait for prices to rally slightly. When they rise above the level of the first bottom, they flash a buy signal. I consider this one of the strongest and most reliable trading signals—a double bottom with a bullish divergence, with the second bottom slightly deeper than the first (see Figures 5.1 and 5.2).

It boggles the mind to think of the thousands of people who, year after year, put their stops slightly below the latest bottom. Why do people put their stops at precisely the level where they are most likely to be hit? Why do they sell at the level where the professionals are likely to be buying?

Crowds crave simplicity. Putting a stop a penny below the latest low is so simple, anyone can do it. And the bulk of trading literature reinforces this pattern.

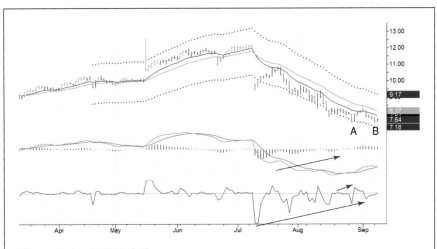

Figure 5.1 CPWR daily

Good trades tend to come together slowly, and this was certainly the case with CPWR. As it slid in July and August, it created multiple bullish divergences, culminating in the bullish divergence of MACD Lines in August. It reached the low of 7.46 at point A in August. Any trader who bought and put his stop "a penny below the latest low" got tossed out in September, when the stock briefly fell to 7.44 at point B. The question at the right edge is this: where will you put your stop if you buy here?

Professional traders exploit the crowd's tendency to place stops a penny below the latest low year after year. They know where those stops are. There is no law that prohibits professionals from looking at charts. Some are even holding stop orders for their clients at those levels. The pros expect to find clusters of stops just beyond the edges of congestion zones.

As a stock sinks towards the level of an important low, its trading volume tends to dry up. All eyes are on that stock, but there is not a lot of activity, as people wait to see whether the support will hold. A small sell order, thrown at the market while buy orders are thin, can push the stock down, below its previous low. That's the area where many serious pros love to operate.

As the falling stock sets off the stops of public customers, the pros snap up shares at a discount. If there are so many shares for sale that the stock accelerates down, they quickly cut their losses and let it

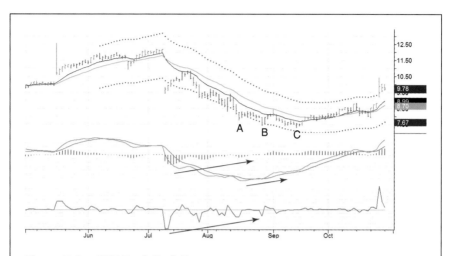

Figure 5.2   CPWR, daily follow-up

The market often meanders while it gathers steam for a dash. CPWR briefly fell to 7.32 at point C, punishing those who casually place their stops immediately below the latest low. That is where beginners cut and run, while professionals tend to go shopping in those areas.

  Was that fishing expedition a crime? Probably not—just a pack of savvy pros trading against the unprepared and fearful amateurs.

slide, but this rarely happens. Normally, the number of shares sold by the people with stops is not that great. As their sales get absorbed and the decline stalls, the pros jump in, joining the feeding frenzy, buying below the lows. The stock rises back into the range, leaving behind a brief downspike—a trace of the pros' fishing expedition. They have just scared a bunch of anonymous amateurs into selling them goods at a discount. Has this ever happened to you?

  Military officers know the value of veteran troops—they hold up under fire. Inexperienced troops are more likely to break and run, but veterans are not easily scared. Time and again they push inexperienced opponents from their positions. The beginners who survive might grow into tough veterans themselves. I hope that working through this book will help you accomplish this goal. And if I have convinced you not to put your stop "a penny below the latest low," then I have not wasted my time writing it.

  So—where should we put our stops? Review Figures 5.3 through 5.6.

Figure 5.3 S&P500 daily

In a sharp mini-crash in February 2007 the Standard & Poor's 500 index fell out of its channel but then appeared to have found a bottom, with the Impulse system turning blue.

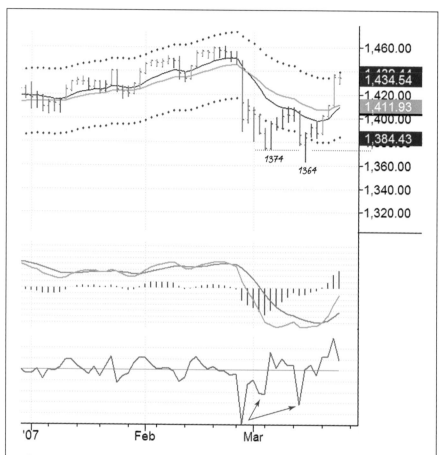

Figure 5.4 S&P500 daily follow-up

Sure enough, prices bounced up strongly enough to hit the upper channel. Unfortunately for many beginners, prices stabbed below the first low before flying off. Their expectation of a rally was correct, but tight stop placement would have led to a loss instead of a profit.

Putting a stop a penny below the latest low tends to be a losing proposition. What are the alternatives? Let us review several possible solutions.

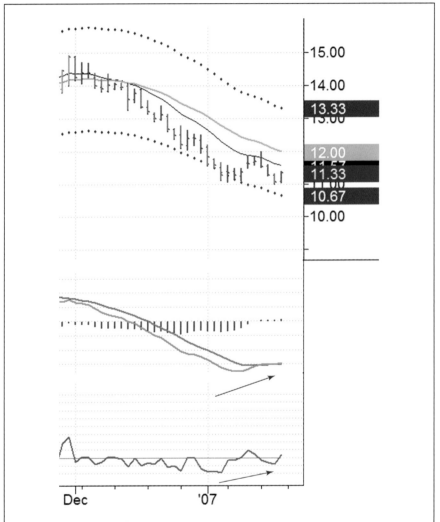

Figure 5.5 TINY daily

A beginner may look at the double bottom in TINY and says: "Wow, look at these divergences! I'll buy and put my stop one tick below the lowest low."

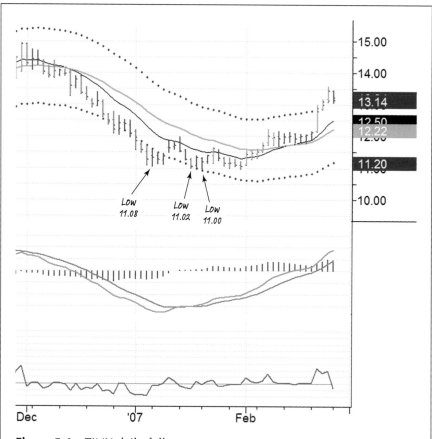

Figure 5.6 TINY daily follow-up

TINY was an exciting stock in an exciting industry, with exciting technical patterns. It did build a base in early January and flew up about 25% before the end of February. Trouble is, it flew up only after it kicked out early buyers who put their stops a penny below the latest low. That low was 11.02, and the stops at 11.01 were taken out when the stock briefly fell to 11.

REDUCING SLIPPAGE—TIGHTER BY A PENNY

Most traders do not use stops. The fact that you are thinking about them and reading this book is a positive sign. Stops improve your chances of rising above the crowd.

Looking at most charts, you can make a fairly good guess about where careless traders would place their stops. When crowd members use stops, they tend to place them at very obvious levels. They slap them immediately below support when long or immediately above resistance when short. Since the crowds lose on balance in the financial markets, it pays to do things differently from the majority. Here and in the next few chapters we will discuss several alternatives to those obvious levels.

If you make your stops tighter, you'll reduce your dollar risk per share, but you'll also increase the risk of a whipsaw. If you place your stops farther away, you will reduce your risk of a whipsaw, but your losses per share will become heavier when your stops get hit. Both approaches have their pluses and minuses, but you must choose only one for any given trade. Like so many choices in the markets, your decision will depend more on your attitude than on any objective study of the market.

My approach to using stops has formed gradually, much of it the result of painful experiences. When I first began to trade I did not use stops. After several beatings from the market I learned that I needed stops for protection. I began using them, but placed them in an amateurish way—a tick below the latest low on long positions or a tick above the latest high when going short. Needless to say, I kept getting stopped out by whipsaws.

To add insult to injury, I noticed that when I placed my stops the usual way, one tick[1] below the latest low, it exposed me to a great deal of slippage. A stock would decline to the level where my stop had been set, but when I received my confirmation, the fill would be several ticks lower. My broker explained that there were so many stops at my level that when the stock hit it, it just went flying. With all those sell orders, including my own, flooding the market, the buyers were momentarily overwhelmed.

What could I do about it? The pain of losing provided plenty of motivation. I decided to tighten my stops and began placing them not one tick below the latest low, but at the actual low level. Looking at many charts, I saw that there had been very few instances when a stock

---

[1]I was surprised by how many people wrote to me after reading my previous books and asked what a tick is. Let me explain it now for those who do not know how to Google their questions—a tick is the smallest price change allowed in a given trading vehicle. As I write this, a tick for most U.S. stocks is a penny. A tick in corn is 1/8 of a penny. A tick in sugar is 1/100 of a penny. Your broker should have a brochure with the information about the tick size for any market you care to trade.

declined exactly to its previous low and held there, without going a tick lower. Normally, it either held well above that low or went well below it. This meant that placing a stop one tick below the low did not add to my safety margin. So I began placing my stop at the actual low, instead of going one tick lower.

This method largely eliminated slippage on my stops. Time after time, a stock would come down to its previous low and just boil there. There would be a great deal of activity but not much movement. Then the stock would fall a tick below its old low and hit an air pocket—whoosh!—falling several ticks within moments.

I realized that the level of the previous low was where the pros re-jigged their positions. The action was tight, and there was very little slippage there. Once the stock fell a tick below its previous low, it was in public stops territory, and the slippage became hot and heavy. With that discovery, I stopped placing my stops a tick below the recent low. I began placing them at the exact level of the previous low—and my slippage on stops drastically diminished. I used that method for many years—until I switched to an even tighter method of placing stops.

NIC'S STOP—TIGHTER BY A DAY

In a Traders' Camp in 2003 I met a trader by the name of Nic Grove. His story, with its colorful personal details, is in some way typical of how people come to trading. As a young man growing up in Australia, Nic was involved in his family's real estate business, then went out on his own as a commercial landscaper. By the time he turned 50, he grew tired of the routine, and sold his business. He flew to Paris, rented a small apartment, and started learning French. Looking for something to do and generate income, Nic stumbled into trading. He happened to read my book, came to a camp, and gradually we became good friends.

During the bull market in 2004 Nic and I were buying stocks that had been temporarily driven down to their EMAs. We wanted to hold them for a rally back to their upper channel line, using a fairly tight stop. Nic suggested looking for the low where most people would place their stops and then examine the bars that bracketed that low on each side. He would then place his stop a little below the lower of those two bars. This concept is easier to illustrate than to describe in words. Please see Figures 5.7 through 5.12.

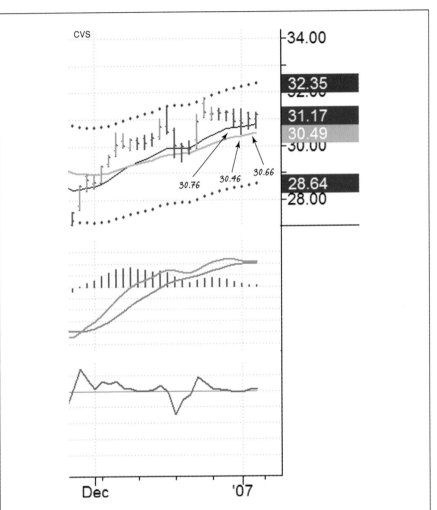

Figure 5.7 CVS daily

CVS is in an uptrend on the weekly chart (not shown). This daily chart shows that it was pulled down into its value zone between the two EMAs. The lowest low of the decline was $30.46, bracketed by two higher lows, $30.76 and $30.66. If we go long CVS, Nic's stop would belong slightly below the lower of those two bracketing lows. Since the lowest of them was $30.66, I would put a stop at $30.64 or even $30.59—on the other side of a round number.

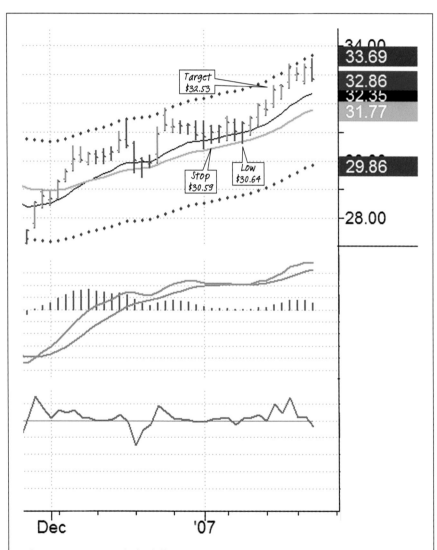

Figure 5.8 CVS daily follow-up

CVS hung around its value zone for a few more days before it took off and hit the target at the upper channel line. The stop below the second lowest low was never endangered.

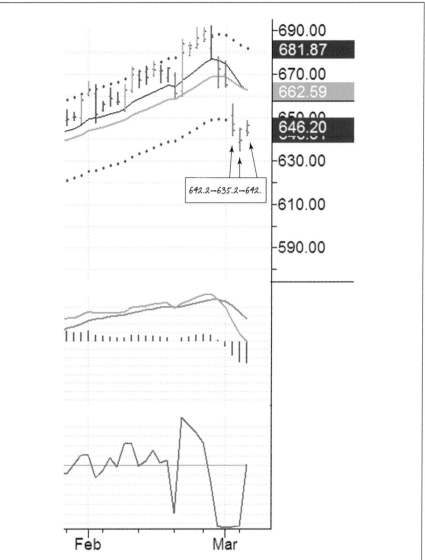

Figure 5.9 Gold daily

Gold, while in a bull market on the weekly chart (not shown), got hit by a
piece of bad news and driven down. It fell below its lower channel line,
a deeply oversold area. The lowest point of the decline was $635.20, brack-
eted by two lows: $642.20 and $642. I would place a stop slightly below
the lower of the two, avoiding the round numbers—$641.90 or $641.40.

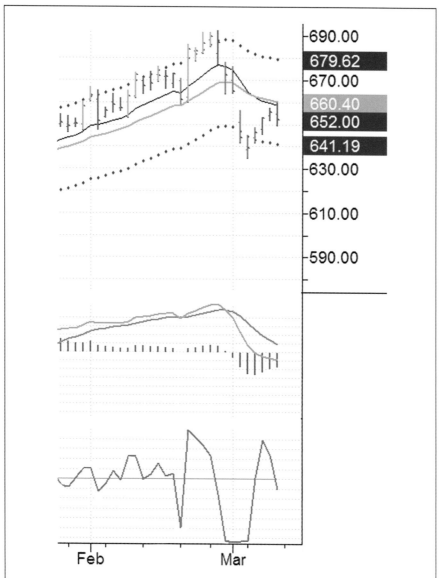

Figure 5.10   Gold daily follow-up

Gold rallied to $659.80, into its value zone between the two EMAs and appears to have stalled. The stop was not hit, but now would be a good time to take profits—since gold is at value and does not seem to be going up.

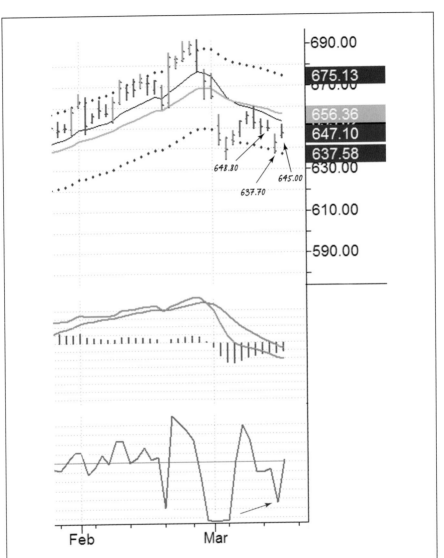

Figure 5.11   Gold—2nd follow-up

Gold punched its lower channel line for the second time. The second decline was less powerful than the first, leading to a bullish divergence of the Force Index. At the right edge, gold looks like an attractive buy again. The lowest low of this decline was $637.70, bracketed by the lows of $648.80 and $645.00. I would put "Nic's stop" slightly below the lower of the bracketing lows, at $644.40.

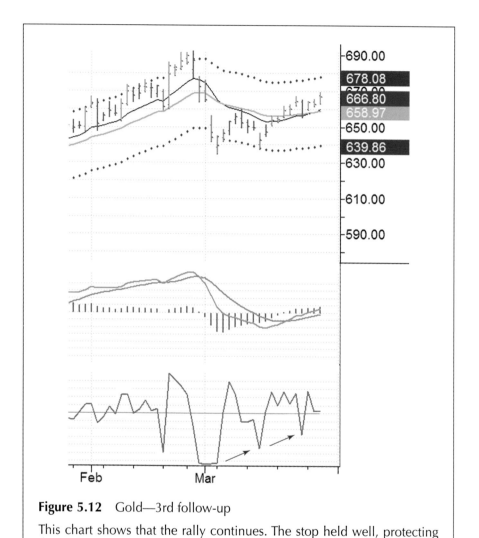

Figure 5.12   Gold—3rd follow-up

This chart shows that the rally continues. The stop held well, protecting the trade.

This very tight method of placing stops is especially suited for short-term swing trading. Trying to catch a bottom tends to be a dangerous business. A very tight stop like this one does not allow any time for dreaming. It tells the market to put up or shut up.

WHEN TO USE WIDER STOPS

The planned duration of your trade helps determine how far from the entry to place your stop. As a rule, a shorter time horizon calls for tighter stops, while a longer timeframe tends to require wider stops.

All timeframes have their advantages and disadvantages. One of the key benefits of longer-term trades is that they give you the time to think and make decisions. At the other end of the spectrum, if you are day-trading and stop to think, you're dead. Every advantage in the financial markets comes at a price. Longer-term trading gives you more time to think and make decisions, but the cost of this luxury is the greater distance from your entry price to a stop. A stock can meander much more in three months than it can in three hours. As traders we shoot at a moving target; given more time, the targets will move a great deal more.

A beginning trader is better off staying away from day-trading. This extremely fast game tends to quickly destroy amateurs. Nor would I recommend long-term trend-trading for those who are just starting out. The best way to learn is by making many small trades, keeping a diary, and practicing your entries and exits. Long-term trades do not provide the necessary level of activity to gain that experience.

Swing trading is a good place to start learning to trade. Once you have a year under your belt during which your equity curve shows an uptrend with shallow drawdowns, you'll know that you are becoming good. Then you can decide whether to continue to focus on swing trading or to expand your horizons. If at that point you decide to learn long-term trading, you will need wider stops.

Why wider stops?

To avoid whipsaws. The only logical place for a stop is the level where you do not expect prices to go.

Think about it—if you go long and place a stop below the market, you want to have it at a level where you do not expect prices to decline. You would not want it where a whipsaw becomes a real possibility. You want your stop at a level that could be reached only if the trend reverses.

If you identify an uptrend and go long, your stop belongs at a level that is safe from the normal chop of prices. A major uptrend is naturally swingier than a little price move. If the noise level is greater, the stops have to be wider.

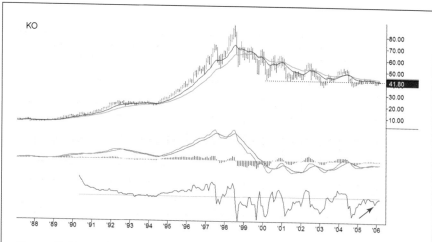

Figure 5.13   KO monthly

When trying to put on a very long-term trade (what used to be called an investment in years past), it pays to begin by analyzing a monthly chart. This chart of KO (Coca-Cola) shows 20 years' worth of history. You can see a bull market that took the stock from under $4 (split-adjusted) to nearly $90 in 1998, followed by a bear market slide to below $40. The area below $40 emerged as strong support which has stopped four declines since 2001. At the right edge of the chart the monthly Impulse system has turned from red to blue, permitting buying.

The principle of Triple Screen is to make a strategic decision on a longer-term chart (Figure 5.13) and execute on a shorter-term chart (Figure 5.14). With the monthly chart permitting us to buy we turn to the weekly chart to decide on our tactics.

Suppose you're trading a $100,000 account and following the 2% Rule. If you place your stop at the closer of the two levels we just discussed, your maximum trade size could be nearly 600 shares. If you chose the wider stop, your maximum permitted trade size would drop to below 300 shares.

Of course every trader must make his own decisions, but I can offer you my take on the situation: a stop on a long-term position must be wide, but not so wide as to kill the trade size. I would be inclined to place my stop at the closer of the two levels—and be prepared to reposition

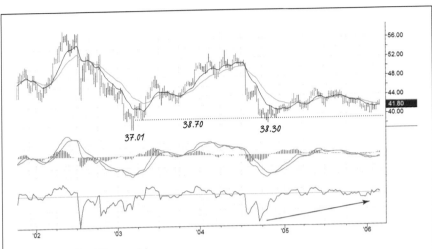

Figure 5.14 KO weekly

As usual, the trend of the shorter timeframe changes ahead of the longer term trend. The upside reversal is already well under way on the weekly chart. A bullish divergence of Force Index helps identify a bottom, and prices have already risen above their EMAs. This chart supports our buying decision. Prices are close enough to value to buy here. To set a price target, I prefer to turn to the longer-term chart. A level of about $60, approximately half-way back up to the top, would seem like a reasonable estimate. But what about a stop?

The latest low was $38.30 and the lowest low next to it ("Nic's Stop") $38.75. If you put your stop at that level, you will risk a bit more than $3 per share. Would that be a reasonable stop?

What if KO fell to its previous low of $37.01 and even violated it by a dollar before reversing to the upside? That would make the bullish picture even stronger but would require a stop of almost $7.

if stopped out. Remember that professional traders will often take several stabs at a trade.

Now let's take a look at what happened to KO going forward (see Figure 5.15).

In summary, wider stops are a feature of long-term trades. If this approach attracts you, the key point to keep in mind is that as the width of your stops increases, the size of your trade must decrease, making sure you stay within the iron triangle of good money management.

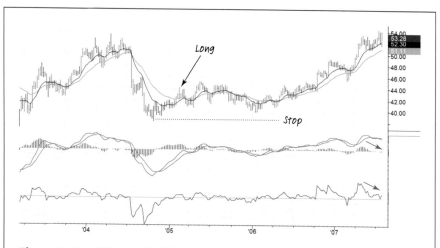

Figure 5.15   KO weekly follow-up

Talk about patience! Had you bought KO at the level we discussed, you would have had to wait nearly a year before the uptrend got going. Prices did sink below the entry level but never violated their stop, even the tighter one. At the right edge of the chart prices have just broken out above their 2004 high. Several indicators are tracing bearish divergences. Shall we hold to our initial target of near $60 or take profits here? This is the sort of dilemma that burdens the lives of long-term traders.

MOVING STOPS

Each trade must be branded with the "iron triangle" that links money management and the protective stop with position size. It makes you enter each trade with a clear stop in mind, but as time goes on you'll face a choice. On the one hand, you may leave both the stop and the profit target in place, and run that trade as originally planned. On the other hand, you may want to move your stop to protect a greater share of your capital or paper profit. Of course, you may only move your stops in one direction—up for longs and down for shorts. You may tighten your grip on a trade but never loosen it.

Some traders use trailing stops which move in the direction of the trade in accordance with some predetermined rule. Others may start out with a traditional stop but then, as prices approach their target, decide that the market wants to go farther. A trader who thinks that the trend is likely to move beyond his initial target can cancel his profit-taking order and switch to a trailing stop. This would allow the trade to run as far as it can before it sets back and hits the stop. Making this switch requires you to make the same calculations as you made when you first got into the trade—balancing the potential reward against the very real risk. When you switch from a target to a trailing stop you must be willing to give up a part of your profit.

There are pros and cons to trailing stops, just like with everything else in trading. On the plus side, a trailing stop can deliver extra profits if the trade moves beyond your target. On the minus side, you risk giving back some profit if the trade reaches the profit target and reverses instead of going any further.

There is a variety of techniques available to traders who like to use trailing stops:

- You can use a multibar low as a trailing stop; for example, you can keep moving your stop to the lowest low of the last three bars (but never against your trade).

- You can trail prices with a very short moving average and use its level for a trailing stop.

- You can use a Chandelier stop—every time the market makes a new high, move the stop within a certain distance from the top—either a specific price range or a number based on an ATR (average true range). Any time your stock makes a new high, you place your stop within that distance from the top, like hanging a chandelier (this method is described in *Come into My Trading Room*).

- You can use a Parabolic stop (described below).

- You can use a SafeZone stop (described below).

- You can use a Volatility-Drop stop (described below, for the first time in trading literature).

- You can use a Time Stop to get out of your trade if it does not move within a certain time. For example, if you enter a day-trade and the stock does not move within 10 or 15 minutes, it is clearly not doing what you expected and it is best to scratch that trade. If you put on a swing trade which you expect to last several days, but then a week goes by and the stock is still flat, it is clearly not confirming your analysis and the safest action would be to get out.

A Parabolic Stop

The Parabolic system, presented in 1976 by J. Welles Wilder, Jr., was one of the first attempts to work the concept of time into the setting of stops. The system moves the stops closer to the market each day. In addition, it accelerates whenever a stock or a commodity reaches a new extreme in the direction of the trade.

$$Stop_{tomorrow} = Stop_{today} + AF \times (EP_{trade} - Stop_{today})$$

Where $Stop_{today}$ = the current stop

$Stop_{tomorrow}$ = the stop for the next trading day

EP_{trade} = the extreme point reached in the market in the current trade. If long, this is the highest since the purchase day. If short, this is the lowest low since the shorting day

AF = the Acceleration Factor

On the first day in a trade, Acceleration Factor equals 0.02. This means you must move your stop by 2% of the distance between the extreme point and the original stop. AF increases by 0.02 each day the rally reaches a new high or a decline reaches a new low, up to the maximum of 0.20.

In the beginning of a trade, Acceleration Factor is small and stops move slowly. As the market reaches new highs or lows, AF increases and stops move fast. If the market does not reach new highs or lows, AF keeps moving stops in the direction of the trade. By doing so, Parabolic forces traders to get out of trades that go nowhere.

Losers go broke by hanging onto losing positions and hoping for a reversal. The Parabolic system protects traders from indecision and imposes discipline on them. It sets a stop the moment you enter a trade and tells you to move it in the direction of that trade.

The Parabolic system is extremely useful during runaway trends. When prices soar or crash without a pullback, it is hard to place stops using normal chart patterns or indicators. Parabolic is a great tool for placing stops under those conditions.

The Parabolic system works well in trending markets but leads to whipsaws in trendless markets. It can generate spectacular profits during price trends but chop up an account in a trading range. Do not use it as an automatic trading method.

Adapted from *Trading for a Living* by Dr. Alexander Elder,
John Wiley & Sons, Inc., 1993

If you become interested in trailing stops, test them like any other method. Begin by writing down your rules, then pull up some familiar charts and apply the rules to the past data. If the system works on paper, begin implementing it with real money, while keeping good records. You want the size of your trades while you test the method to be so small that neither profit nor loss would matter to you. Then you can concentrate on mastering the new approach and leave money-making for later, when you have a higher degree of confidence in your new method.

A SAFEZONE STOP

SafeZone stops are designed to capitalize on the concepts of signal and noise in the financial markets. If the price trend is the signal, then the counter-trend moves are the noise. Engineers build filters to suppress noise and allow the signals to come through. If we can identify and measure market noise, we can place our stops outside of the noise level. This will allow us to stay in our trade for as long as the signal identifies a trend. This concept was described in detail in *Come into My Trading Room* and had since been implemented in several trading programs.[2]

We can define a trend in a variety of ways, including something as simple and straightforward as the slope of a 22-day EMA. When the trend is up, we can define noise as that part of each day's range that protrudes below the previous day's low, going against the trend. When the trend is down, we can define noise as that part of each day's range that protrudes above the previous day's high. A trader needs to select the length of the lookback period for measuring all the "noisy" penetrations. That lookback period must be short enough to make it relevant for current trading—approximately a month of the latest data on the daily charts (Figure 5.16).

To quote from *Come into My Trading Room*:

> If the trend is up, mark all downside penetrations during the lookback period, add their depths, and divide the sum by the number of penetrations. This gives you the Average Downside Penetration for the selected lookback period. It reflects the average level of

---

[2]That book contains step-by-step instructions for calculating SafeZone stops and provides a sample Excel spreadsheet. Elder.com includes SafeZone in its Elder-disks for several popular programs, such as TradeStation, MetaStock, eSignal, and TC2007.

noise in the current uptrend. Placing your stop any closer would be self-defeating. We want to place our stops farther away from the market than the average level of noise. Multiply the Average Downside Penetration by a coefficient, starting with a 2, but experiment with higher numbers. Subtract the result from yesterday's low, and place your stop there. If today's low is lower than yesterday's, do not move your stop lower since we are only allowed to raise stops on long positions, but not to lower them.

Reverse these rules in downtrends. When a 22-day EMA identifies a downtrend, count all the upside penetrations during the lookback period and find the Average Upside Penetration. Multiply it by a coefficient, starting with a 2. When you go short, place a stop twice the Average Upside Penetration above the previous day's high. Lower your stop whenever the market makes a lower high but never raise it.

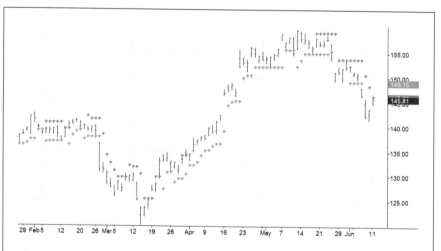

Figure 5.16   DE daily, SafeZone

This chart illustrates a well-known fact about trend-following systems—they shine during powerful trends but lead to whipsaws in trendless markets. You can see how SafeZone caught a powerful upmove in DE in the middle of the chart. This is where a trailing stop performed at its best. In the relatively trendless zones near the left and right edges a trend-following method delivered multiple whipsaws. This chart sends a clear message on choosing stops—use trailing stops only during powerful trends.

Like any other method, SafeZone is not a mechanical gadget to replace independent thought. You have to establish the lookback period
and choose the coefficient by which to multiply the normal noise to obtain the SafeZone stop. Usually, a coefficient between 2 and 3 provides
a margin of safety, but you must research it on your own market data.

VOLATILITY-DROP TRAILING STOPS

One trader who likes to use trailing stops is Kerry Lovvorn, mentioned
earlier in this book. On a visit to New York he showed me a method he
invented. It is designed to keep him in a trade for as long as prices are
running in his favor but prompt him to get out soon after they start
pulling away from their recent extremes. This is the first public presentation of the Volatility-Drop method, offered here with Kerry's permission.

> I do not think of using a trailing stop until my target is hit. At that
> time the trade has fulfilled its duty, but the market may be moving
> in a way that seems to have potential for an additional reward.
> When the market hits my target I have a choice. I can take profits,
> be happy, and go on to the next trade. But then maybe my target
> was too conservative, and there is greater profit potential left in the
> move. I do not want to give all my accumulated profit from this
> trade back but am willing to risk a portion to find out whether the
> move has more life left in it. My decision depends on how much
> profit I am willing to give back to find out. The challenge of a trail-
> ing stop is the same as that of any other stop—where to set it. If
> you set it too tight, you may as well go ahead and exit the trade.
>
> Once the market gets going, it can go much farther than we can
> ever imagine. We can set a trailing stop and let the market decide
> how far it wants to go and when to take us out.
>
> Using trailing stops is my way of saying—hey, if the market is
> willing to give me more, this is how much I am willing to give up
> to find out. I think of it in terms of the price I have to pay to play
> the game. This is similar to the calculations I make when putting
> on a fresh trade—weighing reward against risk. The question is the
> same: How much am I willing to pay? Once I decide to switch to
> a trailing stop, my decision has been made, and I let the market
> decide how far to go next.
>
> I call my trailing stop a Volatility-Drop. If the market is willing
> to go crazy and have this huge momentum move, I am willing to
> stay with it. Suppose I use Autoenvelope to set my price target

when I enter the trade. The normal width of the envelope is 2.7 standard deviations. If I want to switch to a trailing stop once that target is reached, I will place it one standard deviation tighter—at 1.7 standard deviations. As long as the move continues along the border of a normal envelope, I'll stay with it, but as soon as the price closes inside of the tighter channel, I'll be out. A programmer could take it and make it automatic—either intraday, or end-of-day.

How do you decide whether to take profits at the initial target or switch to a trailing stop?

If my target is hit and I see bearish signals, I won't use a trailing stop. If I see a negative price action—like a wide bar closing near the low on heavy volume, I will take my profit at a target and be gone. But when the market is moving well, with higher highs and higher lows, I will follow. It's like a beautiful girl—you are going to follow her along. I make the decision when my target gets hit— I need to see a positive enough action to switch to a trailing stop.

How often do you switch from a target to a trailing stop?

I do it in about two-thirds of my trades. It doesn't always work in my favor. Sometimes I set a trailing stop, and five minutes later I get stopped out. About half the time a trailing stop gives me a little more profit than the original stop. The big payoff comes from those rare cases of oversize profits in runaway moves.

Like any market tool, trailing stops are not for everybody, but they help me in my decision-making. They are good for the people who find themselves struggling to decide whether to get out of the trade or stay in it. Using a trailing stop shifts the decision away from you and hands it over to the market. That's what drove me to use trailing stops so extensively.

This chart (Figure 5.17) illustrates an entry into a trade. The weekly (not shown) was neutral. The daily showed a narrow trading range. I call this pattern "a squeeze play" and try to catch a breakout from it. The recent tall peak of MACD-Histogram led me to expect an upside breakout, and I took a long position inside the squeeze.

Two days later MMM had erupted from its squeeze and flew above my target, which was at the upper channel line, at 80.63 (Figure 5.18). The action was extremely strong, with the entire bar above the channel. I immediately decided to switch to a trailing stop and drew a second Autoenvelope on the chart, at only 1.7

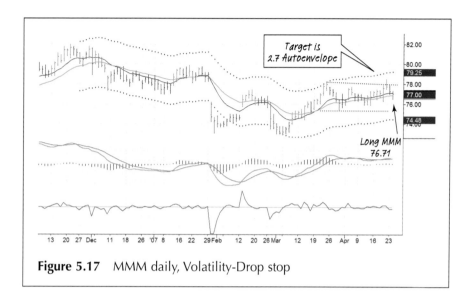

Figure 5.17   MMM daily, Volatility-Drop stop

standard deviations. My plan was to sell after MMM closed inside that narrower channel (see Figure 5.19).

MMM continued to "walk the line" for several more weeks until it finally contracted and closed inside the narrower channel. I exited

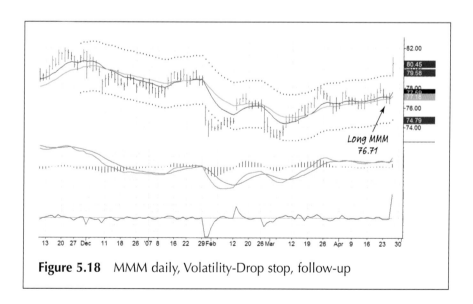

Figure 5.18   MMM daily, Volatility-Drop stop, follow-up

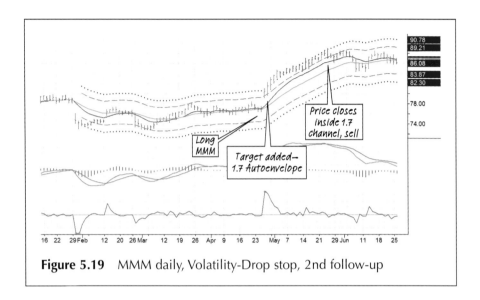

Figure 5.19   MMM daily, Volatility-Drop stop, 2nd follow-up

on May 24 at 87.29, a big improvement over the initial 80.63 target. Notice how different Autoenvelope looks in retrospect—by the time we get to the exit the entry appears quite different. This is because Autoenvelope is based on the last 100 bars action, and as the market becomes more volatile Autoenvelope becomes wider.

Kerry's Volatility-Drop tactic not only provides a useful trading tool but also delivers an important message. Trailing stops are suitable only during certain periods. When the markets are quiet and orderly, a trader is better off with his original profit target and stop. When the markets embark on powerful moves, a trader must use his judgment to recognize them and may switch to a trailing stop.

SELLING "ENGINE NOISE"

I magine driving a car on a routine trip. Gradually, you become aware of a hard rattling noise, which becomes louder whenever you step on the gas. There might be wisps of smoke or steam escaping from under the hood. Will you continue to drive? Will you keep your foot on the accelerator, hoping that maybe the noise is nothing serious and will go away? Or would you pull over and get out of the car to investigate?

Hard noise, smoke, and gradual loss of power could be the signs of engine trouble. Maybe you're lucky and it's no big deal, just a branch caught in the undercarriage or some other nonsense that is easy to remove or fix. On the other hand, something could be seriously wrong with the car. Continuing to drive while ignoring the signs of danger could lead to much worse damage down the road.

You might enter a trade as casually as running an errand. Maybe the trip to your destination will be uneventful, but if you hear hard noise or see steam coming from under the hood, do not press on. Take your foot off the gas pedal, pull over, and step out of the car to investigate what's happening.

There is no reason to hold every trade to its planned target. You have to listen to the market. Perhaps it wants to give you more than you expected, but maybe it wants to give you less. As a trader, you need to keep an eye on what is happening and get out when you suspect engine trouble.

System traders and discretionary traders differ in many ways. For a system trader, a stop is set in stone. He has placed it, along with an order for taking profits at the levels his system gave him; he does not need to look at the screen intraday. A discretionary trader plays a different game. He also has a target and a stop, but he is allowed to exit the market sooner or hold a little longer if his analysis suggests a different course of action.

This permission to change course in the middle of a trade or even in the middle of a trading day has different meanings for different people. My friends among system traders find it stressful. They prefer to perform their analysis in the peace and quiet of their offices and not look at live markets. Discretionary traders, on the other hand, consider this ability to change plans liberating. Yes, I have my plan, yes, I have my stop, but I also have the luxury of choice: I can tighten my stop if I do not like how the market is acting, or take profits early. Or, if I like how the market is acting, I can continue to hold past my profit target and try to take more money from the trade than originally planned.

If you are a discretionary trader, let us review several situations in which you may change your exit tactic in the middle of a trade. I have named these exits "engine noise" because when you first got into a trade you planned to drive somewhere else, but the noise coming from the engine prompted you to change your plans. Please keep in mind that while selling at profit targets or using protective stops works for traders at all levels of expertise, selling in response to "engine noise" requires a much greater level of experience. If you are a beginner, you may want to skip this chapter and return to it later, after you've become a more proficient trader.

WEAKENING MOMENTUM

If you notice that your stock is starting to act sloppy, there is nothing wrong with taking a profit and standing aside, ready to repurchase if and when that stock starts looking firmer. "Looking firmer" does not mean hitting new highs; it means the stock stops declining, flattens out, and starts to pick itself up from the floor.

The time to become suspicious of an open position is when its progress starts slowing down—when the stock starts moving sideways rather than up. There are many measures of market momentum, extensively described in trading books, including my own. The following example uses MACD-Histogram, a popular indicator, to gauge momentum (see Figure 6.1).

Looking at any chart, you must keep in mind that its buy and sell signals seem clear only in retrospect. Buy and sell points are clearly visible on old charts, but the closer you get to the right edge, the foggier

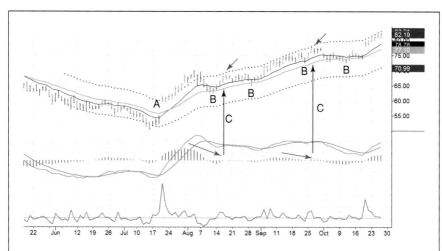

Figure 6.1 AAPL daily

A. Breakaway gap—the start of a new uptrend
B. Pullback to value—buy!
C. Divergence—sell

Here we see how a lengthy downtrend in AAPL ended with a gap to the upside. This breakaway gap flagged a decisive upward reversal, after which it made sense to begin trading from the long side. One way to handle an uptrend is to keep buying pullbacks into the value zone and selling rallies above the upper channel line, in the overvalued territory.

they become. Trends and reversals are hard to recognize in real time. There are almost always conflicting signals at the right edge of a chart, but that is where we must make our decisions. Had we known in advance what was going to happen, we would have bought a load of AAPL and held it. In the real world, every little move could have signaled the start of a reversal. This is why a shorter-term trading approach makes sense—buying near value and selling in the overvalued zone.

If our plan is to buy value and sell above value, what would make us change this approach? What would indicate the loss of momentum?

When a savvy short-term trader sees a divergence between MACD-Histogram and price, he or she is ready to change the plan—sell without waiting for the upper channel to be hit. Maybe prices will reach it or maybe they won't, but meanwhile, it makes sense to grab a profit and re-evaluate the situation from the sidelines. This chart shows how both bearish divergences were followed by pullbacks into the value zone. Those pullbacks created good opportunities to re-establish long positions.

If you do not like how your long position is acting, you have two choices. If you're in a short-term trade, you can just shoot it, accept a lower profit than planned, and move on. If you are in a long-term trade, you probably do not want to sell your entire position. You may want to take partial profits and maintain your core position, with an eye towards repurchasing the shares you've sold at a lower price. This technique allows you to take more than one dollar's profit out of a one dollar move. Let me open my diary to illustrate both approaches.

AN "ENGINE NOISE" EXIT FROM A SHORT-TERM TRADE

One of my favorite sources of ideas for short-term trades is the Spike group. Its members generate two dozen short-term stock picks every weekend, and I almost always select one of them to trade in the week ahead. This particular week, I liked IKN; Jim Rauschkolb who suggested it had sent in the Spike submission form shown in Figure 6.2. This long trade involved risking 25 cents per share to make 57 cents (see Figures 6.3 and 6.4).

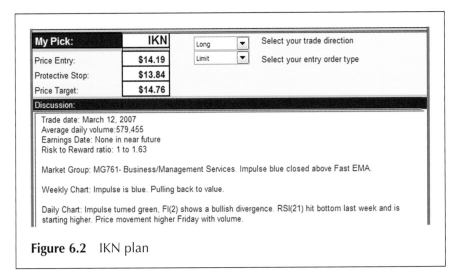

Figure 6.2   IKN plan

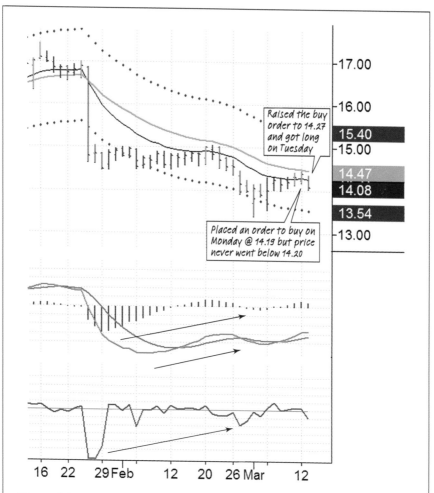

Figure 6.3   IKN entry

I placed my order to buy IKN on Monday at 14.19, exactly where the Spiker who chose it had recommended buying. IKN was strong that day and its low for the day was $14.20. My buy order was not filled, but after the close I felt even more bullish. After studying support and resistance on intraday charts I raised my buy order for the next day to $14.27. The market quickly reminded me that it generally does not pay to move your entries. IKN declined and, after filling my buy order, closed at 14.08, near the day's low. My entry grade was only 31%, as I bought in the upper third of that day's bar.

IKN	long	Date	Upchannel	Downchannel	Day's High	Day's Low	Grade
Entry	$14.27	14-Mar-07	15.4	13.54	$14.37	$14.05	31%
Exit							
P/L					Trade		

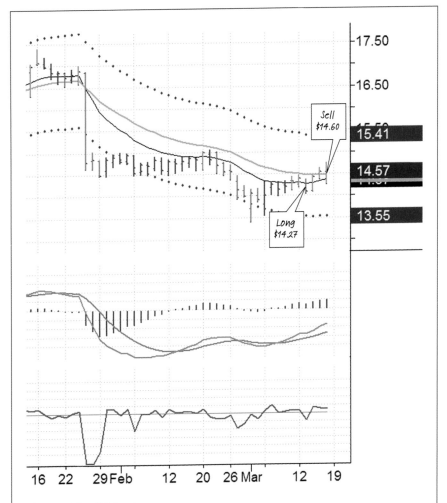

Figure 6.4 IKN exit

On Friday, March 16, IKN took out the previous day's low, then crossed back up above its longer-term moving average (the yellow line). With the weekend approaching and the stock acting inconclusively, I decided not to wait but instead took profits while prices were above value. I sold my IKN at $14.60.

My exit grade was 69%, a high rating, thanks to selling in the upper third of the day's range. The overall trade grade was a middling 18%, reflecting the percentage of the channel I had caught on the daily chart. Since a 20% rating equals a "B", 18% rated a B−. That Spike pick won a Bronze for the week, meaning it was the third best pick of that week, in a very difficult market environment. My discretionary exit led to a profit.

IKN	long	Date	Upchannel	Downchannel	Day's High	Day's Low	Grade
Entry	$14.27	14-Mar-07	15.40	13.54	$14.37	$14.05	31%
Exit	$14.60	16-Mar-07			$14.75	$14.27	69%
P/L						Trade	18%

There is nothing terribly exciting about this trade, which is precisely why it is shown here. There is very little exciting about day-to-day trading, with thrilling trades few and far between. A reasonable trading idea comes in, an entry gets fumbled a bit, the trade does not go as well as expected, but the exit is clean, and in the end a bit of profit drops to the bottom line, nudging up the equity curve. This is what much of trading for a living is about.

A DISCRETIONARY EXIT
FROM A LONG-TERM TRADE

In January 2007 I received an e-mail from a friend who told me about his great bullishness on Ford Motor Company. The firm had just indicated it was likely to announce its biggest quarterly loss in the company's history, but my friend Gerard outlined his reasons why the new CEO would turn the company around. He was a retired money manager whose approach to finding stocks was based on the fundamentals. I respected his judgment and took a look at the stock (see Figures 6.5 and 6.6).

I've already described my approach to trading tips. A tip is merely a trigger for doing one's own research. Even if I were to get a tip from someone like Warren Buffett, I'd still run that stock through my screens. I like it when a tip comes from a fundamental analyst. Since my own work is primarily technical, it provides a multidimensional view of a stock.

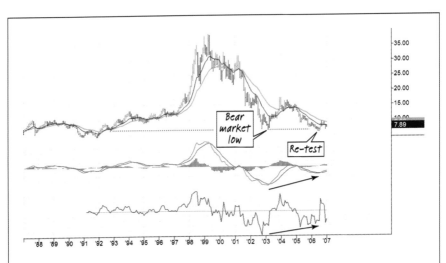

Figure 6.5   F monthly

A quick look at a 20-year long monthly chart of Ford revealed a bull
market top in the 1990s near $40, followed by a vicious bear market,
which took the stock down to $6 in 2003. Ford bounced, then slowly
slid to a slightly lower low in 2006. I love this pattern of a slightly
lower low, accompanied by massive bullish divergences. With the company prospects very appealing, according to my fundamentalist friend,
and a monthly chart very constructive, it was time to look at a weekly
chart.*

---

*There was also a psychological confirmation. That winter I flew to the Caribbean
several times, and on every return the same young man drove the limo from
the airport. He was a nice fellow, interested in stocks, but did not know
who I was. On the last ride, feeling generous, I told him I was buying Ford. He
was so shocked—because of all the bad fundamental news—that he turned
sharply back towards me—and I was afraid he'd skid the limo off the New Jersey
Turnpike. A contrarian loves buying stocks that are hated by the crowd.

I developed a plan to accumulate a fairly large position in F and
hold perhaps for several years, with a tentative target near $20, about
halfway back to the top. Since this plan took a very long-term view, I
had no intention of chasing any rallies, including the one at the end of
January. I was going to wait and accumulate my position during short-
term declines.

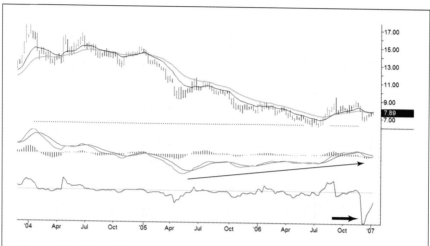

Figure 6.6 F weekly

The weekly chart confirmed multiple bullish divergences at the 2006
bottom and added another strong buy factor—a deep spike of weekly
Force Index in December 2006 marked by an arrow on the chart. Such
a downspike reflects a huge volume of sales, as a mass of traders gives
up on a stock and dumps its shares at the market. This spike of Force
Index revealed that the holders had reached what some call a "puke
point," tossing out their former possessions. After weak hands are
eliminated, only strong holders remain and a stock is ready to advance
(this signal works well at bottoms but its reverse is not useful for calling tops).

My plan continues in effect to this day, as I keep buying on declines,
selling part of my position on rallies, and repurchasing on subsequent
declines. I keep on selling more expensive, recently acquired shares,
while maintaining the core position of older, cheaper ones for the long
haul. Figure 6.7 illustrates the first three steps in this game, while
Figure 6.8 illustrates the fourth.

This long-term position was established on a combination of two
inputs: a fundamental tip and strong technical signals. The buying and
selling campaign depends on keeping an ear out for engine noise
and selling at the slightest signs of sputtering. When the engine sounds
good I repurchase sold shares, at a lower level. All the while, I maintain the core position for the long haul.

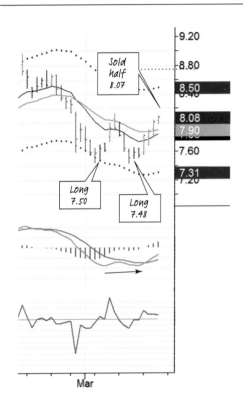

Figure 6.7 F daily

I acquired the first position—about one-fifth of what I meant to accumulate—at $7.50 and the second at $7.48. Both were purchased near the lower channel line on the daily chart, when the Force Index dipped below zero. The two bottoms were separated by a brisk rally. Another rally erupted from the second bottom, but I saw a bearish divergence of the Force Index and a slightly overbought position of MACD-Histogram, which made me concerned that the rally was running into resistance. I implemented my plan by selling the more expensive of the two positions at $8.07, planning to repurchase double its size when prices fell back towards the $7.50 support. The chart above shows these three steps in my Ford campaign—buying at $7.50 and $7.48, then selling half at $8.07.

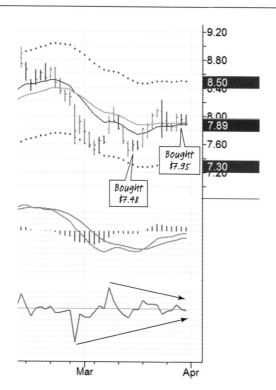

Figure 6.8 F daily follow-up

The day after I sold, F spiked up a little, and then cracked but refused to sink. Its rise had been capped, but there had been no follow-through to the downside. As the days went by I became concerned. My overall stance on Ford was bullish. A stock that refuses to go down probably wants to go up. I thought that the risk of missing a rally was greater than the risk of being caught in a decline, and placed a new buy order.

I bought the same number of shares at $7.95 as I sold at $8.07. My one concession to feeling cautious was that instead of buying back double the position sold, I bought back an identical size. As I write this, F is well above $9, and I continue to use declines to build up my long position, while using rallies to take partial profits.

SELLING BEFORE EARNINGS REPORTS

Traders often wonder how much attention to pay to earnings reports, along with the rest of fundamental data. Before I try to answer this question, let me restate one of the key points about market analysis— our research can never be complete. You cannot be an expert in both fundamental and technical analysis, psychology and cycles, positions of insiders and Federal Reserve policies, and so on. Also, someone who analyses fundamentals, such as earnings, must out of necessity be fairly narrow in his approach; it is difficult to transfer skills of analyzing one industry to another.

When it comes to fundamental analysis, at the very minimum, you need to know to what industry group a stock belongs. Stocks, like people, move better in groups. It is a good idea to go long stocks in strong groups and sell short stocks in weak ones.

Most fundamental information is reflected in stock prices. I sometimes say to fundamental money managers that I feel as though they are working for me. Whenever they buy or sell on the basis of their research, their actions create stock patterns that a technical analyst can recognize.

One problem with fundamental information is that it flows into the markets in bursts rather than in a steady stream. A chunk of fundamental information can hit a stock and make it leap. This is especially likely to happen when a company releases its earnings reports.

Earnings are hugely important because in the long run they drive stock prices. When you buy a stock you are in effect paying for future earnings and dividends. This is why many analysts, fund managers, and traders closely watch the earnings of the companies they follow.

Keep in mind that an earnings report rarely comes as a surprise for those who closely track the company. There are two reasons for that. First, there is an entire industry of earnings watchers and forecasters. Pros with a lot of experience tend to be right about their forecasts. Those who pay them for their research usually buy and sell ahead of the actual reports. Stocks seldom jump on earnings reports because the smart bulls have already bought or the clever bears have already sold. The pros pretty much know what to expect, and the price tends to reflect the mass expectation of what the earnings report will bring. When the report hits the newswires, there is rarely much of a surprise.

The other reason why stocks seldom jump on earnings reports is that the drift of those reports is often leaked in advance of their official release. I think that the volume of insider trading in the stock market is much greater than most people think. When the SEC catches some slob and puts him behind bars for insider trading, that action only shaves the tip of the iceberg. Greedy and stupid guys get caught. The slick types who trade friendly tips in country clubs can benefit from inside information throughout their careers. I learned this when, after only a few years of trading, I was befriended by a man who was on the boards of two listed companies. His boasts of trades based on the inside information passed among corporate buddies has made me very skeptical about market news. News for the masses, not for the classes.

Pascal Willain, a Belgian trader, said in his interview for *Entries & Exits*, "A tiger does not change its stripes. I believe that insider trading is linked to the way the company is managed and its type of business. Large contracts involve multiple participants and take weeks to negotiate, creating more chances for information leaks. A company cannot change the way it does business or its management method—if it leaked information in the past, it will leak in the future. Because of this I like to look at a company's news for the past year to see whether there was a signal prior to its moves."

Those of us who take a fairly skeptical view of companies' ability to keep secrets tend to hold a position, either long or short, straight through the earnings reports (see Figures 6.9 and 6.10). Since the earnings news has already probably been leaked and discounted by the markets, we can expect the pre-earnings trends to continue. On the other hand, those traders who have a greater trust in the system tend to be more cautious and close out their positions in advance of earnings reports.

In my experience, it generally pays to be skeptical about the sudden impact of earnings reports. Companies leak, insiders trade, and earnings reports come and go. Still, once in a while a skeptic gets burned, and the welts can sizzle. Take a look at Figures 6.11 through 6.13, charts of RIMM (Research in Motion), which provided powerful shorting signals shortly before its recent earnings report.

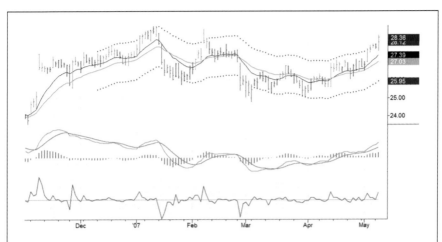

Figure 6.9 CSCO daily

Take a look at this chart of CSCO one day prior to the release of its earnings report. A slow but steady uptrend is in progress, with higher highs and higher lows since March. At the right edge of the chart, prices have risen into the overvalued zone above the upper channel line. Suppose you're holding a long position. What would you do at the right edge—sell or hold through the earnings?

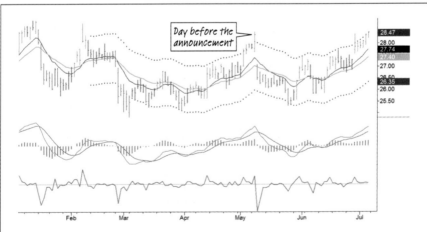

Figure 6.10 CSCO daily follow-up (to 7/8)

As the earnings report was released the stock initially sank, then recovered. Looking at it two months later one message is clear—it pays to sell in the overvalued zone above the upper channel line, earnings or no earnings.

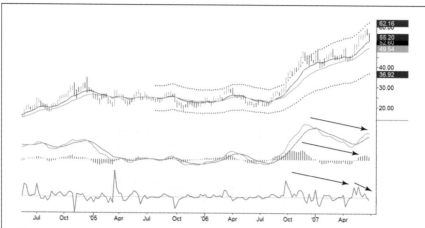

Figure 6.11   RIMM weekly
The weekly chart of RIMM showed a series of gorgeous bearish divergences in all indicators.

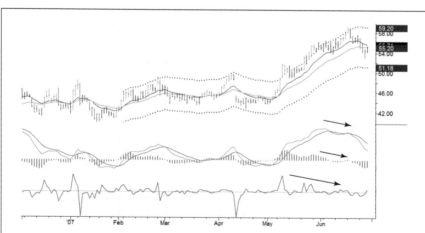

Figure 6.12   RIMM daily
The daily chart confirmed the message of the weekly with its own bearish divergences. A short trade was working beautifully, accumulating profits. At the right edge of the chart, on Thursday, it was hard to make a decision—to cover shorts or take the short trade over the earnings announcement, due after the market close on Thursday. On the one hand, the trade has not yet reached its profit target at the lower channel line but seemed on track to do so. On the other hand, the stock appeared to have recoiled from its Wednesday low.

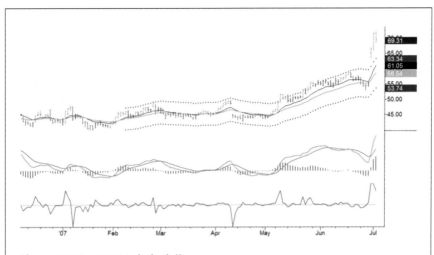

Figure 6.13   RIMM daily follow-up

It is shocking to see what can happen when a company is honest and does not leak! RIMM came out with a triple whammy—it beat projected earnings, raised its projection for the next quarter, and announced a 3:1 stock split. The market was truly surprised—it stood up on its hind legs and roared. The stock exploded on a gap, negating bearish divergences and rising to new record highs.

Dishonesty may be more widespread than many people think but honesty is a more powerful force. The lesson is that if you want to be on the safe side, close out your position prior to an earnings report.

THE MARKET RINGS A BELL

Once in a blue moon the market rings a bell to let you know that a long-term trend is coming to an end. The sound of the bell is hard to recognize amidst the roar of the markets. Most people do not hear it, and only savvy traders respond to it, like a good hunting dog raising its ears to the quiet whistle of its master.

You need a great deal of experience to hear the market ring its bell, and you need a great deal of confidence to act on that signal. You need to be attentive and alert because the market rings the bell very seldom. Your eyes, ears, and mind must be open to recognize those signals. This is not a task for beginners. When you hear the sound of the market bell and act on it, it is a sign that you are becoming a serious trader.

The first time the market rang its bell in front of me I was deaf to it. After several months of watching the wild ride that followed, I could look back and recognize the signal. A major money-making opportunity had slipped away, but I did not miss the major educational opportunity. It sensitized my ears to the ringing of the market bell.

In 1989 I flew to Asia for the first time. The upper deck of the Japan Airlines Boeing 747 felt clubby and comfortable. The lights went out after dinner and most passengers drifted off to sleep, but I felt keyed up on my first flight across the Pacific. I walked over to the galley and fell into a long friendly conversation with a Japanese steward, a man of about 50. He told me how he grew up in poverty after the war, with little education. It took a great deal of hard work to rise to his position

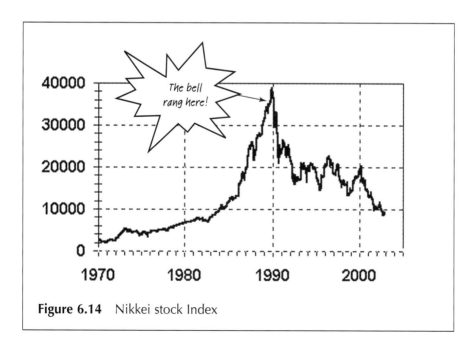

Figure 6.14 Nikkei stock Index

as the chief steward in the business class of the national airline. He was very proud of his accomplishment.

As we continued to chat, he told me he was very active in the Japanese stock market which had been rising for two decades. He said he was making more money in stocks than from his salary and was planning to take an early retirement. He had already selected a Pacific island where he was going to build his villa. There was only one thing that made him angry: the office girls who lived at home with their parents and did not have the family responsibilities of a married man could put even more money into the stock market, making even greater profits!

Several months later the Japanese stock market keeled over and crashed (Figure 6.14). It lost half its value in the first year, and that was just the beginning of a vicious bear market. I had missed a great shorting opportunity right at the top. It was a great lesson that made me determined not to miss such psychological signals in the future.

You can hear the market bell when you recognize an event or a series of events so far outside the norm that it may seem as if the laws of the market have been repealed. In fact the laws of the market cannot go away, no more than the law of gravity can. They can be only temporarily suspended during a bubble, creating an illusion that normal rules no longer apply.

It is not normal for a man who knows next to nothing about the stock market—as my steward told me he did—to be making more money in stocks than from his salary at the pinnacle of a successful career. It is not normal for random office girls to be making even more money than him. The markets do not exist to put money into the pockets of amateurs. When outsiders and latecomers start making a lot of money, the market is near the top. It can only go way down, returning to the equilibrium.

Today, when I think of that conversation, it feels as if someone came up to me with a bell, and rang it next to my ear—sell and sell short! My problem was that because of my lack of experience that sound went in one ear—and out the other.

Bernard Baruch was a famous stock operator in the first half of the twentieth century. He managed to sidestep the crash of 1929, which ruined so many of his peers. He described how one day in 1929 he stepped out of his office, and the man who polished his shoes gave him a stock tip. Baruch recognized the sign—if people at the lowest level of society were buying stocks, there was no one left to buy. He began selling his stocks. In a different era and in a different economy, my Japanese steward had given me an identical signal.

Here's another psychological signal. Having attended traders' expos and shows for many years, I've become aware of a strong inverse correlation between the level of the stock market and the quantity and quality of free gifts that the exhibitors hand out. When the stock market boils at the top you need a shopping bag to hold all the goodies that vendors hand out. A month before the 1987 market top, one of the Chicago exchanges was giving away good sunglasses whose frame was engraved with the saying, "The future is so bright, I have to wear shades." On the other hand, going to an expo near the bottom of a bear market, you'd be lucky to get a free ballpoint pen.

The quantity and quality of free gifts at a trade show serve as useful indicators of the public's mood. When the market is up and the public is happy, people spend money and vendors, feeling flush, hand out more goodies.

On February 24, 2007 I went to a Traders' Expo in New York. The stock market had been rising for nearly four years. It had been going straight up for the preceding seven months with no pullbacks. The richness of the offerings at the trade show was fantastic. I picked up ski hats, baseball hats, a scarf, a stack of T-shirts, and other goodies. But the main gift awaited me at the Nasdaq booth—the exchange was giving away free money (Figure 6.15).

Monday was a holiday, but on Tuesday I began to put out more shorts. My indicators had been flashing sell signals for a month, and now this offer of free money felt as if someone was ringing a bell. The uptrend had overshot any reasonable target, and this free money proved that the uptrend had gone really crazy. I exited almost all my long trades and piled on shorts. I shorted stocks and stock index futures, and even bought some index puts. I did not have to wait very long. The market went up for one day after the show and then it tanked. It was a great time to be short (see Figures 6.16 and 6.17).

Markets are like pumps that suck money out of the accounts of the uninformed majority and flow it into the pockets of a savvy minority. It is a minus-sum game in which winners receive less than what losers lose because the people who run the game siphon off huge sums of money as the costs of doing business—commissions and slippage, fees and expenses. This is why the market always has fewer winners than losers.

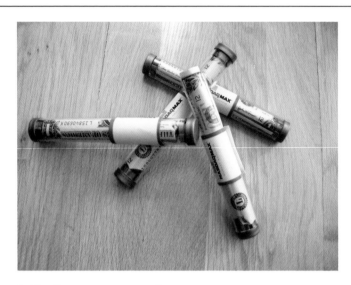

Figure 6.15 Free money at market top

They had dollar bills rolled into plastic tubes, with a little advertisement pasted to them. I could not believe my eyes and asked whether the money was real. They told me to see for myself. I opened a tube and pulled out a crisp new dollar bill. I asked whether I could take two, and they said, go ahead. My companion also got two. When I taught a class later that afternoon, I told my students that the stock market was at a top, and that a loud sell signal was being given right outside the class door, in the exhibit hall.

Professional traders profit from market swings, which move too fast for outsiders. Amateurs profit only from long, sustained trends. Such long, one-way moves are an exception rather than the rule. When everyone becomes bullish and makes money, it is not normal. In the long run, the majority must lose, and only a minority can win. When the market rings a bell it is telling you that an aberration has gone too far, the majority has become very big, and the mass of traders is ready for a nasty fall.

You will not recognize these signals early in your trading career. You can learn to see and hear them only if you are a serious student of the market and keep your mind open. When you start hearing, under-

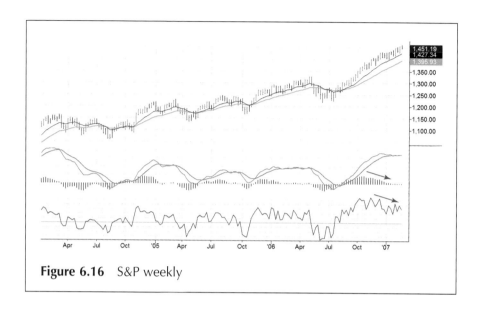

Figure 6.16   S&P weekly

standing, and acting on these signals, that will be a sign that you are no longer a beginner. When you begin acting upon these signals, you'll be among the small minority of traders who are good at the market game.

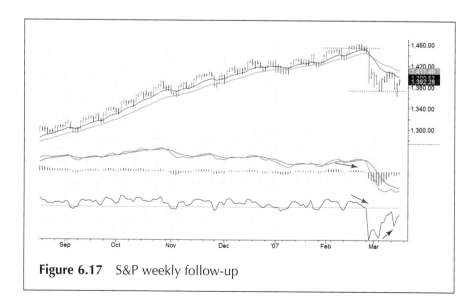

Figure 6.17   S&P weekly follow-up

TRADING WITH
THE NEW HIGH–NEW LOW INDEX

Whether you trade stock index futures or individual stocks, it pays to have an indicator that confirms market trends and warns you of their upcoming reversals. When this indicator starts flashing signals that the stock market is about to turn, you should become especially alert to the technical signals in the stocks you hold.

I've come to believe that the New High–New Low Index (NH-NL) is the best leading indicator of the stock market. New Highs are the leaders in strength—they are the stocks that on any given day have reached their highest point for the past 52 weeks. New Lows are the leaders in weakness—the stocks that have on that day reached their lowest point for the past 52 weeks. The interplay of new highs and new lows provides better information about the health or weakness of a trend than merely looking at market averages.

NH-NL is very easy to construct. Simply take the New Highs for the day, subtract the New Lows, and you'll have that day's NH-NL. Take the sum of the daily NH-NL for the past five days to find the weekly NH-NL.

When NH-NL is positive, it shows that bullish leadership is stronger. When it is negative, it shows that bearish leadership is stronger. NH-NL confirms trends when it rallies or falls in gear with prices. Its divergences from prices help identify tops and bottoms. If the market rallies to a new high and NH-NL rises to a new peak, it shows that bullish leadership is growing and the uptrend is likely to continue. If the market rallies but NH-NL shrinks, it shows that the uptrend is in trouble. The same logic applies to the new lows in downtrends.

I like to view NH-NL on a split screen—the weekly chart on the left, the daily on the right. The weekly chart shows NH-NL as a line, while the daily chart has an additional pane showing New Highs as a green line and New Lows as a red line. Figure 6.18 shows how the chart looked during a recent peak in February 2007.

It does not hurt to know that at the time NH-NL was flashing this sell signal, the market had rung a bell, as illustrated in Figure 6.19. When various indicators, based on different principles, give the same signals, they reinforce each other's messages.

NH-NL helps confirm uptrends and downtrends, or alert us to their impending reversals. While the timing of NH-NL signals is not as precise as other indicators, such as MACD or Force Index, it is very use-

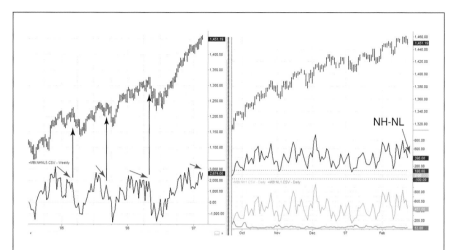

Figure 6.18   NH-NL, February 2007

Red line—new lows.
Green line—new highs.

On the left side of the chart you can see the S&P 500 climb to a new bull market peak while the weekly NH-NL, immediately below, traced a bearish divergence (marked with a red arrow near the right edge of the chart). Similar previous divergences, marked with vertical lines, have identified important tops within the bull market. On the daily chart you can see a minor bearish divergence of daily NH-NL. The main sell signal comes from the weekly chart.

ful because it helps us recognize when it is a good time to accumulate stocks and when to unload them.

While the number of New Highs and New Lows is published in most business newspapers, very few databases include its raw data. I manually input NH-NL readings into TradeStation. Whenever I teach classes abroad, I urge local traders to develop the New High–New Low Index for their local markets. Using NH-NL in a country where other people do not have it would give you a decided advantage.

THE DECISION TREE FOR SELLING

A serious professional in any field, be it auto repair or brain surgery, has a decision-making tree. It is rarely written down, as the pro usually

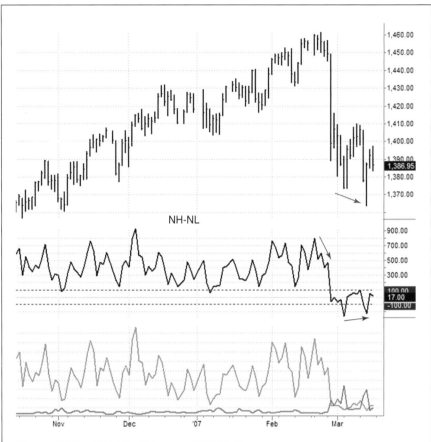

Figure 6.19   NH-NL, February 2007 follow-up

The stock market collapsed following a bearish divergence on NH-NL. It bounced, then sank to a lower low, but the daily NH-NL formed a more shallow low. This bullish divergence indicated that the downside leadership was failing and it was the time to cover shorts and buy again.

keeps it in his head. In fact, it is probably somewhere even deeper—in his bones.

A decision-making tree is a set of rules that helps you decide what to do and what not to do in any given situation. Professionals develop their decision-making trees slowly and gradually, in the course of their training, education, and practice. The best of us continue to develop our decision-making trees as long as we live—this is the value of age and experience. As my late great friend Lou Taylor joked in his late 70s—"If I become half a percent smarter each year, I'll be a genius by the time I die."

Few of us write down our decision-making trees. We tend to develop them imperceptibly, not as a single structure but in bits and pieces that gradually merge into a coherent whole. I grin remembering how, as a greenhorn trader, I decided to write down my decision-making tree during a five-hour flight from New York to Los Angeles. A month later I was still scribbling on a table-sized sheet of paper, crisscrossed with arrows and splattered with whiteout.

The only professionals who always carry printed decision-making trees are airline pilots. They are given manuals that show how to troubleshoot any problem on the plane. If a pilot thinks he smells smoke in the cockpit, he does not just wrinkle his nose and say "Geez, smoke. I wonder what I should do. . . ." Instead of scratching and thinking, he opens his manual to the Smoke page and, with his co-pilot, goes through clearly defined "if–then" questions and answers, which lead to specific actions.

Still, even a printed decision-making tree, approved by the best airline, can never be complete. Reality always has surprises and shocks up its sleeve, and humans have their frailties. In his fascinating book *The Black Box*, Malcolm MacPherson serves up dozens of transcript recordings from the black boxes of crashed airliners. A trader can learn a great deal from watching how some pilots fall apart under pressure while others rise up to the challenge. My favorite chapter in the book is the recording of the black box of a plane whose tail engine had exploded, cutting all hydraulic lines. The onboard manual does not tell the pilot how to control a plane whose controls had been cut, and when he calls the plane manufacturer they tell him that his plane cannot possibly be flying. The pilot hangs up and then figures out how to land by the seat of his pants. His discretionary, as opposed to systematic, flying saved him, his crew, and most of his passengers.

Still, 99 times out of a 100, it is useful to write down your decision-making tree. This is why we will discuss several points that must go into a decision tree for selling.

Before we focus on selling, just a brief reminder about the decision-making tree for buying. It must begin and end with money management. Your first question must be: *Does the 6% Rule allow me to trade?*

A Decision-Making Tree

A discretionary trader's decision-making tree has many branches, and he may follow different ones at different times as market conditions change. Just as all the main branches of a tree are connected to the trunk, a decision-making tree centers around a set of inviolate rules for risk control.

A system trader develops a mechanical set of rules for entering and exiting trades. He backtests them and puts them on autopilot. This is the point, however, where amateurs and pros go in opposite directions. The amateur feels relieved that a system, either his own or bought from someone else, will free him from worry. Since market conditions always change, all systems eventually self-destruct, which is why every amateur with a mechanical system must/will lose money in the end. A pro who puts his system on autopilot continues to monitor it like a hawk. He knows the difference between a normal drawdown and a reading that shows that a system has deteriorated and needs to be shelved and replaced. A professional system trader can afford to use a mechanical system precisely because he is capable of discretionary trading.

A trading system is an action plan for the market, but no plan can anticipate everything. A degree of judgment is always required, even with the best and most reliable plans.

Think of any other plan or system in your life. For example, you probably have a system for taking your car out of the garage. You need to open the garage door, start the car, warm up the engine, and pull the car out into the street without bumping into walls, running over tricycles, or getting hit by passing trucks.

You have a system in the sense that you perform the same actions each time in the same sequence, not thinking of the routine but paying attention to what is important—watching out for dangers, such as kids on bicycles, or freshly fallen snow, or a neighbor crossing the sidewalk. When you detect an obstacle, you deviate from your system, and return to it after the situation returns to normal. You would not try to design a complete system, which would include dealing with the snow, and the bicyclists, and the neighbors, because that system would be too complex; it would never be complete, as a neighbor could come into your car's path from another angle. A system automates routine actions and allows you to exercise discretion when needed.

And that's what you need in the markets—a system for finding trades, setting stops, establishing profit targets—all the while paying attention

to a heavy truck headed for you in the shape of a Federal Reserve announcement or a kid on a tricycle in the form of a disappointing earnings report. Many beginners set themselves the impossible task of designing or
buying a complete trading system, which is just as impossible as a complete system for pulling your car out of a garage.

Adapted from Come into My Trading Room by Dr. Alexander Elder,
John Wiley & Sons, Inc., 2002

Your last question before putting on a trade must be what size the 2%
Rule allows you to trade. We discussed these rules in Chapter 2 and
returned to them in Chapter 5, in the Iron Triangle section (page 103).

If you buy well, it becomes much easier to sell well. If you buy in
accordance with your money management rules, you will not be
stressed by carrying a size that is too large for your account.

To draft a decision tree for selling you need to consider several
questions:

1. **Is this a short-term or a long-term trade?**
   Your tactics for setting a target will depend on the answer to this
   question. If this is a short-term trade, you would need a nearby
   target in the vicinity of a channel or an envelope. If it is a long-
   term trade, you can set the profit target farther away, in the vicinity of major support or resistance. Trends go farther and last longer
   than ordinary price swings. As a general rule, trend traders tend to
   be long-term oriented and swing traders short-term oriented.

   Sohail Rabbani, a trader interviewed in *Entries & Exits,* com-
   pared the two types of traders to elephant hunters or rabbit
   hunters. One shoots only rarely, at a big target, while the other
   shoots often at a small target. There are vast differences between
   the two hunters' equipment, as well as their entire hunting process.
   Many beginners go out into the bush with some random guns,
   sold to them by some fast-talking dealers. They have a vague idea
   of shooting something—maybe an elephant, or maybe a rabbit,
   but they are most likely to shoot themselves in the foot.

   Do you know what target you are trying to shoot? Have you
   written down at what level you expect to take profits? Have

you written down for how long, approximately, you expect to be in this trade? A short-term trader must keep especially close track of his trade grades and be quick to exit soon after his stock hits an A level, after traveling 30% of the channel on the daily chart. A longer-term trader needs to hold until his trade hits a much more remote profit target.

2. **Where will you place your stop?**
   In short-term trading, not only will you have a nearby profit target—you will also have a reasonably tight stop. With trend trading, the target is farther away, the estimated time to the target is measured in months if not years. Since an elephant may meander, hunting him requires much wider stops.

   As a general rule, stops should be tighter for short-term trades and more relaxed for long-term trades. Occasionally you may be lucky to find a stock that sits very quietly on rock-solid support. You may acquire a large long-term position with very low dollar risk. Still, the majority of long-term trades require more leeway. A long-term trader may well consider a fairly loose stop on his position while shorter-term traders tend to use tighter stops on their trades.

   Since the iron triangle limits your total risk per trade, the greater the distance to the stop the fewer shares you may carry. As the risk per share goes up, the number of shares you buy must come down, keeping your total risk within your money management limits.

   If you trade a small account, you pretty much have to go to the maximum 2% risk limit on most trades. For someone who trades a good-sized account the situation is somewhat different. A trader with a large account might limit his risk on short-term trades to 0.25% of trading capital, but go up to 1% on long-term trades. This means that even though his risk per share is greater on long-term trades, his position size can still be fairly large.

3. **Listen to different types of "engine noise" for short-term or long-term trades.**
   When a trade starts sputtering and jerking instead of pulling towards the target, a discretionary trader might decide to hop off. He does not have to wait until the trend turns on him and hits his stop. He may well grab a small profit and move on to greener pastures. The type of noise that causes alarm is different for short-term and long-term traders.

A short-term trader may watch the daily charts and indicators for any signs that his trade is becoming overbought and topping out. He would almost certainly run from a bearish divergence of daily MACD-Histogram, but he might also scramble after seeing a fairly minor sign, such as a bearish divergence of the Force index or even a simple downturn of daily MACD-Histogram. With his short-term outlook, any subtle sign of tiredness, the slightest engine noise may be taken as a signal to hop off while there is still good profit on the table.

A long-term trader has to be more tolerant of minor noise. He should not jump in response to signals on daily charts. If he does, he is almost certain to lose his grip on a good trade. He needs to focus on the weekly charts and wait for much louder "engine noise" before getting out of his trade. He may look for signals similar to those a short-term trader looks for, but on the weeklies rather than on the dailies. It is not a good idea for a long-term position trader to keep too close an eye on the daily chart.

An experienced trader can actually combine long-term and short-term approaches in a single campaign. He or she may apply short-term trading skills to long-term trades by trading around a core position. You can maintain a core long-term position through thick and thin but keep trading shorter-term in the direction of that trade with a portion of your account.

Let's say you are trying to hold 1,000 shares of an $8 stock with a target in the low 20s. You may want to consider 500 shares of that position as a long-term hold. The rest may be optional and depends on the behavior of your stock. You may build up your position to 1,500 when the stock pulls back to a moving average, sell down to 500 on a rally above a channel. You may keep buying and selling while holding your long-term position. If this sort of activity appeals to you, be sure to keep good records. You must measure which is more profitable—the core position or your little dance around it.

Whatever you do, keep a visual diary of your decisions and actions. Keeping good records will help you accelerate your learning, survive the inevitable hard times, and claw your way to profitability.

PART THREE

HOW TO SELL SHORT

Pssst! Want to hear a secret?

Here it is, but please promise to keep it very quiet: Stocks sometimes go down.

Yes, really! Everybody keeps buying them but sooner or later every stock suffers a price drop.

If living well is the best revenge, then one of the sweetest things you can do in the markets is to take something that hurts everybody—price drops—and turn that into a source of profits. Think of all those times you bought a stock and it crapped out on you. Imagine if you had been on the opposite side of that trade, making money instead of losing on every downtick.

Would you like to profit from price declines? If so, we need to talk about selling short.

First, a few basic definitions. Everybody understands how to make money from buying low and selling high, but many have no concept of how to profit from price drops. To make sure we are on the same page, let's run through a basic explanation.

Suppose you look at IBM, trading at $90, and decide it is going to $99. You buy a hundred shares, hold, and sell when the stock reaches your profit target. You make $9 per share, for a total of $900 on 100 shares, minus commissions and fees. This is so simple, a child could understand it. But what if you look at IBM at $90 and conclude that it is overvalued and likely to drop to $80? How can you possibly profit from that?

A short-seller enters a trade by borrowing someone else's shares and selling them in the market. Later on he buys back the same number of shares and returns them to his lender. This is possible because one share of IBM is just like any other share. It does not matter which shares you borrow, sell, and return—as long as the numbers match. If you can buy those shares back at a lower price you'll make money.

Your friendly broker will handle the entire transaction. If you tell him to sell short 100 shares of IBM, currently trading at $90, he'll begin by making sure you have $9,000—the cost of 100 shares—in your account. He'll set that money aside as a security deposit (for simplicity's sake we will not discuss margin here). Then he will put on a green eyeshade and shirt-sleeve protectors and shuffle into the back office where there are rows of folders with clients' stock certificates. As he goes through those folders, he finds that Aunt Millie has a few hundred shares of IBM that she inherited and not touched in years. He borrows 100 shares from her folder, leaving a note that you owe her those 100 shares. He then turns around, sells 100 borrowed shares in the market, and puts the proceeds into his safe deposit box with a note about the transaction. Now you owe Aunt Millie 100 shares, while the proceeds from selling them are sitting in your broker's safe, with your name pinned to the envelope of cash. You can always use that money to buy back IBM and return shares to Aunt Millie.

Suppose your analysis was on target and IBM declines to $80. You call your broker and tell him to cover your short position. He takes the envelope with $9,000 cash from the safe and buys 100 shares of IBM. Now, with the share price down to $80, he needs only $8,000 to buy those 100 shares. There will be $1,000 left over. That money, minus commissions and fees, will be your profit. Your broker will put it into your account and release your security deposit that he held during the short trade. With 100 shares of IBM in hand, he will shuffle into the back room, find Aunt Millie's folder, put 100 shares back, and remove the note that you owe her those shares.

Now the transaction is over—you have your profit as well as your security deposit, the broker has his commission, and Aunt Millie has her shares back. Why would she lend them out to you? A standard agreement for a margin account in the United States automatically gives a broker the right to lend out shares from the account. Or maybe Aunt Millie was savvy enough to negotiate a small fee with the broker for giving him the right to lend out her shares. There is really no risk to her because the money from the sale is held by the broker and that plus your security deposit is enough to buy her shares back at a moment's notice.

Of course, the sequence we just reviewed is a cartoon-like simplified picture. There are no green eyeshades, shirt-sleeve protectors, or back rooms with dusty share certificates. Nowadays every step of selling short is performed electronically.

What can go wrong with selling short? When you buy a stock, it can go down instead of up. Just as the stocks you buy can go down, the stocks you sell short can rally. For example, IBM, instead of declining from $90 to $80 might rally to $95. If you decide to cover your short at that point, it will cost you $9,500. Since the proceeds of the short sale brought only $9,000, the broker will take an additional $500 from your security deposit to buy back enough shares to make Aunt Millie whole. Also, if IBM declares a dividend, Aunt Millie will expect to receive it because she owns the stock. Since you borrowed her shares and sold them, you'll have to pay that dividend to her out of your own pocket.

These two risks—the price risk and the cost of the dividend—pretty much cover the waterfront. You can evaluate your risks in advance and decide whether you can live with them. People are usually much more afraid of fantasy than reality—and the scariest fantasy in shorting is the idea of unlimited risk.

If you buy IBM at $90, the worst thing that could happen would be for it to drop to zero, wiping out your investment. That would be bad, but you know your maximum risk before putting on a trade. If, on the other hand, you short IBM at $90, and it begins to rise, your loss would be unlimited. What if it went up to $1,000 per share? $2,000? You could be financially wiped out.

Right, and a meteorite could also fall on your head while you're walking down the street.

It is a well-known fact of human psychology that people underestimate common dangers and overestimate unusual dangers. In the city of New York, where I live, a murder on the subway becomes front-page news. It obscures the fact that many more people get killed by slipping and falling in their own bathrooms. A zoo animal that mauls its keeper makes national news, while thousands of fatal auto accidents pass virtually unnoticed.

Every serious trader must have an action plan. An important part of that plan is to define your risk and set a stop-loss order. The stops on purchases go below the market, on short sales above the entry price.

Occasionally you will encounter a fast market. There will be slippage and your loss may be bigger than anticipated. Still, if you short large, liquid, actively traded stocks, such unpleasantness will occur very rarely.

For any person who can imagine shorting IBM at $90, not using a stop, and then watching it climb to $1,000, I have only one piece of advice. It is the same advice I'd give to his counterpart who buys IBM at $90 without a stop and watches it slide down to zero, wiping out his investment: "Don't be an idiot. Use stops."

Instead of shivering and imagining fantastic risks of shorting without stops, let us discuss the practical do's and don'ts of shorting stocks, futures, and options. Let us discuss real risks, as well as very real opportunities.

All stock market beginners come in as buyers. Most short-sellers are pros. Why do you think they keep shorting, year after year? Do they do it out of civic-mindedness, as a public service? Do they do it because they like to gamble? Or do they sell short because the money can be much better there than in buying? Think about it.

Let us now take a closer look at shorting.

SHORTING STOCKS

Stocks do not move in straight lines. They rise and fall as naturally as humans inhale and exhale. Some of their rises and declines are minuscule, but others are quite large, presenting attractive trading opportunities.

There is one common prejudice from which you must free yourself in order to sell short. Most people feel comfortable buying but feel uneasy profiting from declines. I think they acquire this prejudice as young adults. When I taught a class on trading at a local high school, the kids took to shorting like fish to water. They were responsible for bringing in trading ideas, and we would discuss them in class and trade them in the account I had opened for that class. On any given day the kids would make as many suggestions to sell short as to buy. Often the same kid would bring up both a long and a short.

The kids got it. They understood that trading means betting on moving objects. It matters little whether you bet on a rise or a decline. You only need to get the direction right and determine the most promising entry point, profit target, and where to place a protective stop. The kids came to the market without prejudices and had no inhibitions against shorting. The class bagged some profits on the way up and on the way down. It also took some losses in both directions, but we made sure they were smaller than our wins. We played the game in both directions.

It is my belief that short-sellers, while pursuing their own self-interest, provide an important public service in the markets. First of all, by selling overvalued shares, we increase their supply and dampen excessive market volatility. Extremely volatile markets tend to hurt public investors. Selling more stock when prices are high tends to smooth out wild peaks. Second, when a stock is in a severe decline, short-sellers are among the first to step in and buy, cushioning that decline. Buyers tend to grow skittish and hang back during severe drops. It is short-sellers, flush with profits, who step in to buy in order to cover and turn paper profits into real money. Their covering slows down the decline, and that's when the bargain hunters step in. Next thing you know, a bottom is in place and the stock is going back up again. Short-selling dampens excessive price swings and benefits the public.

I do not want to imply that short-sellers are a bunch of social workers, running around to help others. We aren't. But as the great economist Adam Smith showed two centuries ago, people in the free market help others by doing what is best for themselves. Bears help the markets, as long as there is no collusion between them—no "bear raids." This caveat applies equally to buying, to manipulating stocks upward.

While the government has a legitimate role in policing the market, it appears to have taken things a little too far. In its zeal the government slapped several illogical restrictions on short-sellers. The worst of them was "the uptick rule," which said you may only sell short if the previous tick—a minuscule price change—was an uptick. In other words, you may only sell short a rising stock. Ostensibly this was done to protect buyers from the packs of short-sellers hammering their stock with an avalanche of sell orders. I have only one question for these protectors of the public—why not have a downtick rule as well, to protect the innocent from being swept away in a bubble? To carry the uptick rule to its logical conclusion, a downtick rule would permit buying only on a downtick, when prices decline.

A tremendously positive development occurred in the U.S. stock market while I was working on this book. Shortly before I submitted the manuscript to the publisher, the government did a sensible thing and rescinded the uptick rule. The silly rule that was a part of the trading scene for some 70 years is finally gone! Of course, the futures markets never had a downtick rule.

Shorting has one massive advantage over buying and one massive disadvantage. The great advantage of selling stocks short is that they tend to go down about twice as fast as they rise. This applies to all timeframes—to monthly (Figure 7.1), weekly (Figure 7.2), and daily (Figure 7.3), as well as intraday charts.

Traders say that it takes buying to put the stocks up but that they can fall under their own weight. This greater speed of declines creates

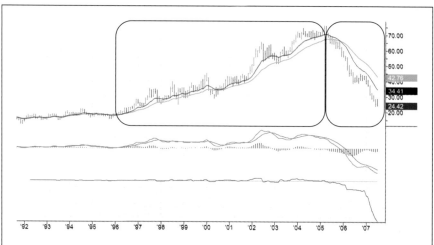

Figure 7.1 MNI monthly

MNI monthly: from 23 to 76 in 10 years, from 76 back down to 23 in 2.5 years.

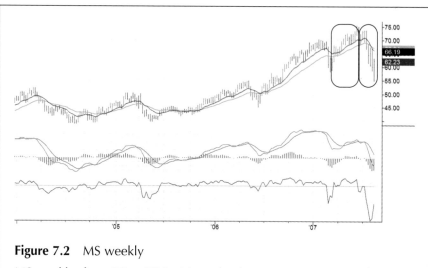

Figure 7.2 MS weekly

MS weekly: from 58 to 75 in 14 weeks, from 75 to 58 in 8 weeks.

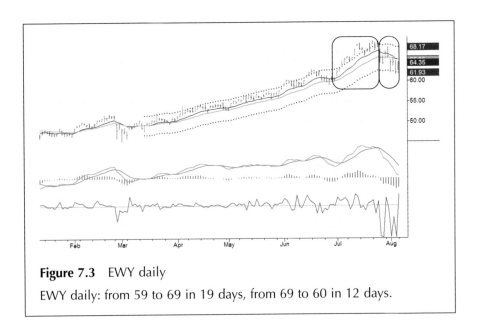

Figure 7.3 EWY daily

EWY daily: from 59 to 69 in 19 days, from 69 to 60 in 12 days.

a real advantage for experienced traders. Your money is safe in a money market fund, but the moment you use it to trade, you expose it to risk. Both opportunity and risk are in the markets. Of course, you look for the areas where the opportunity outweighs the risk, but generally, the faster the trade, the less time you spend exposed to market risk. Selling short allows you to profit faster—or to leave sooner if you find you've made a mistake.

Every action in the stock market has two angles—one helpful, the other dangerous. You can never fully separate the two or have one without the other. It is essential that you keep your eyes open to both sides of the coin and be realistic. What should we do in response to the advantage and disadvantage we just discussed?

In general, you want to be more short-term oriented in shorting than in buying. You are surfing against the gently rising tide, the downtrends are faster and more furious than the uptrends, and there is no point in giving a short trade too much time to "work itself out." Give the downtrends less time to put up or shut up than you would give to an uptrend.

The one great disadvantage of selling stocks short is that the broad stock market has a centuries-old tendency to rise over time (Figure 7.4). The estimates of the angle of this so-called "secular rise" vary, clouded

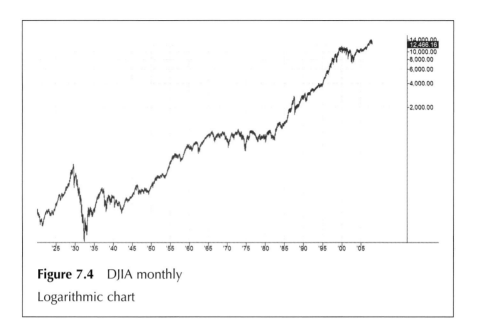

Figure 7.4   DJIA monthly
Logarithmic chart

by many old stocks disappearing and new stocks being listed. Still, an average 3% rise per year seems like a reasonable estimate. This means that in shorting you are swimming against a gently rising tide.

YOUR FIRST SHORTS

Whenever I talk about shorting in a class, hands go up and beginners ask how to find stocks to short. I suggest thinking of all those stocks they bought and lost money on. Think of the stocks you expect to decline. Find the stock you hate the most and sell it short.

A friendly reminder: do not try to make a lot of money on the first short, or on the second short for that matter. Go short just a few shares.

Take your first baby steps without having to worry about money. You'll have plenty of other things to think about—selecting a stock to short, choosing a profit target, setting a stop, as well as learning the mechanics of placing an order. Be sure to work out these and other issues while trading a size so small that neither gain nor loss will matter much at all.

Trade size serves as a huge emotional amplifier. The bigger the size, the greater the stress. To reduce stress, especially early in the game, when you are still learning to short, trade a small size. There will be plenty of time to increase the size of your trades once you grow more comfortable with shorting.

Several weeks prior to writing this chapter, I was at home one morning in front of a live screen. My laptop beeped, signaling an incoming e-mail. It came from Zvi Benyamini, a recent Traders' Camp graduate who wrote that he had implemented much of what we had discussed and was ready to begin shorting. I replied with a suggestion that he write up his analysis of the stock he wanted to short, using the format we discussed in the Camp. Several minutes later an e-mail (Figure 7.5) came in:

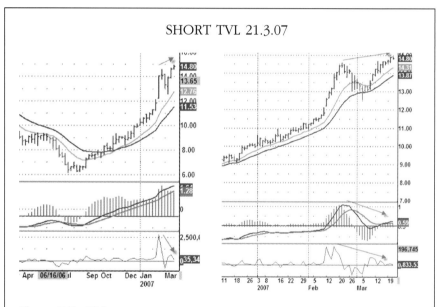

Figure 7.5   TVL entry

Weekly double top, blue for a while, diverging FI. Daily major MACD divergence, FI major divergence from a month ago, this peak also losing force. Ticked blue today.
Shorted 100 @ 14.79
Stop: hard at 15.2, bail if turns green.
Target: 12.77 weekly fast MA. Partial around 13–13.5 if stalls.
Note—Alex's warnings: strong MACD-Histogram on the weekly chart, and stock visibly strong (not affected by the recent crash).

After the market closed for the day, I received a follow-up (Figure 7.5):

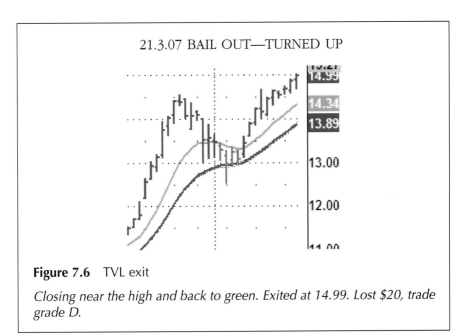

Figure 7.6   TVL exit

Closing near the high and back to green. Exited at 14.99. Lost $20, trade grade D.

This is a good example of how an intelligent person learns to short and how little he pays for his lessons. This camper found a stock and worked it up independently. He created a good Trader's Diary entry and documented his decision-making process. He even wrote down my objections to his trade. As an independent man, he put on the trade anyway, but made its size very small. His loss cost him 20 cents per share on 100 shares, or $20 plus commissions. Yet he received a lot of educational value from this trade, with tiny financial risk. He can afford many such lessons, without becoming stressed by losses.

I did not like TVL as a short pick that day. First of all, the time was not right for shorting. The stock market had just established an important double bottom and rallied from it. The tide of the market was moving up, and I had already covered almost all of my own shorts. Furthermore, it did not feel right to short a stock that kept reaching new highs almost every day for several weeks.

When you go long, it is not a good idea to buy a stock that keeps making new lows. It is OK to buy low, but not OK to buy down. Similarly, when you want to go short it is not a good idea to sell short a stock that keeps making new highs. You want to see some evidence that the uptrend has hit the ceiling, stopped rising, and is ready to turn down.

My camper made two mistakes by shorting a rising stock in a strong market. At the same time, he got two important things absolutely right. He made excellent notes that he can review again and again. And he traded a very small size, so that his mistakes cost him next to nothing. He paid cheap tuition for a lot of serious learning.

THE ASYMMETRY OF TOPS AND BOTTOMS

When we talked about buying stocks, we focused on two main approaches—value buying and momentum buying. When we look for stocks to sell short, we cannot simply flip these methods. Shorting is different from buying because mass psychology is different at tops and bottoms, in uptrends and downtrends. Stock market bottoms tend to be narrow and sharp, while the tops tend to be broad and uneven.

Stock market bottoms are built on fear. When longs can no longer take the stress of losing, they panic and dump their shares with little regard to price. Their fingers have been caught in the door, and the pain is so bad that they want to get out at any price.

Fear and pain are sharp and powerful emotions. A selling panic shakes out weak holders, and once they are out, the stock is ready to rise again. As long as you do not buy prematurely and then panic and sell at the bottom, buying tends to be fairly permissive (Figure 7.7).

Tops are built on greed, a happy emotion that can last a long time. As bulls make money, they call their friends and tell them to buy, even after their own money runs out. That's why the tops tend to last longer and be more irregularly shaped than the bottoms. You can see that the upward spikes of Force Index do not identify tops but rather confirm the ongoing uptrend.

While the bottoms tend to stand out clearly on the charts, the tops tend to be broad and less defined, with many false breakouts. Whenever the bulls find more money, they toss it at their favorite stock, making it rise above a seemingly well established top. Those brief, upward fake-outs are very typical of market tops.

Figure 7.8 comes from my trading diary. I shorted RL in June, after it staged a false upside breakout that was accompanied by a slew of bearish divergences. I thought that the false breakout had cleared the air for the decline, but it was slow in coming. Instead of collapsing, the stock continued to percolate at high level, sorely testing my patience, before

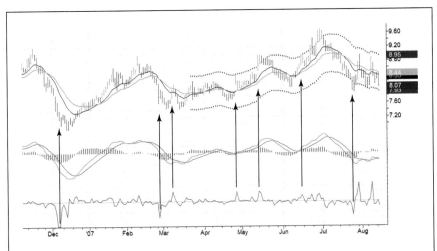

Figure 7.7   F daily

The fundamental asymmetry of tops and bottoms is clearly reflected by the Force Index. Its downspikes tend to serve as good markers of public panics that clear the air and augur new advances. A downspike of Force Index does not necessarily nail the exact day of the bottom, but it shows where the weak holders are dumping their shares, and the buying opportunity tends to come within days.

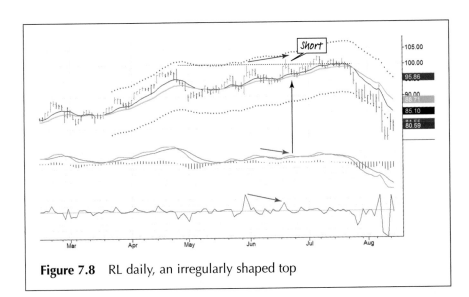

Figure 7.8   RL daily, an irregularly shaped top

it finally did what I expected. It stayed up like a bull that has had a sword plunged through its heart yet continues to run during a bullfight.

This kind of behavior at the tops makes shorting much harder than buying. Tops demand wider stops, increasing the risk per share. If you use tight stops, your risk of a whipsaw is much greater with shorts than with longs.

Let us review some of the major opportunities and dangers of shorting.

SHORTING TOPS

If you can profit from buying low, you ought to be able to profit from shorting high. Keep in mind that shorting near the top tends to be harder than buying near the bottom. At the end of a downtrend, markets often appear exhausted and listless, with low volatility and tight price ranges. On the other hand, when prices are boiling near the top, you can expect high volatility and wide price ranges. If buying can feel like climbing on a horse that is standing by a fence, shorting can feel like trying to mount a horse running in the field.

One of the key solutions for this problem, as for so many others in trading, is money management. You need to short smaller positions and be prepared to re-enter if stopped out. If you commit all your permitted risk to one entry, a single false breakout will kick you out of the game. It pays to trade a size smaller than the maximum permitted by your money management rules. It makes sense to keep some risk capital in reserve. You can either use wider stops or be prepared to re-enter if stopped out. You need to be able to hold on to your bucking horse (Figure 7.9).

During a monthly webinar in January 2007 a trader named Deborah Winters asked me to analyze JCP. I had not looked at the stock in years but became very excited once I saw its chart. I had become very bearish in the beginning of 2007, and some of my reasons for that I've already discussed in the chapters on the market bell and on the New High–New Low Index. Against the background of a toppy stock market, the weekly chart of JCP looked like a screaming short:

- The stock was expensive, just below its all-time high.
- It had broken out to a new high two weeks earlier; that breakout failed and the stock fell back into the trading range. A false breakout to a new high is one of the strongest shorting signals in technical analysis.

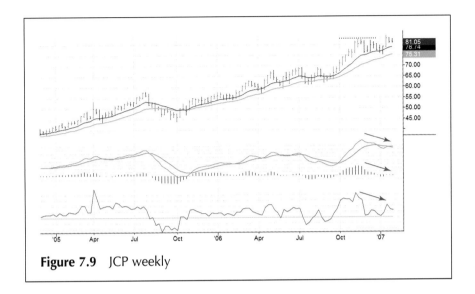

Figure 7.9   JCP weekly

- The weekly price was above value—above both moving averages.
- There were clear bearish divergences in MACD-Lines and Force Index; MACD-Histogram, while not diverging, was declining.

The daily chart of JCP confirmed the message of the weekly, suggesting that the stock was near its top (see Figure 7.10). It showed the same false upside breakout—a sharp spike to a new high, followed by a slide back into range. There were bearish divergences of MACD-Lines and the Force Index, but not MACD-Histogram. Whenever a webinar pick appears especially attractive, I announce to the group that I might trade it in the days to come. That is exactly what I did with JCP. My profit target was about $75, in the value zone on the weekly chart. I was not going to continue holding the stock much above $88. It was not a very appealing reward-to-risk ratio, but the technical signs led me to believe that the likelihood of a price break was much greater than that of a rally. The reward-to-risk ratio on a well-thought-out trade is not like a coin toss with a 50/50 chance of winning or losing. In such a trade the likelihood of the reward is higher than that of losing.

JCP	short	Date	Upchannel	Downchannel	Day's High	Day's Low	Grade
Entry	$81.45	30-Jan-07	84.09	76.56	$81.79	$80.66	70%
Exit							
P/L						Trade	

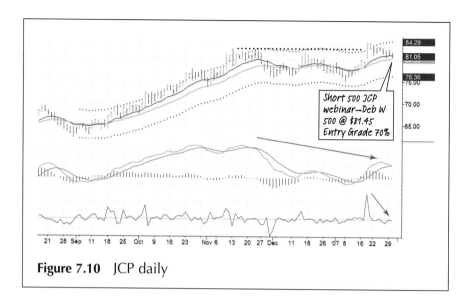

Figure 7.10   JCP daily

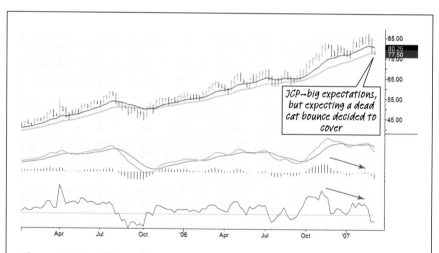

Figure 7.11   JCP weekly exit

This weekly chart reflects profit-taking in the vicinity of the initial profit
target. Prices fell below the fast red EMA and even the slower yellow
EMA, but their decline appeared to have slowed down. At the same time,
the weekly Force Index had produced a downspike, a likely sign of a
bottom. Weekly MACD-Histogram fell to the level at which it could be
expected to make a bottom. The sweet part of a downmove appeared to
be over; there was no point waiting for prices to hit the initial $75 target.

The ideal place to sell or sell short is near the upper channel line. I try to avoid shorting below value, below the daily EMAs. I refuse to sell short at or below the lower channel line because there prices are overextended to the downside. Here I was so bearish on the market and so concerned about not missing a big downmove that I shorted near value, a little low for my liking. It was not a very good entry, because when you short at value you give up the help of the rubber band that has been overextended to the upside and can help snap prices down. Still, it was a nice entry into a short trade—selling closer to the day's high than to its low, scoring a 70% sell grade.

The daily chart helps understand some of the psychological pressure associated with shorting. The exit charts (Figures 7.11 and 7.12) show that my shorting was quite premature, and there were several weeks when holding short felt very hard. There were two strong reasons why I was able to hold. One was that I was extremely bearish on the market at that time and was heavily short across the board. Many of my shorts were turning out a lot better than the one for JCP, reinforcing my confidence in the bearish view.

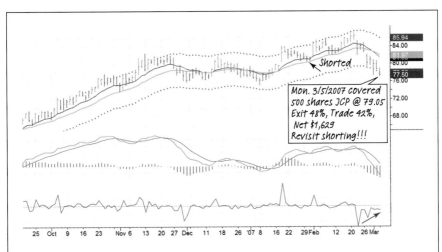

Figure 7.12   JCP daily exit

Shorting at a level that had turned out to be too low reduced profits from this trade. While my exit grade was a reasonable 49% and the trade grade of 44% well above the "A level," I took less profit from this trade than was available. A good trading idea with a middling implementation produced a profitable, but not a spectacular, trade.

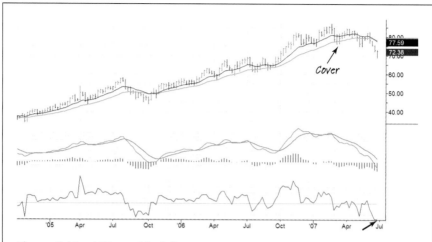

Figure 7.13 JCP weekly follow-up

One of the advantages of keeping a visual diary is that it allows you to look back and learn from your successes and failures. Returning to JCP two months after the trade, I could see that continuing to hold the short would have sharply increased my profits. It's a question of what you prefer—fast dimes or slow dollars. If only we could make our decisions in the middle of the chart and not at its right edge, we would always make the best choice!

The second reason was that the size of my short position was minuscule relative to the size of my trading account. If I had to use a tight stop, I would have been stopped out of this trade. A trader who is not greedy and has a bigger account has an advantage. If you risk 0.25% of your capital on a trade, and it starts going against you, you may increase your risk on that trade to 0.5% and still be well within the 2% maximum risk limit. A small trader who throws a full-size position at the market all at once has no such option. Having a large account is like driving a powerful car—you do not want to put the "pedal to the metal" all the time, but it is comforting to know that you have a power reserve.

Throughout this trade I remained in touch with Deborah, who had brought JCP to my attention. I encouraged her decision to hold, especially when she felt like throwing in the towel several times during the trade. One of my rules is that when I trade a friend's pick I tell that friend when and where I get in or out. Sharing a trade is like sharing a meal or going on a trip together—you do not want to do it in silence (Figure 7.13).

JCP	short	Date	Upchannel	Downchannel	Day's High	Day's Low	Grade
Entry	$81.45	30-Jan-07	84.09	76.56	$81.79	$80.66	70%
Exit	$78.15	5-Mar-07			$79.05	$77.21	49%
P/L						Trade	44%

SHORTING DOWNTRENDS

Several years ago, at a dinner in Sydney held by the Australian Technical Analysts Association, I found myself sitting next to an architect who told me that every year he flew to Spain and ran with the bulls in Pamplona. As a herd of bulls destined for bullfights are released from their pens, they run to the bull ring through the narrow streets of this medieval town. A crowd of men race in front of the bulls, taking the risk of getting gored or trampled if they do not run fast enough. I asked him why he did it, and he said that nothing else made him feel as alive as flirting with mortal danger.

I sometimes wonder whether trying to short market tops is similar to running in front of a thundering herd. This pursuit attracts us not only with its great potential profits, but also with the emotional satisfaction of having challenged and outrun the crowd.

There is another approach to shorting. Instead of tangling with a running bull you can wait until a bull is going down the chute at a slaughterhouse. There are men who stand by the side of that chute, zapping bulls dead. Their level of emotional satisfaction is probably a lot lower than that of the man running in front of the herd in Pamplona. But their success rate in bringing home a steady paycheck is probably a lot higher.

Let us keep in mind that the slaughterhouse job is not without its risks. A bull can lurch at the side of a chute and crush the worker's arm. We need to take a look at how to position ourselves outside of that chute and zap the bull with the least risk. Let us now take a look at shorting stocks that are already in downtrends (Figure 7.14).

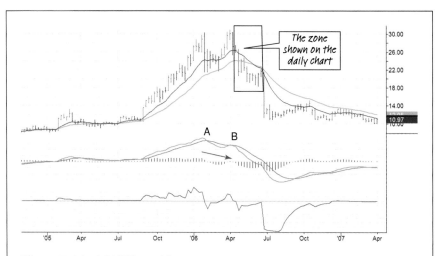

Figure 7.14 NWRE weekly

This weekly chart of NWRE shows a terrific opportunity to sell short near the top in early 2006. A false breakout to a new high, accompanied by a bearish divergence A-B, rang the bell for short-sellers. The wonderful thing about the middle of any chart is that trading signals stand out so clearly. The problem is that the closer we get to the right edge, the foggier the market becomes. I have not yet found a broker who will take my orders in the middle of the chart—they all want me to trade at the right edge.

If, as often happens, you have overlooked a shorting signal at the top, how can you take advantage of the decline that follows? Let us zoom into the area highlighted on the weekly chart and examine it using a daily chart (Figure 7.15).

That chute is the envelope on the daily chart.

The idea is to sell short when prices are near value, in the middle of the chart. The time to cover shorts and take profits is when prices fall to or below the lower channel line. We want to short value and cover in the undervalued zone.

After NWRE collapsed from its top in early April, it pulled back up to value. The space between the two moving averages is the value zone, marked "value—short" on the chart. That pullback provided a shorting opportunity. NWRE gapped down and fell below its lower channel line. That area is marked "oversold—cover" on the chart. In May, prices pulled back up to value again, creating another shorting opportunity. By mid-May prices slid into the oversold zone below the lower channel line, giving the signal to cover. This pendulum-like motion—the rise to the value zone, followed by a subsequent drop to the oversold level below the lower channel line—continued up to the right edge of the chart and beyond.

Selling short within a channel provides a series of clearly defined trading opportunities. Still, nothing in the markets is completely simple; there are always hidden dangers. For one thing, the depth of the

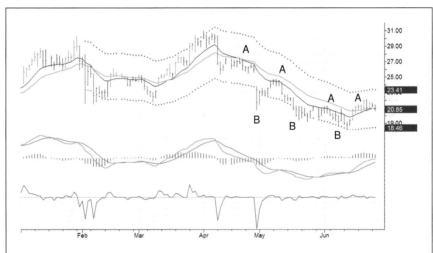

Figure 7.15 NWRE daily

A. Value—short   **B.** Oversold—cover

The same false breakout to a new high that we saw on the weekly is also clearly visible in the middle of the daily chart. Here we see no bearish divergence of MACD-Histogram, only a short-term bearish divergence of the Force Index. What is extremely useful about the daily chart is that it allows us to see the chute through which the bulls are going to their slaughter.

penetration of both the value zone and the oversold zone varies from week to week and from month to month. You cannot afford to be greedy inside the chute. You must be satisfied with grabbing a quick profit and moving on.

This is where the practice of grading your trades by the percentage of the envelope you capture becomes extremely useful. Remember, an A trade captures 30% or more of the envelope height. A third of any envelope equals two-thirds of the distance from the EMA to the channel line. This is the distance you must consistently catch to consider yourself an A trader. Technically, this is not such a hard task. Psychologically, it tends to be excruciatingly difficult, especially for those who have not yet mastered their greed or gotten rid of a perfectionistic streak.

To trade successfully within a channel, you must set a realistic goal, take your profit at that level, and be satisfied with it. Kicking yourself when you occasionally miss an opportunity to catch a bigger move is counterproductive and absolutely forbidden.

Let us return for a moment to the weekly chart, to see what happened beyond the right edge of the daily. NWRE collapsed, garnering further profits for the bears. Near the right edge of the weekly chart it appears to have made a false downside breakout, accompanied by a bullish divergence of MACD. The Force Index points to a near-total absence of bears. They cannot drive this sensitive indicator anywhere near the levels reached during previous declines. When the bears appear exhausted, it is time to start exploring the bullish side.

To summarize the lessons from this trade:

- Make a strategic decision on the weekly chart, tactical plans on the dailies.

- A divergence of MACD-Histogram is one of the strongest signals in technical analysis.

- Trading within a channel lowers risk but also reduces potential rewards.

- You must rate all your short-term trades by the percentage of the channel captured in that trade.

- Trading within a channel, you must have your finger on the trigger, ready to exit with a good grade, without waiting for super-profits.

SHORTING FUNDAMENTALS

Fundamental and technical analysts approach the markets from different angles. Fundamentalists explore supply-demand relationships in futures and the financial data for companies whose shares they want to trade. Technicians follow the trails left by buyers and sellers on their charts. A savvy trader can rely on both types of analysis and profit from their combination.

You must realize that you cannot become an expert in both fields. You will always be stronger in one than the other. Your guiding principle when using both fundamentals and technicals should be to make sure that their signals do not contradict one another. If one screams to buy while the other yells to sell, the safest course of action is to step aside.

Fundamental analysis is the more narrow of the two. You can apply the same technical tools to stocks and futures, to indexes and forex. A fundamental analyst cannot possibly be an expert on both bonds and crude oil, or on stocks in biotech and defense.

There are two main approaches to using fundamental analysis in trading—one broad, the other narrow. First of all, it pays to have a general understanding of the major fundamental trends that affect your market. For example, if you are looking for stocks to buy, you want to know that biotech or nanotechnology have greater potential for new advances than commodity chemicals or household appliances. This basic understanding can help you focus on the more promising areas of the market.

A more focused approach is to take a specific trading idea from fundamental analysis and put it through the filter of technical analysis. The key principle is to use fundamental information as an idea generator and technical studies as a trigger. The technicals can either release you to pursue that trade or stop you from going any further.[1]

---

[1] I believe in this idea so strongly that for years I have been telling friends who like to buy stocks without any knowledge of technical analysis: "Go to a free website, pull up a weekly chart of your stock and overlay it with a slow moving average; do not buy a stock whose slow moving average is pointing down, indicating a downtrend."

No matter how good a fundamental story, if the technical factors do not confirm it, there is no trade. This rule applies to both bullish and bearish fundamental information. When the fundamentals suggest a trade and technical factors confirm that signal, you have a very powerful combination. Here is an example of a trade that illustrates this approach.

During the weekend of February 10, 2007, I received an e-mail from Shai Kreiz, a member of our Spike group (Figures 7.16 through 7.22). The group's members compete for prizes each weekend by sending in their best picks for the week ahead. Every member receives everyone else's picks. On most weekends I select a favorite and trade it myself.

Many picks are technical, but this one had an unusually high volume of fundamental information. Shai wrote:

> Weight Watchers International looks like it's time to lose weight. There is a massive bearish divergence on the daily chart, and price is overextended on the weekly, with MACD about to turn down.
>
> WARNING: Earnings report and conference call is scheduled for Tuesday, February 13, after the market close.
>
> Normally I wouldn't stay in a trade on an earnings day, but there is an interesting situation in this case and I am willing to risk

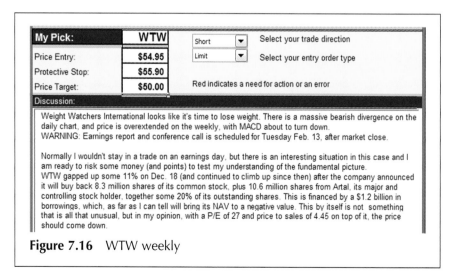

Figure 7.16   WTW weekly

some money (and points) to test my understanding of the fundamental picture.

WTW gapped up some 11% on December 18 and continued to climb since then, after the company announced it would buy back 8.3 million shares of its common stock, plus 10.6 million shares from Artal, its major and controlling stock holder, together some 20% of its outstanding shares. This is financed by $1.2 billion in borrowings, which, as far as I can tell, will bring its NAV to a negative value. This by itself is not something that is all that unusual, but in my opinion, with a P/E of 27 and price-to-sales of 4.45 on top of it, the price should come down.

Shai wrote that he was going to short at $54.95, with a stop at $55.90 and a profit target of 50. I understood his fundamental note as saying that this bird was flying higher and higher despite a major bloodletting of capital; a further flight would be unsustainable. Technically, the weekly chart looked awful (Figure 7.17).

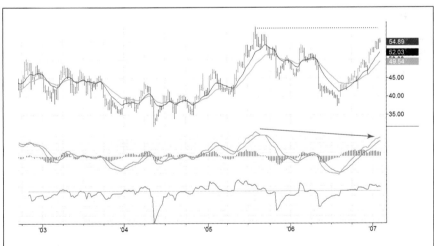

Figure 7.17 WTW weekly

WTW was approaching major resistance in the vicinity of its 2005 top while MACD Lines were tracing a bearish divergence and Force Index was sagging.

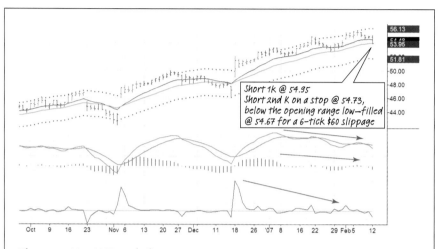

Figure 7.18 WTW daily entry

The daily chart showed massive bearish divergences of MACD Lines, MACD-Histogram, and Force Index. The stock appeared poised at the edge of a cliff, ready to tumble down.

WTW	short	Date	Upchannel	Downchannel	Day's High	Day's Low	Grade
Entry 1	$54.95	12-Feb-07	56.85	51.09	$55.14	$53.95	84%
Exit							
P/L						Trade	

WTW	short	Date	Upchannel	Downchannel	Day's High	Day's Low	Grade
Entry 2	$54.67	12-Feb-07	56.85	51.09	$55.14	$53.95	61%
Exit							
P/L						Trade	

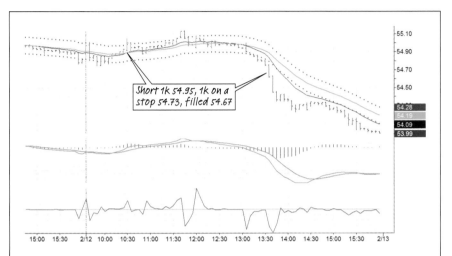

Short 1k 54.95, 1k on a
stop 54.73, filled 54.67

Figure 7.19   WTW entry, 5 minute chart

This combination of ominous fundamental and technical signs looked
so bearish that I decided to double the size of my short position. After
shorting 1,000 shares at the level recommended by Shai, I placed
another order to short 1,000 shares at $54.73, at the low of the open-
ing range. WTW had opened flat, tried to rally but then reversed, and
accelerated on its way down. My second order to short was filled at
$54.67, inflicting $60 worth of slippage, six times greater than the commission cost.

The amount of money a trader commits to a trade can stress him
and impair his decision-making. As noted above, I carried double my
normal position size in WTW. I was still well under the 2% Rule risk
limit, but at double the normal risk this trade certainly had more than
its share of my attention. The money was clouding my judgment.

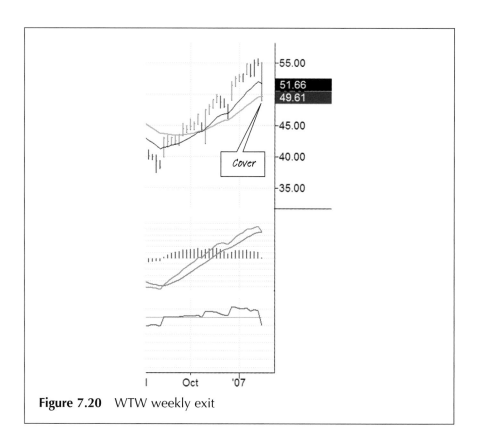

Figure 7.20   WTW weekly exit

WTW	short	Date	Upchannel	Downchannel	Day's High	Day's Low	Grade
Entry 1	**$54.95**	12-Feb-07	56.85	51.09	$55.14	$53.95	**84%**
Exit	**$50.39**	14-Feb-07			$51.38	$49.03	**42%**
P/L						**Trade**	**79%**

WTW	short	Date	Upchannel	Downchannel	Day's High	Day's Low	Grade
Entry 2	**$54.95**	12-Feb-07	56.85	51.09	$55.14	$53.95	**84%**
Exit	**$50.40**	14-Feb-07			$51.38	$49.03	**42%**
P/L						**Trade**	**79%**

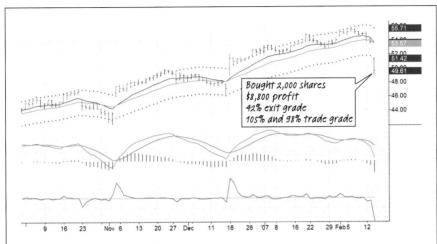

Figure 7.21   WTW daily exit

WTW closed near the low of the day on Monday. It stayed near that level on Tuesday. On Wednesday the market did not like what the management had to say in their earnings report and conference call. The stock gapped down, hitting Shai's target for the trade.

The price of WTW on the weekly chart stabbed down, below the slow yellow EMA. For me, the trade had completed what it was supposed to accomplish. Just a few days prior, WTW was above value on the week-lies. It made sense to sell short an overvalued stock for a trip down into the value zone. Now that the destination had been reached, it made little sense to stick around. Yes, of course, the stock could continue even lower and become undervalued, but that would be a different trade. There are many concepts for trading the markets, and you have to choose the ones with which you are comfortable. This trade was based on a con-cept I liked—shorting above value and covering at value. Now the choice was between staying and trying to trade the downtrend or getting out and moving on to look for another trade with a similar pattern. My choice was to exit and take profits.

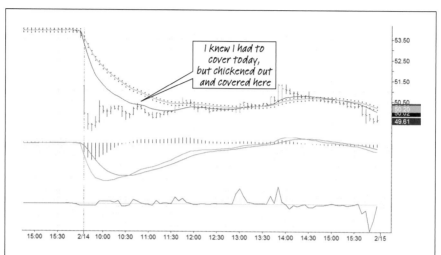

Figure 7.22   WTW exit, 5-minute chart

As a discretionary trader, I did not have a standing order to cover shorts below the market. When WTW overshot Shai's target at the opening, I waited to see whether the downmove would continue. When WTW began to rally, I covered both positions in two separate orders, within a penny of each other.

Normally, when prices open down on a severe gap, there is no great rush to cover shorts. Prices tend to hang around the gap level for a while, testing lower ground and giving plenty of opportunity to cover. But here, trading a double position size, I had a quick $10,000 profit within 48 hours of entering the trade. I felt anxious not to let it slip away, and as soon as prices began to rally from their gap opening, I felt jittery and covered.

It was a fairly sloppy exit, with only a 42% rating. The trade itself had an excellent 79% rating, but it could have been higher had I let it run a little longer instead of jumping to protect my early profits (Figure 7.23).

To summarize the lessons from this trade:

• Fundamental information can provide useful trading signals, as long as technical analysis confirms them.

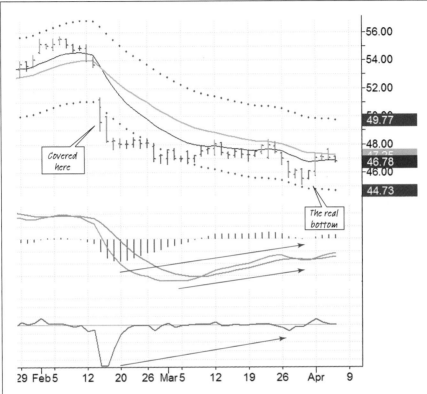

Figure 7.23 WTW follow-up

Keeping a visual diary encourages you to return to completed trades at regular intervals and learn with the benefit of hindsight. This follow-up chart, from some 8 weeks later, shows that the profit per share could have been just about doubled by a patient trader. I did not need to carry a double-sized position to make more money. Normal size, coupled with peace of mind, would have worked just as well.

- The value zone between two moving averages serves as a magnet for prices—they tend to return to it from above and from below.
- The amount of money we have riding on a trade tends to negatively impact our decisions.
- It pays to keep good records.

A visual diary is a valuable learning tool. If you keep records like the one shown here and return to review them, you will profit from your experience. Reviewing your diary will help you become a better trader. The profits may have been banked long ago, but the learning process still continues.

FINDING STOCKS TO SHORT

I have two main ways of looking for stocks to short—one is easy and the other requires hard work.

The "easy" way is not all that lazy, of course. It involves looking at short candidates from the Spike group, as well as other sources. I have already described my approach to trading tips. They provide ideas for possible trades, but I analyze the stocks myself and make my own decision whether to trade them or not. Each tip must be processed through my own trading system. That system, described earlier in the book, must confirm the tip in order for me to trade it. Still, with 20 smart people in the Spike group scanning and researching the stock market, and sending in their picks, there are often attractive short candidates. I put them through the Triple Screen and Impulse systems to decide whether to trade those picks and what parameters to use.

The "hard work" approach involves looking at the entire universe of stocks. With thousands of shares listed on the U.S. market and even more overseas, it is impossible to review all of them with any degree of thoroughness. This is why, over the years, I have developed a short-cut that allows me to zoom in on the most promising stocks. I use it in my search for both long and short candidates. Here we will focus on looking for stocks to short.

Begin by scanning stock industry groups and subgroups, looking for those that look attractive for shorting (Figure 7.24). If you like to short the tops, look for the groups that appear toppy. If you like to short the downtrends, look for the groups that are already moving within established downtrends. Once you find an attractive group or subgroup, open up the list of its component stocks and look for shorting candidates among them.

Looking at a hundred or more stock industry groups keeps you in touch with the entire stock market. Analyzing individual stocks within selected groups allows you to efficiently allocate your time. Several friends have offered to automate the entire process for me, but I do not feel comfortable with shifting the responsibility for finding trades to a computer. I want to look every group and subgroup in the face, so to speak. I try to go through this scanning process at least twice a month, and more often when the market appears ready to turn.

The program I like to use for this is TC2007[2] (www.tc2000.com). I like how it breaks the entire stock market into 239 industry groups and subgroups and makes it easy to switch from any group or subgroup to its component stocks. The chart above shows the beginning of a scan. Select "Industry Groups" from the directory of securities. Then select

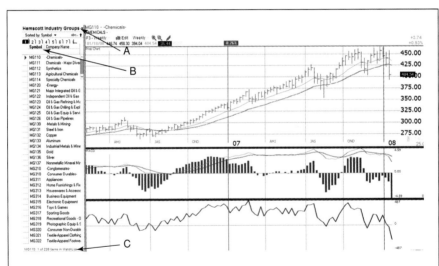

Figure 7.24 Scanning groups in TC2007

A. Click on this menu to select Industry Groups.
B. Click on this menu to sort them by the symbol.
C. The watchlist has 239 groups and subgroups.

---

[2] I have used TC2007 (Copyright © 1997–2007 Worden Brothers, Inc. All rights reserved.) to draw Figures 7.24–7.28).

"Symbol" from the list of sorting options. Since I run these scans on weekends, I want to look at the weekly charts whose template includes my favorite indicators: two moving averages, MACD Lines and Histogram, and Force Index.

Of course you can implement these ideas in many other software programs. After all, on a journey to some remote point, the skill of the driver counts for a great deal more than the brand of his car.

During today's scan we find an attractive group, MG135—Gold (Figure 7.25). The weekly chart had recently broken out to a new high but could not hold that level and sank back below resistance, leaving behind a false upside breakout—a great sign of weakness. MACD-Histogram traced out a bearish divergence. That was another great sign of weakness, marking an attractive subgroup in which to look for shorting candidates.

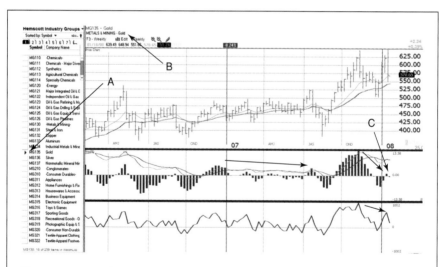

Figure 7.25   Selecting a group in TC

A. Highlighting an attractive group
B. Click here to switch to subindustry components
C. Missing right shoulder

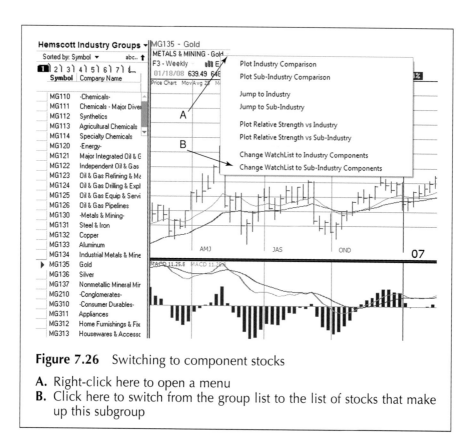

Figure 7.26   Switching to component stocks

A. Right-click here to open a menu
B. Click here to switch from the group list to the list of stocks that make up this subgroup

Two clicks take us from the selected subgroup (which TC calls Sub-Industry) to its component stocks (Figure 7.26). Here we will look for a shorting candidate.

First, a bit of housekeeping is in order. We need to sort the stocks (Figure 7.27) within a group or subgroup by price rather than by symbol. When looking for stocks to sell short, I want to look at the most expensive stocks first. When looking for stocks to buy, I want to begin with the least expensive stocks. Buy low, sell high! (See Figure 7.28.)

At this point in my own trading, I would switch from TC to Trade-Station (www.tradestation.com). The first has a much better scanning capability, while the latter has greater technical tools. Again, the sequence of steps is more important than any specific software. The search pro-

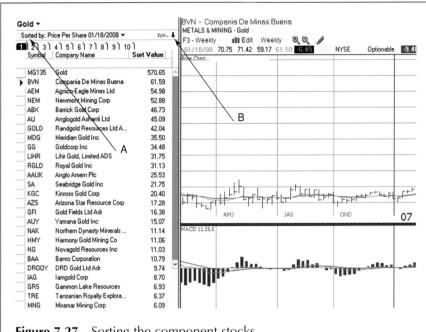

Figure 7.27 Sorting the component stocks

A. Click here and sort the component stocks by share price
B. Click here to display the component stocks from the most expensive down

cess we've just discussed allows you to keep tabs on the entire stock market but zoom in on specific stocks and dedicate the bulk of your time to them.

SHORT INTEREST

If misery loves company, what does happiness love? Solitude, perhaps?

We know that most traders lose money, and only a minority makes steady profits. A successful trade is likely to run in the direction opposite to that of the majority of traders. This is why it pays to know how much or how little company you will have when you short a stock.

Most traders only buy stocks. Very few people sell short, and the total number of shares shorted usually represents only a tiny percentage of any company's shares. If you want to measure the intensity of short-

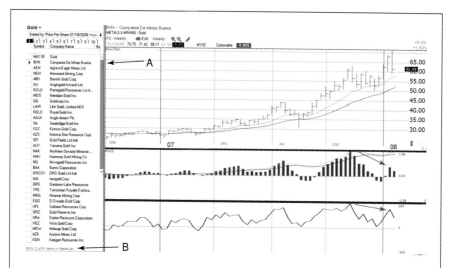

Figure 7.28 Finding a shorting candidate

A. BVN is the most expensive stock in this subgroup.
B. There are 50 stocks in this subgroup.

The pattern of BVN—Compania de Minas Buena—appears remarkably similar to that of the entire subgroup. You can see several strong sell signals on this weekly chart. Now is the time to switch to the daily chart and make tactical decisions on where to enter, where to set a target, and where to place a stop. Now is also the time to use money management rules to decide on position size. Finally, you should create a visual diary for your planned trade.

sellers' involvement in any given stock, you have two indicators available to you—the Short Interest Ratio and Days to Cover.

The Short Interest Ratio compares the number of shorts held by the bears with the "free float" in any given stock. The free float is the number of shares available for shorting. You find it by taking the total number of shares issued by the company and deducting three share groups: the restricted stock granted to executives, shares held by "strategic shareholders" who own more than 5% of company shares, and, finally, insiders' holdings. When you subtract the number of shares that cannot be easily sold from the total number issued by a company, you find the number of shares that are in play—the free float.

Brokers report the number of shares that have been shorted and not covered to the exchanges, which summarize this information for every stock and disclose it to the public. If you divide the total number of shares that are being held short by the total free float, you'll have the Short Interest Ratio. It reflects the intensity of shorting in any given stock.

When the Short Interest Ratio rises, it shows that the bears are becoming angrier and louder. You must keep in mind that every short position must eventually be covered. When shorts panic and run, they will cover at any price. Short-covering rallies are notorious for their speed. A growing Short Interest Ratio delivers a warning that the bears are becoming too numerous. When this happens, a stock becomes subject to a violent upmove.

There is no clearly defined safe or dangerous level of the Short Interest Ratio. It varies from stock to stock, especially in optionable stocks, where speculators may sell the stock short and at the same time write a put, in effect balancing the two, trading a spread rather than expressing any great bearishness. As an estimate, a Short Ratio of less than 10% is likely to be tolerable, while a reading of over 20% marks a suspiciously large crowd of short-sellers.

Another useful measure of the level of bearishness is the Days to Cover indicator. To calculate it, divide the total short interest in a stock by its average daily volume. It shows how many days it would take for all the short-sellers to cover their positions if they all panicked and decided to cover at once.

When someone yells "Fire!" in a crowded movie theater, it matters little whether that fire is real or not, as people rush for the exits. Similarly, it takes surprisingly little to touch off a panic in the stock market—either up or down. The shorts may become lazy and complacent on the way down, but they are prone to dash for the exit in a wild short-covering rally, creating a panic rally that feeds on itself.

When a crowd panics in a movie theater, people get trampled at the door. If the number of Days to Cover is less than one, you have a small crowd at a wide door, and a panic is unlikely. If Days to Cover rises above 20 (it sometimes goes above 50), it tells you that the stock has become a safety hazard for the bears—it would take many days for them to escape, and some of them are sure to get killed as they try to push through the narrow doors.

Keep in mind that the door can quickly become wider, making it easier to escape and reducing the number of Days to Cover. For example, if there are 10 million shares of outstanding shorts and the average daily volume is 1 million, then Days to Cover equals 10. If the volume zooms up to 2 million, Days to Cover will drop to 5—without any change in the number of shorts. As a rule of thumb, when the Days to Cover indicator is below 10 the danger of a squeeze is low, while a reading above 20 sends a definite warning.

There are several ways to obtain Short Interest Ratio and Days to Cover for most stocks. For example, you can go to the popular Yahoo Finance website, type in a symbol and click "Get quotes." Scroll down the page and click on "Key statistics." There you will find "Shares short" and "Short ratio."

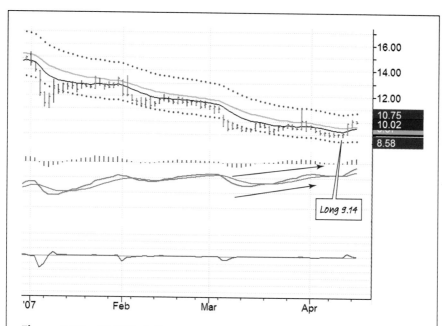

Figure 7.29   NURO daily

I traded NURO from the long side because I liked the divergences and the fact that the stock was in a tight price squeeze. Still, there were other attractive stocks at the same time. What clinched the deal for me was that NURO had a very high level of shorts, with a Short Interest of 50% of the float and 20 Days to Cover. Needless to say, the first little strength in the stock triggered short-covering, and there was a very satisfying price pop.

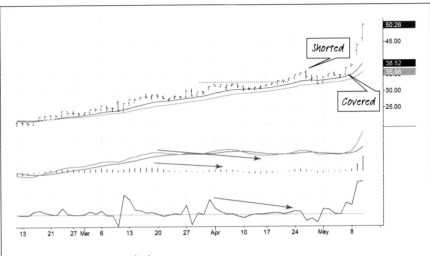

Figure 7.30 HANS daily

The divergence looked beautiful, and the stock started curling down. What we overlooked at the time was its high short interest. The stock just started going up and up, and we had to cut losses. Then it gapped up on a major distribution agreement with an industry leader. Several weeks later it became a great short, but by that time we were out.

Kerry Lovvorn, a trader mentioned earlier in this book, has said:

> I do not trade specifically on short interest. I work up all my trades the way I usually do, but then look at Short Interest to help rule trades in or out. Given two trades of equal attractiveness, I am more apt to buy a stock with a higher Short Interest Ratio. I know that the people who are short will have to come in and buy it—that there will be willing buyers. But I will not buy a stock simply because it has a high Short Interest Ratio (see Figure 7.29).
>
> I also pay attention to short interest when looking at potential shorts. Here I primarily use the Short Interest Ratio as a filter to help me stay away from certain stocks. I do not want to be a part of the crowd, trying to pass through that door. Remember when both you and I were shorting HANS? (See Figure 7.30.)

Misery loves company and happiness loves solitude. Short Interest Ratio and Days to Cover help you find stocks whose short side is not overcrowded.

SHORTING NON-EQUITY INSTRUMENTS

It goes without saying that whichever trading vehicle you buy you must eventually sell. Most markets also allow you to sell short. The exceptions are few and far between. U.S. stock market authorities used to throw some sand into the gears with their "uptick rule," which made it a little more difficult to short stocks. The regulators in several less developed markets went so far as to outlaw shorting stocks, in a misguided attempt to support their markets.

While there are restrictions on shorting stocks, the entire trading world is free to short futures, options, and forex. Those markets simply could not exist without shorting. Since we have already discussed methods for shorting stocks, we will now look into shorting non-equity instruments.

As a stock trader, you must learn to buy and sell, but shorting is optional. You can be a successful trader without ever shorting. Over decades and even centuries, the gently rising tide of the stock market, mentioned earlier, slightly slants the board in favor of the bulls. Even in bear markets, where buying opportunities are few and far between, a savvy bull can find an industry group that rises while others sink. Still, a stock trader who knows how to sell short has a definite advantage over a perma-bull, especially during bear markets. This is why I encourage you to learn to sell short.

While only a small minority of stock traders sell short, a vast amount of shorting takes place in forex, futures, and options. As a matter of fact, the volume of shorting in futures or forex is exactly equal to that of buying! For every contract bought there is also a contract sold short. A futures trader who never sells short is a curiosity. An options trader who never sells short (i.e. writes options) is most likely a loser. And a forex trader who does not sell short simply does not exist. If any of these statements seem incorrect to you now, you will fully understand what I mean by the end of the chapter on shorting non-equity instruments.

Shorting is an integral part of the derivatives markets, but this creates a problem for the author. The only way to completely cover shorting futures, options, and forex is to write an entire book on these markets. Such enormously broad coverage is outside of the scope of this project. How shall we resolve this dilemma?

Instead of teaching you the A-to-Z of futures, options, and forex, I will begin each chapter by referring you to what I think are the best books on each market. They will help you learn the basics of futures, options, or forex before delving into how to sell them short. Then, as we get into each chapter, we will jump right into shorting, without becoming bogged down in the mechanics of each trading vehicle.

If you understand futures, options, or forex, you can take the methods you've learned in the stock market and apply them there. Here we will focus on the unique features of those markets that impact shorting.

Ready?

Then let's move on!

SHORTING FUTURES

When you buy a stock you buy a share in an existing business. When you go long a futures contract, you buy nothing but simply enter into a binding contract for a future purchase of a commodity. The person on the opposite side of your trade enters into a contract for a future sale. For every long there is a short, for every promise to buy a promise to sell. Those promises are backed by margin deposits on both sides.

Nobody expressed the philosophy and the basic principles of futures trading better than the late Thomas Hieronymus in his *Economics of Futures Trading*. One of the deepest and wisest books on futures, it

Futures: Recommended Literature

Winning in the Futures Markets by George Angell is the best introductory book for futures traders (and the only book by that author I recommend). *The Futures Game* by Teweles and Jones is a mini-encyclopedia that has educated generations of futures traders (be sure to get the latest edition). *Economics of Futures Trading* by Thomas A. Hieronymus is a profound book, but it's long been out of print—try finding a used copy. Last but not least, there is a chapter on futures in my book *Come into My Trading Room*.

unfortunately has been out of print for many decades. Probably because this is not a "how to" book, nobody cares to reprint it, with only an occasional used copy turning up on book-selling websites. Leafing through my old copy, I want to share with you several quotes, before we turn to the topic of shorting futures.

Hieronymus on Futures

The market is a balance of judgments, so that for every good judgment there is a poor judgment. Futures trading is an exciting game, the score of which is kept with money.

A commodity contract has a short life span. Thus, speculative fictions in securities can be long perpetuated but speculative excesses in commodities, up or down, are soon pricked by the test of the first delivery day.

The supply harvested during a short period of time must be made to last until the next crop is available. There is one and only one average price that will make the supply just clear the market.

The current price reflects the composite judgment of the traders in forecasting the equilibrium price. The composite judgment of all the market participants is that the equilibrium has been found and that prices will not change. But none of the individuals who make up the composite think that the equilibrium has been reached, else they would not have a position. Obviously, the composite is always wrong.

To take a position in a market is to challenge the aggregate judgment—to say that the market is in error.

Each speculator must identify and do his own thing. Perhaps more importantly, he must stay out of someone else's game. The market will tell its own story and your only task is to hear it fast.

To try to squeeze out the last bit of opportunity is to get too cute with the market; to be too disdainful of the intelligence of the market. The locals are in the business of fine-tuning.

In the aggregate, the participants break even gross and lose net by the amount paid in commissions, brokerage, and clearing fees.

The big contributors to the game are the people who badly overstay positions.

The people who do not trade regularly and consistently are among the biggest contributors to the game.

The existence of inventories creates a carrying charge. The effect is to force a continually rising price of futures. But if the basic value is unchanged over time, a continual rise in futures is not possible. Accordingly, the total price structure must periodically collapse.

From Hieronymus, Thomas A., *Economics of Futures Trading*, 1971

Of course, in shorting futures there is no silly "uptick rule." When you place an order to sell a future, it makes no difference whether it is an order to sell a long position or to open a new short trade.

There is no prohibition against insider trading. You can track the behavior of the insiders through the "commitments of traders" reports regularly published by the CFTC (Commodity Futures Trading Commission).

Most shorts in most futures markets are held by the commercials or hedgers who are the true insiders. You can try to explain those findings away, saying that most insiders are producers who sell futures as a hedge for being long inventory, but that would be a superficial explanation. Do you really think that hedgers as a group keep positioning themselves to lose money on futures, month after month and year after year? Far from it! What does it mean then that they tend to be heavily short?

For example, a major agribusiness may sell futures to lock in a good price for a harvest that has not yet been gathered. But that is only part of the game. Any hedger worth its salt runs its futures division as a profit center and not merely as a price insurance office. They expect to make money on those shorts.

Futures, unlike stocks, have natural floors and ceilings. A stock may fly to the moon or get delisted and disappear. This cannot happen in futures, where the cost of production creates a price floor and the price of substitution a price ceiling. Those levels, however, are somewhat flexible rather than totally rigid.

As futures prices swing between those two levels, a hugely important factor, pointed out by Hieronymus, comes into play. Commodities incur carrying charges, as the cost of storing, financing, and insuring them gets worked into their price. If this process were to continue unabated, month after month, prices would gradually climb to dizzying heights. What happens instead is that relatively slow and steady price increases get punctuated by brief violent drops, returning the price to a realistic level—and then the process begins again.

On Futures

Buying a stock makes you a part-owner of a company. When you buy a futures contract you don't own anything, but enter into a binding contract for a future purchase of merchandise, be it a carload of wheat or a sheaf of Treasury bonds. The person who sells you that contract assumes the obligation to deliver. The money you pay for a stock goes to the seller, but in futures your margin money stays with the broker as a security, ensuring you'll accept delivery when your contract comes due. They used to call margin money honest money. While in stocks you pay interest for margin borrowing, in futures you can do the opposite, collecting interest on your margin.

Each futures contract has a settlement date, with contracts for different dates selling for different prices. Some professionals analyze the spreads between the months to predict reversals. Most futures traders do not wait and close out their contracts early, settling profits and losses in cash. Still, the existence of a delivery date forces people to act, providing a useful reality check. A person may sit on a losing stock for ten years, deluding himself that it is only a paper loss. In futures, reality, in the form of the settlement date, always intrudes on the day-dreamer.

Futures can be very attractive for those who have strong money management skills. They promise high rates of return but demand ice-cold discipline. When you first approach trading, you are better off with slower-moving stocks. Once you have matured as a trader, take a look at futures. They may be right for you if you're very disciplined.

Futures, unlike stocks, have natural floors and ceilings. Those levels are not rigid, but before you buy or sell, try to find out whether you're closer to the floor or the ceiling. The floor price of futures is their cost of production. When a market falls below that level, producers start quitting, supply falls, and prices rise. If there is a glut of sugar, and its price on the world markets falls below what it costs to grow the stuff, major producers are going to start shutting down their operations. There are exceptions, such as when a desperately poor country sells commodities on the world markets to earn hard currency while paying domestic workers with devalued local money. The price can dip below the cost of production, but it cannot stay there for long.

The ceiling for most commodities is the cost of substitution. One commodity can replace another if the price is right. For example, with a rise in the price of corn, a major animal feed, it may be cheaper to feed animals wheat. As more farmers switch and reduce corn purchases, they take away the fuel that raised corn prices. A market in the grip of hysteria may briefly rise above its ceiling, but cannot stay there for long. Its return to the normal range provides profit opportunities for savvy traders. Learning from history can help you keep calm when others are losing their heads.

Adapted from *Come into My Trading Room*,
by Dr. Alexander Elder, John Wiley& Sons, Inc., 2002

Visualize the dunes at an ocean shore. As the waves pound the sand, they build up the dunes. At some point the dunes fall under their own weight, and the whole process begins anew. This is exactly what you see in most futures markets—slow build-ups followed by quick collapses.

While there are many great opportunities for buying in the futures markets, this is a book about selling and selling short. This is why we will bypass buying and take a closer look at shorting futures (Figure 8.1). Here we can take advantage of their propensity for relatively slow and steady rises and sharp declines.

Cocoa is a notoriously difficult market to trade. An American journalist who used to write under the pseudonym of Adam Smith in the 1970s quipped that if you ever feel a desire to trade cocoa futures, just lie down and wait until the feeling passes. Cocoa is notorious for its brief violent moves. As you can see on this chart, most of its violence is to the downside.

Even in a relatively peaceful stock market, rallies tend to last longer than declines. Here, in futures, declines tend to be compressed into sharp shakeouts. Even in this fairly flat range in cocoa, you can see that

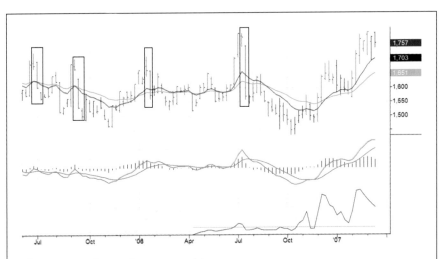

Figure 8.1 Cocoa futures weekly

Here cocoa appears to have settled into a long-term price range, roughly between $1,800 and $1,500 per ton. When it declines to or below $1,500, it is near a bottom, and when it rises above $1,700 it enters the zone in which it faces a definite risk of getting hit on the head.

most rallies take several weeks or even months, while most declines are over in a single week. They cover a great distance like a speeding bullet, terminating old bulls and clearing the path for a new gradual advance.

Slow and shallow rises make beginners think that their longs are safe, that prices will continue to rise. Then some sudden event, like an unexpected blow, punctures their balloon, and the air escapes with a great *whoosh!* The shorts, many of them professional traders, clean up while public traders get taken out feet first, and the next round of the game is ready to begin. At the right edge of Figure 8.2, gold is in the midst of a slow and steady rise, looking very peaceful, as if saying "everything's nice, come here, chicky-chicky."

A savvy trader looks at the time scale at the bottom of the daily chart (Figure 8.3) and notices that the rise has been going on for a month and a half and covered a distance of $42. He knows that if he buys gold here he absolutely must use stops—and hard stops at that. Furthermore, it may make sense to use stop-and-reverse orders. I am not a huge fan

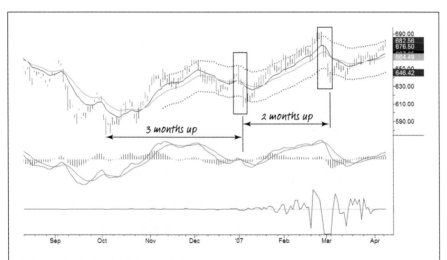

Figure 8.2   Gold futures daily

Crawl up slowly and tumble down fast: it took gold over three months to rise from $575 to $660—but only three days to slam down to $606, retracing 64% of the decline. The next rise, from $607 to $692, went on for over two months—followed by a drop to $635, a 67% decline, in only four days. Those long, gradual rises lull most traders into a false sense of security.

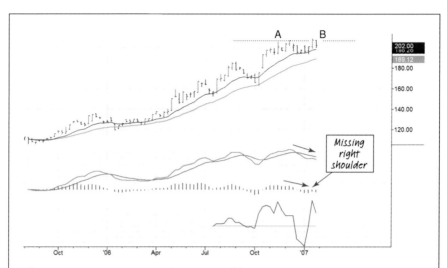

Figure 8.3 Orange juice futures weekly

The weekly chart of OJ showed a false breakout to a new high accompanied by a bearish divergence—one of the most attractive patterns in technical analysis. At point B, OJ broke above the level of the top A but could not hold the altitude and dropped back into range. MACD Lines traced a bearish divergence. MACD-Histogram showed an extremely powerful pattern that Jackie Patterson, a member of the Spike group, has named "a missing right shoulder" (actually, Jackie used a more colorful term that I slightly toned down).

In area A, MACD-Histogram rallied well above the zero line, creating a left shoulder. Then it cracked below zero, "breaking the back of the bull." Later, at point B, MACD-Histogram could not lift itself above the zero line. It just pulled up towards zero and then ticked down. This weekly chart was a screaming sell. The rally had been going on for a while and the clock was ticking for one of those downdrafts that occur when the bubble gets pricked.

of such orders, but they can make sense during slow rallies, since they can be stopped into a short position simultaneously with the closing of the long one.

In conclusion, let me pull up a record of a futures trade from my diary (Figure 8.4). This trade shows how a trader can capitalize on futures' tendency for quick deflationary moves.

OJ drew my attention while doing my weekend homework. On most weekends I take about an hour to review all the major U.S. futures markets. One of several advantages of futures is that there are so few of them. It is easy to keep track of all futures, unlike the many thousands of stocks.

The price balloon got pricked soon after the opening on Monday. The slow sluggish uptrend was punctured, letting out the hot air that had held up OJ (Figure 8.5).

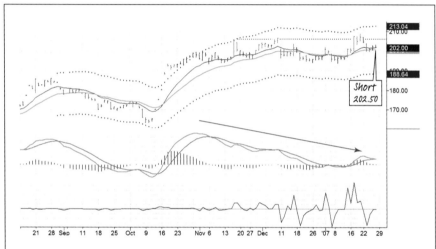

Figure 8.4   Orange juice futures daily, entry

The daily chart also showed a failed upside breakout accompanied by a bearish divergence of MACD Lines. While this signal was not as strong here as on the weekly charts, it certainly did not contradict the weekly. It is quite normal for either the weekly or the daily to send a better signal— and whenever that happens, the weekly trumps the daily. I decided to short OJ soon after the opening on Monday, unless there was an extremely strong rally at the open or if price collapsed before I could get in.

OJ 3/7	short	Date	Upchannel	Downchannel	Day's High	Day's Low	Grade
Entry	$202.50	29-Jan-07	212.50	188.25	$203.80	$195.25	85%
Exit							
P/L						Trade	

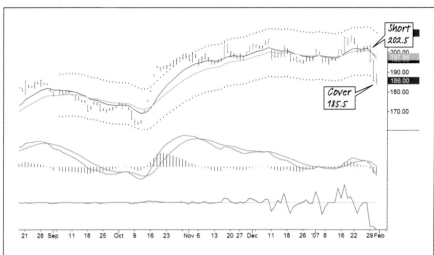

Figure 8.5   Orange juice futures daily, exit

When prices stabbed below their lower channel line on the daily charts, my target was reached and I covered my shorts in OJ. The trade was over and done within two days. Perhaps the collapse would continue, but with my profit target already hit, I had no further reason to stay in the trade.

OJ 3/7	short	Date	Upchannel	Downchannel	Day's High	Day's Low	Grade
Entry	202.50	29-Jan-07	212.50	188.25	$203.80	$195.25	85%
Exit	185.50	31-Jan-07			$189.25	$184.20	74%
P/L						Trade	70%

This was an emotionally as well as financially satisfying trade—I wish more of my trades were like this (Figure 8.6). The entry made logical sense and the exit signals were very clear.

Some professional futures traders say that the big money is on the long side of the market—buying cheap and holding through thick and thin. Whether you are a long-term or short-term trader, it pays to be aware of the fact that futures tend to have long slow rises and quick violent declines that hurt slow bulls and offer fantastic rewards to quick bears.

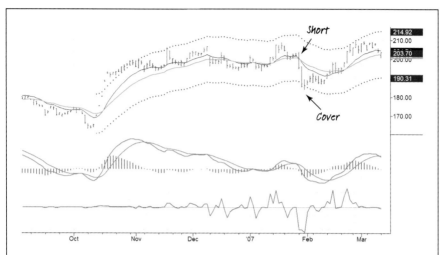

Figure 8.6 Orange juice futures daily, follow-up

In retrospect, looking at OJ almost two months later, both the entry and the exit made a lot of sense. At the right edge of the chart, OJ is starting to sink again, indicating another likely spell of trouble.

WRITING OPTIONS

In options, as in no other field, there is a sharp dividing line between two groups of people. On the one side are the beginners and gamblers who lose money year after miserable year. On the other side are the pros, making a steady living in the options market.

Do you know where that line is drawn?

Options: Recommended Literature

Every options trader should own Lawrence McMillan's *Options as a Strategic Investment.* You will probably use it as a handbook rather than read it from cover to cover. Many professionals read Sheldon Natenberg's *Option Volatility and Pricing Strategies.* Harvey Friedentag's *Options: Investing Without Fear* has a nice angle on covered writing.

The great Warren Buffett is a witty man and, like so many successful money managers, he is a games player. He even used to publish a newsletter on handicapping horses. Buffett chuckled when he said that when you sit down to a game of poker, you must know within fifteen minutes who is going to supply the winnings. If you do not know the answer, that person will be you!

The great dividing line in options is between the buyers and the writers. On the one side of the line are the winners who write options. On the other are the losers who buy them.

I have never in my life met a person who built equity buying options.

Oh, every option buyer can tell you about a successful trade or even a few trades in the options market. But those are merely flashes in the pan—totally different from having a long-term positive equity curve. Those occasional wins are like payouts from a slot machine—enough to keep losers motivated to throw more money away.

Options tend to attract poor beginners because the game is cheaper than stocks. Many buy options as a substitute for stocks, and I always tell such folks that they are chasing a deadly illusion. The key difference between options and stocks is that options are wasting assets. When you buy an option, you have to be right on the stock, right on the extent of its move, and right on your timing. This would be like trying to toss a ball through three moving rings at an amusement park.

A beginner can be bullish on a stock, buy its calls, watch that stock go up, and still lose money. He might be right on the trend, but if the stock takes longer than expected to hit his target, the option will expire worthless. After taking his lumps a beginner may decide to shop for a longer-term option next time. Then he discovers that longer-term options are ruinously expensive.

A woman who was a market maker on the floor of the American Exchange once said to me: "Options are a hope business. You can buy hope or sell hope. I am a professional—I sell hope. I come to the floor in the morning, find out what people hope for, price that hope, and sell it to them."

Profits in the options business are in the writing, not in buying.

When you write options, you begin every trade by taking in someone else's money. A hopeful buyer forks over some money to a writer who is almost always a much more experienced trader. As lawyers say, possession is 90% of the law. It is easier to hold on to the money that other people give you. The job of options writers is to hang on to buyers' money and not let it slip away.

Poor option buyers are twisting in the wind as they keep trying to convert hope into money. Meanwhile, options sellers lean back and enjoy the passage of time. An options writer had shorted a wasting asset, and as time chips away at its value, it will cost him less and less to cover his short. Its value might even go down to zero, and then he will not have to pay a commission to cover his short position.

It is easy for a successful option writer to feel magnanimous and give a little money back to the poor buyer. If he has sold an option for a dollar and now that option is quoted for a dime, there is not much reason to hold it to expiration. He has already earned the bulk of what was available from that trade and there is no need to try and squeeze out the last cent. If he buys the option back for ten cents, he will close the trade, escape any future risk, and will have the peace of mind to look for another option to write.

In options, as in so many things in life, it pays to do things differently from the crowd. Since the mass of traders is a heavy buyer of options, it is a good idea to take a contrary tack and write options.

Living well is the best revenge. As you become more experienced, it will feel very sweet to take what kills most options traders—time—and convert it into a source of profit.

The main choice to make when selling options is whether to write them covered or naked. In covered writing, you write options against the stocks you own. In naked writing, you create options out of thin air, backing them with the capital in your trading account. Let us review these choices in writing options.

Covered Writing

If you hold a stock whose upside potential appears limited, you may sell calls on your shares. You will immediately collect cash from the sale and then wait for one of three things to happen:

- If the stock stays relatively flat and does not reach the option's exercise price, you will pocket the premium, boosting your total return.
- If the stock falls, you will also pocket the premium, cushioning the fall in your stock.

- If the stock rises above the option exercise price, it will be called away. You'll keep the premium in addition to the capital gain from the purchase price to the exercise level. Since there is a big universe of interesting stocks out there, you take your freed-up capital and look for new opportunities.

After you sell a stock short, you can sell puts against your short position, selecting an exercise price below your target for the downmove. If the stock stays flat, you keep the option premium. If it rises, you also keep the premium, reducing your loss on the short position. If the stock falls below the exercise level for the put, your position will be called away. You'll keep the premium and also pocket the capital gain.

The main use of covered writing is to boost returns and reduce losses in a large stock portfolio. It is a labor- and capital-intensive business. It is not enough to go out and write covered calls on a single stock—that would be too much work for a small reward. To make economic sense, covered writing needs to be done for a large number of stocks. As your stock portfolio gets bigger, covered writing makes more and more sense. The manager of a multimillion-dollar diversified stock portfolio owes it to his investors to explore putting that portfolio into a covered writing program.

Naked Writing

The edgy, highly promising, but potentially dangerous, area of the options business is writing naked options. While conservative investors write covered calls against their stocks, naked writers create options out of thin air. Naked writers walk a narrow line, protected only by their cash and skill; they need to be absolutely disciplined in taking profits or cutting losses.

We all have our favorite markets and methods, and serious people tend to specialize. When I began working on this chapter I called Dr. Diane Buffalin in Michigan, an experienced options writer, and asked for a few examples of her trades.

Diane sounded bubbly when she talked of her love of writing options.

> I am doing lots of boring options trades. It's so simple, I could teach my granddaughter to do it. I said to her—you go to an art high school, you can recognize lines. I can show you—when those lines stop going down, it is time to sell a put.

I like taking money in and do not like paying it out. Happiness is selling an option that expires worthless. I had taken my Schedule D to several accountants who said there was a problem with it; buy prices were missing. I had to explain to them that I had sold options and they expired worthless.

I love naked selling. The problem with covered selling is that to make money on an option you have to lose some on a stock, and I don't like that. I look for stocks that I would like to own which are declining. When they stop going down I sell their puts and collect a 10% premium.

I feel like a dealer in a casino, making money off the players' egos. Those flashy guys keep coming in, wearing gold chains. They throw hundreds of dollars on my table for some plastic yellow chips. The wheel keeps spinning and they have fun, but on the third Friday of the month the wheel stops, and that's when I collect. I try not to smile too much, not to show them how happy I am to have their business.

I am a professional psychologist, but the insurance company pays the same rate whether I give a patient good advice or not. Trading is the only business where you get paid in proportion to how smart you are. But you have to work hard. People keep asking me to teach them to write options. I give them a few stocks to follow and tell them to keep a daily list of their prices, along with several options prices. Not one person who came to me could keep that list up for a month. Lazy.

A stock can go up, down, or sideways. If you buy a stock or an option, you have one way to make money and two ways to lose. When I sell an option, I have two ways to make money, and sometimes even three. The time to sell an option is when a stock stops moving, and the sharper its move has been, the more they will pay you for the option.

Here are two simple current option trades on two popular stocks: ATI (Allegheny Technologies) and CHL (China Mobil). On March 6, 2007, both stocks showed a pattern I like. I visually scan my charts for this pattern because I am not computer-savvy enough to create an electronic scan.

The stock market had dropped precipitously on February 27 and was still forming a bottom. Because of the high volatility, puts had a bit more of a premium. That was good. Better to sell more expensive merchandise than cheap merchandise—there is more profit built into the price (Figure 8.7).

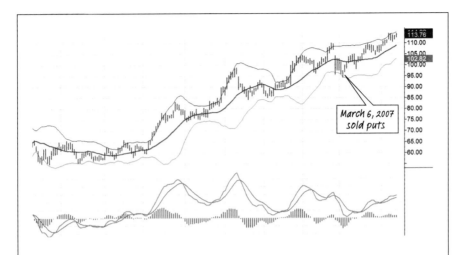

March 6, 2007
sold puts

Figure 8.7   ATI daily

ATI hit the bottom of the Bollinger band on March 5th and was rebounding: The MACD had stopped going down—that was my trigger. At that time I had two choices. I could buy 1,000 shares of the stock at 97, but that would put $97,000 of my money at risk after a precipitous drop in the market. Alternatively, I could sell a put and take in about $4,800 for my promise to buy a good stock at a $2 discount from its current price. I sold the April 95 put for $4.80, taking in $4,800. It is now worth only 5 cents, and I will let it expire and have another zero in my "Paid" column.

The downside was that I could have made a lot more money buying the stock, which is now at 113, but then I would have had to put $97,000 of capital at risk, and I like to sleep at night and not live on antacids. Actually, I did make a lot more money on the stock by continuing to sell puts at higher strike prices, much the way you would add to a stock position.

I also sold the puts on China Mobil on the same day, for the same reason (Figure 8.8). The stock was at $44.5, and its June 45 put was at $4.80. I selected June because that's how far I had to go to make 10%, which is what I like to get. I'm really selling time, thinking that in three months the stock will not drop below 45. If it drops and I have to buy it, I'll receive a 10% discount.

People ask me all the time, "If selling options is so great, how come more people don't do it?" I think it's because most options

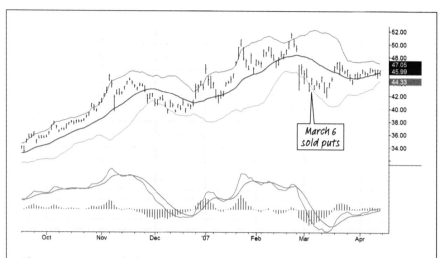

Figure 8.8 CHL daily

Initially, it appeared I was wrong about this stock, as it fell further during the Asia sell-off. It dropped to $41.70 a week later, but I didn't fold my position. The option was showing a $300 loss, but the stock was still above my break-even point and time was definitely on my side. Currently, the stock is at $45.90, the option shows about $1,500 profit, and it still has two more months to make the other $1,500. It looks as if the only thing better than being right and making money, is being wrong and making money anyway!

traders like to gamble. They look for tips, but have little patience to play options like chess. Buying options takes little money (about 10% of the stock price), but selling them takes considerable cash. Most brokerage houses won't let you sell puts unless you have at least $100,000; some require $250,000 and two years' experience. Brokerage houses say they are trying to protect you, but they let you buy options which have a high probability of losing money; they won't let you sell options, which have a much lower probability of losing money.

If you sell a put, the worst thing that can happen is that you will buy a stock at a predetermined price. How awful is that? Don't millions of investors and traders do exactly that every day? So I just sell puts on stocks that I would buy anyway, at a price that I would gladly pay. The only difference is that I get to make the profit without putting my capital into the market. I actually have it in secure bonds, earning interest. And what is the worst thing that can happen if you sell a naked call? You end up with a short position on a volatile stock. Isn't that exactly what many professional traders do anyway? I love options because I get my profit up-front. And "the worst thing that could happen" is just fine with me.

FOREX

Whereas the chapters on futures and options began with lists of recommended books, I cannot offer such a list here. There is not a single book on trading forex that I can confidently hand to you and say "It is good; read it." You will have to pick bits and pieces from among the yards of books on forex.

The forex market has several distinct segments, and your choice of where to trade will have a huge impact on your chances of winning or losing. The differences between traders in the forex market remind me of the class system in a Third World country. There are a few rich citizens, the great unwashed masses of poor people who are not likely to ever get a fair shake, and a tiny middle class, trying to hold on to its tenuous gains.

The big money plays in the interbank market, where dealers trade tens of millions of dollars at a clip. The middle class is in forex futures, getting battered by gap openings because futures trade almost 24/7. Down at the bottom of the pyramid are the poor folks with small trading accounts at forex houses.

Gamblers, losers, and poorly capitalized beginners are always on the lookout for the next big chance to get rich quick. Years ago they used to trade odd lots on the stock exchange, from where they moved to buying options. After they lost their shirts and many other garments, the get-rich-quick crowd migrated into the forex market.

The trouble with forex is that a great many forex houses operate as bucket shops. When you place an order to buy or sell, they give you what they call a confirmation. In fact, there is almost never a real trade, merely a bookkeeping entry at the forex house. Whatever you want to trade, the forex house will take the opposite side of the trade, knowing full well that the clients will lose on balance. Starry-eyed dreamers are hit with multiple charges which help them go down faster.

Forex houses offer wild margins, as high as 400:1. Remember, you need to pay 50% as a margin in stocks, perhaps as low as 5% in futures. The 0.2% margin in forex ensures that no meaningful money management is even remotely possible.

Aside from charging you a spread when you buy or sell, a forex house charges interest on your nonexistent "position." In fact there is usually no real position, only a bookkeeping entry, since your order has not gone anywhere. When you trade a cross, a forex house will pay less than base rate on the long leg of the currency trade and charge more than the base rate on the short leg of the trade.

When you trade stocks, a brokerage house does not care whether you make or lose money. They merely execute your orders and collect commissions. In many forex houses, instead of transmitting orders to the markets, the brokers simply play against their customers. The forex shops are betting against you on every trade. This means that in order for you to make money the broker has to lose. This is a deeply flawed system. The stock market was purged of this malignancy nearly a century ago, but the broom has not yet reached the forex shops.

The proprietors of forex houses know that most turkeys are doomed because of lack of skill, emotionalism, and poor capitalization. Why transmit an order to the market and share the money with someone else? Spreads, commissions, and interest charges on bucketed positions drive the nails into gamblers' coffins.

Savvy dealers monitor their clients' total positions, and when those become too one-sided in any given market, say by $1 million, they lay off that risk in the interbank market. Some houses go a step further—when clients' positions reach an extreme, they trade against them.

A really honest house, transmitting trades for execution, would suffer from a terrific disadvantage in comparison to the bucket shops. Bucket shops can always underprice an honest house because they do not have to pay the execution costs. I am sure there are some decent and properly run forex houses, but the deck is stacked against them.

Governments around the world have certainly failed to clean up the forex business. I hope that in the future some private entrepreneurs using Internet technology can create a more even playing field for small forex traders. Until such a transparent system emerges, I have only two words for you—buyer beware!

If you do not have tens of millions of dollars to play the interbank market and are too smart to use a bucket shop, you're left with only one choice—forex futures. These were first traded in the pits of the Chicago Mercantile Exchange in the 1970s. It commissioned the late Milton Friedman, a Nobel-prize winning economist, to write a paper that explained the economic need for forex futures. Now, of course, forex futures trade in many countries on different continents.

More importantly, they trade electronically, providing access to a well-established and transparent business virtually around the clock.

Why would anyone go to a bucket shop instead of forex futures? Perhaps for the same reason people buy lottery tickets with poor odds but big promises. To trade a forex future, you might need to lay down a couple of thousand dollars margin. At the same time, some forex shops allow you to open an account with as little as $50, while offering a "shoulder" of 100:1, meaning you can buy $5,000 worth of forex with your measly deposit. Of course, you "buy" nothing except for a receipt from that bucket shop which then charges you interest on the entire $5,000.

Needless to say, to trade forex futures you must understand how to trade futures in the first place. As mentioned above, this book is not designed as an introductory text for futures traders. There are many books on this topic, and my favorites are listed in the previous sections. My goal here is merely to point out the differences between shorting forex and shorting stocks.

Shorting is an integral aspect of forex because every forex trade is a spread trade. Whenever you buy one currency, you automatically go short another. Buying forex without shorting at the same time is impossible, like finding a coin with only one side.

All trades are measured in money. Depending on where you live, you deal in dollars or pounds or yen, and so on. If your trading account is in dollars and you buy the euro, then as you go long the euro, you automatically go short the dollar. If you short the Swiss franc in that same dollar account, you automatically go long the dollar.

A forex trader can go outside of his home currency by trading the so-called "crosses." For example, EURAUD means long the Euro, short the Australian dollar. SWFJPY means long Swiss, short Yen. Every forex trade is a spread trade. When you speak of buying forex it automatically means shorting some other forex—you cannot buy or sell just one side of a coin.

Study after study has confirmed that the forex market is among the most trending in the world (Figures 8.9 and 8.10). Once a currency gets into a major trend, whether up or down, it might stay in it for years. This is due to the fact that in the long run the value of a country currency depends on government policies. When a new government comes to power and starts implementing its economic policies, a currency is likely to enter into a long-term trend. No trend, of course, proceeds in a straight line. In the short- and even intermediate-term there

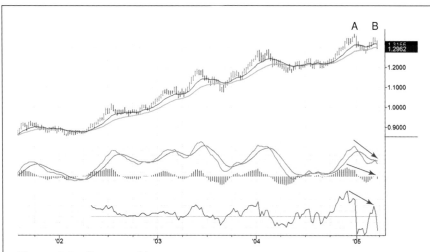

Figure 8.9 Euro weekly

This chart shows a four-year upmove in the euro against the U.S. dollar. The trend, driven by economic fundamentals, appeared unstoppable. One could buy and hold or try to play the swings (a friend of mine fell madly in love with a woman and found himself unable to trade; he put his assets into the Euro, and by the time of the wedding was $300,000 ahead of the game). At the right edge of the chart there are multiple and severe bearish divergences. The bulls are healthy and powerful at peak A, which was followed by a normal pullback to the value zone. The rally to peak B was accompanied by prominent bearish divergences in MACD Lines and Force Index; the divergence of MACD-Histogram was of a particularly ominous type—a missing right shoulder. The signals to sell and sell short were loud and clear.

is a lot of backing and filling. Those counter-trend moves are frequent enough and large enough to provide short-term trading opportunities, as well as a killing ground for the poor turkeys with no holding power.

When you start planning your forex trades, it is important to keep in mind that one type of trading that works well in the stock market is likely to be very problematic in the forex market. Swing trading, which involves holding a position from several days to a couple of weeks, is much more prone to whipsaws in forex than in the stock market.

The reason for this difficulty is that forex trades essentially 24/7, and what you see on the charts in your time zone is just a segment of total

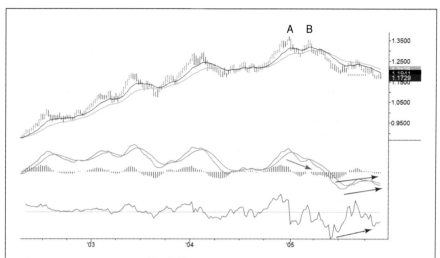

Figure 8.10 Euro weekly follow-up

The euro's downward reversal was initially pooh-poohed by the bullish crowd. As the downtrend deepened, the crowd woke up and started looking for a bottom, to load up for the next upleg. When the euro fell below its latest bottom, they threw in the towel. That's where the buy signal emerged, almost a mirror image of the sell signals at the top: a false downside breakout, with bullish divergences in all the indicators. One could not hope for a better set of signals to cover shorts and go long.

worldwide activity. The bulk of trading takes place while you are asleep or away from the screen. It is hard to bet on a horse that keeps running around the track while you're dreaming in your bed.

To sidestep this problem you can move into either very long-term or very short-term trading. You can put on a small position with a very wide stop and try to hold it through thick and thin, riding a long-term trend. Alternatively, you can zoom into the right edge of the chart and day-trade forex, closing your positions at the end of the day and avoiding overnight risk.

CONCLUSION

Many traders buy in a very soggy way. When a stock goes their way they tend to take profits too soon, out of insecurity and fear. When a stock goes against them, they grimly hold on, not knowing what to do with a puppy that is fouling up their living room and chewing up their couch. They do not set profit targets or think about stop-losses.

This vague and indecisive approach to trading and investing tends to reflect how many people live their lives. They postpone making hard decisions, as if they had all the time in the world. While their current situation is a mess, they keep dreaming that, in the words of a Broadway song, "the sun'll come out tomorrow." In fact, their time is limited, and, with their kind of decision-making, tomorrow is likely to be even worse than today.

While structuring your life is outside the scope of this book, we can certainly begin by structuring your trading. What are your profit goals and loss tolerance? How will you manage risk and keep records? When will you sell every stock that you own? How will you capitalize on declines by selling short? These are the key questions you should be able to answer much better now, after you have worked through this book.

Trading is not a trivial pursuit. Earlier in this book we discussed the need for a strict control of your risks, by applying the 2% and the 6% Rules. You should feel perfectly free to tighten those numbers, as many professionals do, but you can never loosen them.

I have shared with you a discovery that took me more than a decade to make and which had a hugely positive impact on my own trading and that of my students. The single most important factor in your success or failure is the quality of your records. Beginners spend endless hours playing with the time window of Stochastic or the settings of Relative Strength Index. Those issues are chickenfeed in comparison to the importance of good trading records. In this book I have shown you what records to keep and how to use them. Will you follow these instructions? Will you try to improve on them?

We've taken a quick look at buying but have spent the bulk of our time on selling and shorting. It is essential to establish profit targets as well as stop-loss levels for every stock you buy. We have discussed several methods of setting both. You need to choose the techniques that fit your personal style and incorporate them in your trading.

If, like most traders, you have never sold short, I encourage you to find a stock that you hate, a stock that you think is going sharply lower, and sell a few shares short. Do it a few times, practice shorting a small size. You are not obligated to become an active short-seller, but if you decide to specialize in buying rather than shorting, I want you to make that choice as a free person, and not out of ignorance or fear.

One topic we have not touched upon is the tax aspect of trading. I am not an expert on this topic and can only suggest that you read up in this area and seek competent advise.

One of the great attractions of trading is its promise of freedom. Another is that trading is a lifelong pursuit in which you can grow better as you grow older. Memory, patience, and experience—the virtues of age—are the essential assets of trading. But first, in order to benefit from your experience, you need to survive and stay in the game long enough to learn to play it well. You need to set up your money management so that no premature loss or a string of losses can kick you out of the game. You need to set up your record-keeping system in order to learn from your experiences.

If you take the message of this book seriously and apply its rules, instructions, and lessons, you have a fascinating road ahead of you. I wrote this book to help you make the correct choices at several crucial forks in the road.

I wish you success.

HANDLING PROFITS—
THE PERSONAL DIVIDEND

As Oscar Wilde said over 100 years ago, "Every true idealist is after money—because money means freedom, and freedom, in final analysis, means life." Money can be a powerful motivator—I remember being driven hard by my desire to be able to spend more time with my children instead of being on call at the hospital; to live in a nicer house; to go to the Caribbean to escape the northern winter, and so on.

When you begin making money, it is important to know what is enough, when it is the time to jump off the carousel. There is always a bigger carrot to chase—a bigger house, a nicer villa, a shinier toy. If you do not shift gears when you are good and ready, you can spend the rest of your life chasing the almighty buck—and that would be a sad life. Remember, the goal is freedom and not a shinier toy.

Your solution to this challenge is going to be as unique as you are. I can tell you a bit about my choices, but when you begin to implement your own solutions I would like to hear from you.

One thing I continue to do, unrelated to the pursuit of money, is write books. Their royalties cannot begin to cover the profits that I give up by taking thousands of hours and a lot of energy away from trading. I like the work of writing and the reward of dealing with readers who are attracted by it.

My other pursuit is teaching. A couple of years ago I volunteered to teach a class called "Money and Trading" at a local high school. To make the experience more real for the kids, I opened up a $40,000 account for my class. I told the kids that if our account showed a loss at the end of the school year, I would eat it, but if it showed a profit, I would donate one-half to the school and distribute the other half among members of the class.

As the year went on, I was surprised to discover that I often focused with greater intensity on this small account than on my own. We ended up having a good year. The kids loved the experience, and the school keeps inviting me back. Teaching a class and making decisions in front of a group reminded me of those athletes that get an extra edge from playing a game in front of their fans.

The Personal Dividend

One of my early priorities was making best use of any trading profits, which included building my equity base and paying down my mortgage. A number of factors led me to re-think the method by which I was spreading around my success. Based on my treat-it-like-a-business philosophy, I thought, "successful businesses issue dividends." I set very aggressive goals each quarter—basically trying to bring home more money trading than I earned in my job. As long as I achieve 100% or better of the goal I set for myself each quarter, I create a pot of 5% of quarterly profits as the dividend. That is then divided equally among the recipients who can do what they want with the money.

No one was told about the dividend program at first. The first dividend for Q4-2002 was issued in person, by surprise. My presentation approach was to staple a bunch of hundred dollar bills into a card. The impact sure had its desired effect!

The recipients now include 6 key constituents, plus a local charity where they do an amazing job focusing on specialist palliative care. The 5% dividend does not change the world, but it is appreciated by the recipients!

Some quarters I don't meet my goal, and that keeps each quarter fresh, with everyone keen on knowing how well I am doing! I let people know during the 3rd month each quarter if the dividend is "likely or not." It has certainly helped me be more focused, and helping my family in a methodical way adds a very rewarding dimension to the work. I like having my "shareholders."

From *The Unconventional Trader* by Robert Bleczinski

In February 2007, Bob Bleczinski, one of my Camp graduates, came from London to New York to collect an award. I asked him to make a brief presentation at our monthly campers' meeting. Bob, a very focused and intense man, gave a quick overview of his approach to trading, which included what he called "the personal dividend." He had set a profit target for each quarter and whenever he reached it he took a percentage of that profit and distributed it to the people on his list.

Bob had a sister who at one point was very sarcastic about his trading, calling it simple gambling. That sarcasm quickly evaporated after

Bob drew a list of his half dozen nearest and dearest, and his sister started receiving her dividend. She went from being a critic to being a fan.

Bob's idea appealed to me, but I modified it to suit my personal style. I set a very modest, non-stressful target for myself—four percent per quarter (a little more than 16% annualized). Those first four percent per quarter are mine to keep, but anything above that I consider super-profit and share 10% of the amount with the people on my list. I created my list differently from Bob—it includes people towards whom I feel cordial, who can use the money, and who have been kind or helpful to me in some way.

Trading is a very private pursuit. I found that by sharing the fruits of my success with the people I care about I have created a group of fans who have a positive impact on my performance. Just as I focused so intensely on the small school account, I am pushed to exceed the 4% target in order to be able to deliver the personal dividend to those on my list.

It is a great pleasure to face the people I like and who have been kind to me and hand them envelopes with a friendly card and a few hundred dollar bills. I explain to them how the dividend came about and why they are on the list. Now I no longer play the trading game in solitude but in front of a bench of cheering supporters.

References

Allen, David. *Getting Things Done*. New York, NY: Penguin, 2002.

Angell, George. *Winning in the Futures Markets*. New York, NY: McGraw Hill, 1990.

Appel, Gerald. *Technical Analysis: Power Tools for Active Investors*. Financial Times, Ramon, CA, 2005.

Bade, Margret. Personal communication, 2003.

Benyamini, Zvi. Personal communication, 2007

Bleczinski, Robert S. *The Unconventional Trader*. An unpublished paper, 2007.

Buffalin, Dr. Diane. Personal communication, 2007.

Deffeyes, Kenneth S. *Hubbert's Peak: The Impending World Oil Shortage*. Princeton, NJ: Princeton University Press, 2003.

Elder, Alexander. *Come into My Trading Room*. New York, NY: John Wiley & Sons, 2002.

Elder, Alexander. *Entries & Exits: Visits to 16 Trading Rooms*. Hoboken, NJ: John Wiley & Sons, 2006.

Elder, Alexander. *Trading for a Living: Psychology, Trading Tactics, Money Management*. New York, NY: John Wiley & Sons, 1993.

Faith, Curtis. *The Way of the Turtle*. New York, NY: McGraw Hill, 2007.

Friedentag, Harvey Conrad. *Options—Investing Without Fear*. Chicago, IL: International Publishing Corporation, 1995.

Gajowiy, Nils. Personal communication, 2007.

Grove, Nicholas. Personal communication, 2004.

Hieronymus, Thomas A. *Economics of Futures Trading*. New York, NY: Commodity Research Bureau, Inc., 1971.

Kreiz, Shai. Personal communication, 2007.

Linenberger, Michael. *Total Workday Control Using Microsoft Outlook.* Ramon, CA: New Academy Publishers, 2006.

Lovvorn, Kerry. Personal communication, 2007.

MacPherson, Malcolm. *The Black Box: All-New Cockpit Voice Recorder Accounts of In-flight Accidents.* New York, NY: Harper, 1998.

Mamis, Justin. *When to Sell: Inside Strategies for Stock-Market Profits.* New York, NY: Simon & Schuster, 1977.

McMillan, Lawrence G. *Options as a Strategic Investment.* Upper Saddle River, NJ: Prentice Hall, 2002.

Natenberg, Sheldon. *Option Volatility and Pricing.* New York, NY: McGraw Hill, 1994.

Pardo, Robert. *Design, Testing and Optimization of Trading Systems.* New York, NY: John Wiley & Sons, 1992.

Parker, Jeff. Personal communication, 2007.

Patterson, Jacqueline. Personal communication, 2006.

Rauschkolb, James. Personal communication, 2007.

Rhea, Robert. *The Dow Theory.* New York, NY: Barron's, 1932.

Smith, Adam. *The Wealth of Nations.* New York, NY: Bantam Classics, 2003.

Steidlmeier, J. Peter. Presentation at a TeleTrac conference, 1986.

Teweles, Richard J., and Frank J. Jones. *The Futures Game*, 3rd ed. New York, NY: McGraw Hill, 1998.

Weis, David. *Catching Trend Reversals*: a video. New York, NY: elder.com, 2007.

Weissman, Richard L. *Mechanical Trading Systems: Pairing Trader Psychology with Technical Analysis.* Hoboken, NJ: John Wiley & Sons, 2005.

Wilder, J. Welles, Jr. *New Concepts in Technical Trading Systems.* Greensboro, SC: Trend Research, 1976.

Winters, Deborah. Personal communication, 2007.

ACKNOWLEDGMENTS

In January 2007, as the bull market kept hitting new highs, I had dinner in Manhattan with Kevin Commins, my editor at Wiley. He asked what area was not well covered in trading literature, and I told him it was selling. There are hundreds of books on buying, but there hadn't been a good book on selling in decades, I told Kevin. The time to publish one is now, because this bull market is getting old; my indicators show that the next year we are likely to be in a bear market. People do not buy books on selling in bull markets. If you have someone write this book fast, it will come out in the right climate—in the midst of a bear market. "Who do you think could write such a book" asked Kevin—and from that point until now my life was taken over by this project.

I am grateful to the good folks at John Wiley & Sons, with whom it has been my good fortune to produce a number of trading books. Joan O'Neil, the publisher, has made me feel very welcome there. The production crew is absolutely professional and a pleasure to work with. Paul diNovo, the art director for my books, has impeccable taste. Emilie Herman, Laura Walsh, and Todd Tedesco are highly productive and helpful. Outside of Wiley, working on this book with Joanna V. Pomeranz, Gabriella Kadar, Nancy W. Dimitry, and Matt Kushinka felt like repeating a journey with a group of old friends. Ted Bonanno, my agent, helped ensure the smoothness of this as well as many other projects.

Both my daughters helped edit this book. Miriam is a journalist in Moscow and Nika is working on her doctorate at Princeton, but both found the time in their busy schedules to review the manuscript and make constructive suggestions. Carol Keegan Kayne, the reliable guard against sloth and imprecision, performed the final check of the book, weeding out mistakes that had eluded everyone else's eyes.

Kerry Lovvorn, a trader in Alabama and my co-manager of the Spike group, generously helped produce many charts for this book. Jeff Parker, a trader and a member of the Spike Group in North Carolina, has read the manuscript and asked tough questions that helped improve the book. Patricia Liu was an invaluable sounding board, as I read the manuscript out loud to her, making sure it flowed just right. All the while, Inna Feldman, my manager at elder.com, ran the company alone for weeks, making sure I had enough time to write and edit.

I am grateful to you all. Without your help this book would probably not see the light of day, or if it did, its quality would not be the same. Thank you very much.

Dr. Alexander Elder
New York City
March 2008

ABOUT THE AUTHOR

Alexander Elder, M.D., is a professional trader and a teacher of traders. He is the author of *Trading for a Living* and the *Study Guide for Trading for a Living*, considered modern classics among traders. First published in 1993, these international best-sellers have been translated into more than a dozen languages and are being used to educate traders around the world. His *Come into My Trading Room: A Complete Guide to Trading* was named a 2002 Barron's Book of the Year. His *Entries & Exits: Visits to 16 Trading Rooms* was named a 2007 SFO Magazine Book of the Year. He also wrote *Rubles to Dollars: Making Money on Russia's Exploding Financial Frontier* and *Straying from the Flock: Travels in New Zealand*.

Dr. Elder was born in Leningrad and grew up in Estonia, where he entered medical school at the age of 16. At 23, while working as a ship's doctor, he jumped a Soviet ship in Africa and received political asylum in the United States. He worked as a psychiatrist in New York City and taught at Columbia University. His experience as a psychiatrist provided him with unique insight into the psychology of trading. Dr. Elder's books, articles, and reviews have established him as one of today's leading experts on trading. Many of his own trades are featured in this book.

Dr. Elder is the originator of Traders' Camps—week-long classes for traders. He is also the founder of the Spike group, whose members are professional and semi-professional traders. They share their best stock picks each week in competition for prizes among themselves. Dr. Elder continues to trade, conducts webinars for traders, and is a sought-after speaker at conferences in the U.S. and abroad. Readers of this book are welcome to request a free subscription to his electronic newsletter by contacting his office:

elder.com
PO Box 20555, Columbus Circle Station
New York, NY 10023, USA
Tel. 718.507.1033
e-mail: info@elder.com
website: www.elder.com

INDEX